TREASURES OF THE

BRITISH
MUSEUM

Edited and Introduced
by Sir Frank Francis, KCB
Director and Principal Librarian
of the British Museum 1959–68

TREASURES OF THE

BRITISH MUSEUM

with 439 illustrations, 64 in colour

THAMES AND HUDSON · LONDON

Text filmset in Great Britain by Keyspools Ltd, Golborne, Lancs
Printed in West Germany by K. G. Lohse, Frankfurt am Main
Bound in Holland by Van Rijmenan NV, The Hague
ISBN 0 500 18125 x clothbound
ISBN 0 500 20119 6 paperbound

Contents

INTRODUCTION

> 'On the 7th of June 1753 . . . His Majesty, being seated on the Throne adorned with his Crown and Regal Ornaments, and attended by His Officers of State; the Duke of Cumberland in his Robes sitting in his Place on His Majesty's Left Hand; the Lords being also in their Robes . . . the Clerk of the Crown read the Titles of the Bill to be passed as follows . . . An Act for purchasing the Museum or Collection, of Sir Hans Sloane, and of the Harleian Collection of Manuscripts and for providing one general Repository for the better Reception and more convenient Use of the said Collections, and of the Cottonian Library, and of the Additions thereto.
>
> 'To this Bill the Royal Assent was pronounced and in these words; videlicet, *Le Roy le veult.*'

This was the legal instrument setting up the British Museum. The collections of its sister institution, the British Museum (Natural History), not dealt with in this book, were originally an integral part of the original British Museum. They were moved *en bloc* to South Kensington in 1887.

There has never been a general history of the British Museum. A glance at the chapters that follow, with the accompanying illustrations, will go far to explain why this is so. The collections at Bloomsbury are so large and so multifarious and the activities of the thirteen various departments so diverse that it would be a task as vast as all the twelve labours of Hercules combined to encompass it in one general study. The department by department survey, by senior officers, here presented, is probably the best approach to a general history that can be offered.

One of my most eminent predecessors as Director and Principal Librarian once put forward the view that the British Museum is, next to the Royal Navy, the national institution which is held in most universal respect. Time is no respecter of reputations, but there can be no doubt that the British Museum has the material resources to justify continued acceptance of this idea and, given the developments foreshadowed in plans put forward in the 1960s, will have ample means to display its treasures and bring them into full use for the general public.

The British Museum at Bloomsbury is unique in that it comprises under one roof and in one organization a national museum of antiquities and a national library. It was founded in 1753, following the Will of a well-known eighteenth-century physician, Sir Hans Sloane, who bequeathed his extensive collections 3

◀ 1 The British Museum, the Ionic colonnade and portico completed in 1847

2 Humfrey Wanley (1672–1726). In 1708 he was employed to catalogue the Harleian library and became 'library-keeper' to the first and second Earls of Oxford. The preservation and recording of many early manu-scripts is due to his diligence

of books and antiquities to the British Nation in return for a payment to his daughters of £20,000.

The range of the collections which came to the British Museum from Sir Hans Sloane is reflected in the collections as they are today in the British Museum and the British Museum (Natural History), otherwise known as the Natural History Museum. They comprised some forty thousand printed books, seven thousand manuscripts, including fine early Chinese drawings of plants and flowers, prints of natural history interest by Albrecht Dürer, extensive natural history specimens, and antiquities from Egypt, Greece, Rome, the Middle and Far East and America. At the beginning the 'artificial repro-ductions', as the objects of antiquity were designated, were but an insignificant appendage to the natural history collections or, to give them their contemporary title, the 'natural productions'.

To Sloane's collection the Foundation Act added two other important collections, the Cottonian, collected by Sir Robert Cotton, the Elizabethan antiquary, who set out to gather and preserve the records of English literature and history dispersed at the dissolution of the monasteries in 1535 and the Harleian library collected by Robert and Edward Harley, first and second Earls of Oxford, under the guidance of their 'library keeper' Humfrey Wanley. A third collection, the Royal Library, the library assembled under various monarchs and maintained in the royal palaces of St James and Westminster, was given to the British Museum by King George II in 1757.

These three libraries with the Sloane Library, are regarded as the 'Foundation collections', and because of the richness and variety of their contents have assured a pre-eminent place for the Museum among the world's libraries. From them the Museum received such treasures, to name only a few, as the Gospels written and decorated about AD 698 in the monastery at Lindisfarne, the unique copy of Beowulf (written about AD 1000), two of the four extant copies of Magna Carta, fine manuscripts of Chaucer, Lydgate, Gower and Hoccleve, the invaluable Bagford collection of fragments of early printing, many volumes from Archbishop Cranmer's library and the fifth-century *Codex Alexandrinus* of the Bible, presented to Charles I by Cyril Lucar, Patriarch of Constantinople. (This Bible manuscript was to be joined, 310 years after the original gift, by the fourth-century *Codex Sinaiticus*, purchased from the Soviet Government in 1934.) The Royal Library had the right to a copy of every book printed in the British Isles, and this right was transferred to the British Museum with the gift of the library; it has been maintained through the deposit clauses in successive Copyright Acts.

204

184

As the range of Sloane's collections influenced, if it did not dictate, the scope of the British Museum as it is today, the wishes he expressed in his Will for its government were in part responsible for the form of its constitution for over two hundred years. From 1753 to 1963 the British Museum was controlled by a body of trustees, headed by three *ex officio* Principal Trustees, representing the three estates of the realm, the Archbishop of Canterbury, the Lord

3 Sir Hans Sloane (1660–1753), a physician by profession, his extensive collections of books and antiquities became the basis of the British Museum

4 The Old British Museum, Montagu House, from the north-east, *c.* 1800

Chancellor and the Speaker of the House of Commons, and including, also *ex officio*, most of the senior government ministers and other holders of important official positions, representatives of the families of the principal early bene-factors of the Museum, and an additional sixteen trustees elected by the official and family trustees. Trustee business was entrusted to a Standing Committee which, at any rate in recent times, tended to consist of the elected trustees.

The Trustee body, owing to the old-fashioned nature of its constitution, became in recent times the object of largely mistaken criticism and, by an Act of Parliament passed in 1963, it was replaced by a body made up as follows: sixteen nominees (one by the sovereign, fifteen by the Prime Minister), four appointees from the Royal Society, the Royal Academy, the British Academy and the Society of Antiquaries respectively and five members elected by the Board itself. The Board elects its own chairman. The chief officer of the Museum is the Director and Principal Librarian and there are thirteen keepers who are the heads of the thirteen departments, which include the Research Laboratory, into which the Museum is divided; one of the keepers, the head of the Department of Printed Books, has the rank of Principal Keeper.

The search for a building to house these collections ended with the choice of Montagu House, a mansion belonging to the Montagu family in the Blooms-

4

bury district of London on the site occupied by the present Museum building. Buckingham House, now Buckingham Palace, was also considered, but was thought to be too expensive and not as well situated. The British Museum was opened to the public in its new quarters in 1759.

Once the British Museum was established it soon became the natural depository for collections of all kinds and it attracted many gifts. These are described in the pages that follow. All that is necessary at this point is to draw attention to some of the most significant, especially those that have played a part in influencing Museum policy over the years. Among the earliest was the Thomason collection, bought and given by King George III in 1762, after nearly a century of neglect. This collection, among the Museum's treasured possessions, was made by a far-sighted bookseller, George Thomason, during the Civil War; he collected conscientiously copies of books and pamphlets published during the whole of this period from 1642 to 1660, thus providing a superb reference library for the period of something like twenty-two thousand items. Eighteen years later another significant addition was made by the bequest by David Garrick, the actor, of his library of one thousand printed

5 The garden of the Old British Museum, Montagu House, from the north-east, by Paul Sandby, 1780

plays from which Charles Lamb culled 'the flowers of a thousand dramas'. The Library also benefited richly by the bequest in 1799 by the Reverend C. M. Cracherode of his collections which included fine printed books, bindings by Roger Payne, superb drawings by the great masters and fine specimens of the coinages of Greece and Rome.

The first notable addition to the scanty 'artificial productions' came in 1782, with the purchase of a collection of Greek vases and other antiquities mostly from Southern Italy from Sir William Hamilton, Ambassador to Naples.

It was the first two decades of the nineteenth century that saw the real foundations laid of the Museum's great collections of sculptures. By the Treaty of Alexandria, following the defeat of the French at the Battle of the Nile in 1801, the Museum acquired many of its fine Egyptian sculptures and the

65   Rosetta Stone. In 1805 the Towneley collection of Greek and Roman sculptures, bronzes and terracottas was purchased; in 1815 the sculptures from the
168   temple of Apollo at Bassae were bought, and in 1816 came sculptures from the
167   Parthenon at Athens acquired in the early years of the century by Lord Elgin.

So numerous were the acquisitions at this time that a series of extensions to the building had to be built. The first, consisting of a suite of rooms projecting
5   northwards into the garden from the north-west corner of Montagu House, was built in 1804 and 1805. Even while this Gallery of Antiquities, as it was called, was being put up, additional space had to be provided for the Towneley collection. The Towneley gallery was constructed in the years 1806 to 1808, to be joined, to the west, in 1816, by a temporary building for the Elgin marbles.

Some idea of the amount and the variety of these additions can best, perhaps, be indicated, albeit sketchily, by a chronological list of some of the significant purchases and gifts during this period:

1807: Purchase of the manuscripts of the Marquess of Lansdowne, which brought to the Museum the political papers and a mass of correspondence of William Cecil, Lord Burghley, Queen Elizabeth I's chief minister, and the
407   official papers of Sir Julius Caesar, the statesman active during the reign of James I.

1810: Purchase of the Greville collections of minerals.

1813: Purchase of the considerable Hargrave library of legal manuscripts and printed books.

1814: Purchase of the music collection of the historian of music, Dr Charles Burney, thus adding substantially to the music from the Old Royal Library, the Harleian collection and music books presented by Sir John Hawkins in 1778.

1815: Purchase of the collections in zoology formed by Colonel George Montagu of Lackham.

1815–16: Purchase of the herbarium and other natural history collections, including a library of over fifteen thousand volumes, formed by Baron von Moll of Munich.

1817: Purchase of the collections of the younger Charles Burney, son of the historian of music, and brother of Fanny. His large library included the famous eleventh-century Towneley Homer; he also had over five hundred volumes of classical manuscripts, mostly humanist copies of the fifteenth century, and a large library of printed texts, many of them copiously annotated by famous scholars. From the point of view of modern students, the most significant part of Burney's collection was the seven hundred volumes of seventeenth- and eighteenth-century newspapers, which has formed the substantial foundation of the Museum's newspaper collections.

This same year the Museum acquired the first of its three collections of French Revolution 'tracts' – the name given to the fugitive literature, pamphlets, fly-sheets and periodicals published during the Revolutionary period. This collection, formed by Colin, Marat's publisher, was later to be expanded by two further collections bought from John Wilson Croker in 1831 and 1856 respectively.

1818: The collections of antiquities and printed books of Miss Sarah Sophia Banks, given by her brother Sir Joseph Banks, President of the Royal Society from 1778 to 1820, and one of the Museum's most active Trustees.

1820: Shortly after Banks's death in 1820, the Museum became legatee of all his collections, his extensive natural history library, his manuscripts, drawings and engravings, and his herbaria, comprising his own botanical collections and those of a number of famous botanists.

1822: Purchase of the Monticelli collection of minerals, mostly of volcanic origin.

It is small wonder that when in 1823 the British Government, with the concurrence of the Trustees, agreed to accept for transfer to the British Museum the 65,000 volumes, 19,000 unbound pamphlets, the maps, charts, plans and topographical drawings and the prints and drawing of which the library of King George III was composed, a new building for the Museum became essential. Montagu House had lasted for fifty years and was already 'in a decaying condition', and so congested that Banks's library, bequeathed in 1820, was still awaiting reception. The Trustees, disturbed both by the Museum's rapid growth and the dilapidated condition of their building had already – some two years earlier – appointed an architect, Robert Smirke, to prepare plans for an extension northwards from the east end of Montagu House. What had been urgent had now, with the impending arrival of King George III's books, become imperative. Parliament, with commendable promptitude voted £40,000 in 1823, to be followed by further sums amounting to £80,000 in the years 1826–8. Smirke, the young architect chosen by the Trustees, designer of the rebuilt Covent Garden Theatre and the main portion of the Royal Mint, had a ready-made style for a building which had to house, among other things, the famous Elgin marbles from Athens. Smirke's plans, ready by the first months of 1824, provided for a new wing to be built out into the gardens from the north-east corner of Montagu House and similar ranges of

6

15

6 Sir Robert Smirke (1781–1867), chosen as the architect of the New British Museum, was noted for the fact that most of his buildings were in either Doric or Ionic style. His British Museum is pure Ionic (*Pl. 1*). He was knighted in 1813

galleries on the west and the north; the quadrangle was to be completed by demolishing Montagu House and substituting for it a new front conforming to the rest of the design. After which the colonnade separating the original Montagu House courtyards from Great Russell Street was to be replaced by a railing. Thus the plans for the building as it is, broadly speaking, known today, were already in existence in January and February 1824 and were to be carried out in the following thirty years.

The foundations of the new east wing to house the 'King's Library' and at the south end to provide two new reading rooms, were laid in the autumn of 1823 and the wing completed before the end of 1826, a temporary passage- way being provided to connect the new wing with the existing library. The upper floor of the new wing was originally intended for the national collection of pictures, but it was eventually devoted to the collections of minerals and geological specimens. The King's books were transferred from Kensington Palace in July 1828.

The remaining stages of the construction of the building can be briefly sketched at this point: By 1831 the temporary Elgin marbles gallery had become a public scandal and money was voted by Parliament for a new building, a projection, by itself, parallel to the west wing of the new building. At the same time, the northern half of the west wing, continuing the line of the

8

gallery erected in 1804 to 1808 was begun, to be followed in 1833 by the new northern or library wing, at an estimated cost of £70,000. The new reading-rooms ('rooms', according to *The Times*, 'almost too spacious for quiet study and literary repose'), provided in the northern wing were opened to the public in this year, with a separate entrance of their own from Montagu Place. There were now places for 168 readers as against the 120 previously available.

By 1838 the quadrangle was in a sense complete, but Montagu House had still to be demolished and the new front substituted. The cost of this part of the operation was estimated at a quarter of a million pounds spread over five or six years. 'Poor condemned Montagu House' was finally pulled down by 1845 and the new entrance hall opened in April 1847. The wall and railing along Great Russell Street were erected in the autumn and winter of 1850-1.

Shortly after it received the conventional acquisitions described above, the Museum acquired a most significant addition in the shape of an Italian refugee revolutionary who had left his home-town of Modena with a price upon his head. It was in 1831 that Antonio Panizzi, later to be described as the second founder of the British Museum, joined the staff as an extra assistant. He had come to England in 1820 and after short periods of teaching Italian in London and Liverpool, where he had such powerful friends as Ugo Foscolo, William Roscoe and Henry Brougham, he became Professor of Italian at the then University of London. His rise in the Museum was rapid: he became Keeper of Printed Books in 1837 and Principal Librarian in 1856. As early as 1835, in his evidence before a Parliamentary Committee of Enquiry, he propounded

1

7

7 Sir Antonio Panizzi (1797–1879), the second founder of the British Museum as he has been called, infused it with a new spirit, believing that 'a museum is not a show but an institution for the diffusion of culture'. He was knighted in 1869

8 The King's Library, built by Smirke between 1823 and 1826 to house George III's library given to the nation by George IV in 1823

the idea of a national library in terms which would be understood at the present day, and throughout his time in the Museum he pursued with characteristic vigour his ideal of the British Museum as the national library, as 'an establishment for the furtherance of education, for study and research', where a poor student could 'have the same means of indulging his learned curiosity, of consulting the same authorities, of fathoming the most intricate inquiry as the richest man in the country.'

He perceived that a library such as he envisaged needed a worthy catalogue. Soon after his accession to the keepership of Printed Books he was able to propound his famous code of ninety-one rules for cataloguing, the first thorough code ever made. The resultant catalogue, compiled in manuscript on separate slips for each entry, which could be duplicated (thus in a way anticipating the card catalogue), and inserted by the 'movable method' in large folio volumes, was placed in the Reading Room in 1850. It consisted of 150 volumes; by 1875 the catalogue had become so large (2,250 volumes) that printing became inevitable.

During his official lifetime Panizzi transformed a rather haphazard printed books library of about 200,000 volumes into a well-organized methodical

9 The circular Reading Room, built in the great quadrangle of Smirke's original design

collection of about a million. The basis for this achievement was a survey of the British Museum Library, conducted by him in 1845, which disclosed the gaps in collections which had grown with no thought-out plan; his survey resulted in a substantial increase in the annual grants made by Parliament, and thus became in large part responsible for the Museum library's pre-eminent position at the century's end. It was also largely due to Panizzi's friendship with Thomas Grenville that Grenville's magnificent library was bequeathed to the Museum in 1847.

Once again substantial acquisitions forced attention on the need for an enlargement of the building. As Esdaile says, 'in 1850 Panizzi reported that in view of the difficulty of storage he could only usefully spend £2,500 in place of the £10,000 voted in 1846, and this reduction held in the following year also. The Grenville books and many others as well, were stacked on the floor.' The problem for the Library was solved by the erection of the circular Reading Room surrounded by book stacks (constructed of cast-iron) in the great quadrangle which had been a feature of Sir Robert Smirke's original design. Time had shown that the space taken in by this quadrangle was wasted, since it had been provided with no obvious approach for the public

9

and could be seen from the ground floor only through a hole specially cut in the north wall of the entrance hall. The new Reading Room and book stacks completed by 1857 put the Department of Printed Books in a far better position than most of the other departments, which, as will appear later, were by this time desperately short of space.

Panizzi retired in 1866. He had shown himself to be a superb library administrator; he had transformed the British Museum library and laid down the lines along which not only this library but other great libraries were to develop. The momentum he supplied lasted the Museum three quarters of a century and the changes that took place in the next seventy years were largely developments of initiatives started by him.

In the meantime the collections of antiquities had been growing enormously both in bulk and in significance as the result of the excavations of a remarkably successful series of archaeologists: Sir Charles Fellows at Xanthus, the ancient capital of Lycia, and at other centres in Asia Minor in the 1830s and 1840s; Sir Henry Layard in Mesopotamia in the forties and Sir Charles Newton at Halicarnassus in the fifties. Through the efforts of these men the Museum acquired some of its best-known sculptures including the Nereid Monument, the Assyrian reliefs, the remains of the Tomb of Mausolus and the Demeter of Cnidus.

169

83, 170

The acquisition of such vast and varied collections underlined the need for a change in the internal organization of the Museum. Antiquities had originally been lumped together with 'natural productions' to form one of the three 'departments', the others being printed books and manuscripts. 'Antiquities' was made a separate department in 1807 but as time went on it became obviously too large and too all-embracing to provide efficient administration and desirable specialization. The retirement of Edward Hawkins, for thirty-four years the Keeper of this Department, provided, in 1860, the opportunity for change. The Department of Antiquities was split into three: Oriental Antiquities which comprised Egyptian and Assyrian, with British and Medieval and Ethnography; Greek and Roman; and Coins and Medals. The surprising association of British and Medieval with 'Oriental' antiquities was perhaps a reflection of Panizzi's belief that the British Museum should concern itself only with 'classical' antiquities, which he put before the Trustees in a report in 1857. As for ethnographical collections, including (to quote his recent biographer) 'not only the arts and crafts of primitive peoples, but also the treasures of the civilizations of China, India and the New World, all *that* could go anywhere, as long as he was no longer responsible for it'. Panizzi revised this opinion, however; and it was on his recommendation a matter of months before his retirement, that a new department of British and Medieval Antiquities and Ethnography was created. The brilliant Augustus Wollaston Franks was its first Keeper.

The Department of Natural History had earlier been divided: a Botanical Department being created in 1827 when the Banksian collections were incorporated and by 1857 there were also departments of Zoology, Palaeonto-logy and Mineralogy. A further development had taken place shortly after Panizzi's appointment as Principal Librarian: a new office of Superintendent of the Natural History departments had been created under the Principal Librarian. The first incumbent of this post, Richard Owen, lost no time in drawing attention to the growth of his collections and the difficulty of providing adequate space for their proper exhibition. The solution of the problem presented by the size and the growth of this part of the British Museum was the subject of heated debate for the two decades following Panizzi's appointment to the Principal Librarianship. He himself had long held the view that the scientific collections should be moved from Bloomsbury and he lost no opportunity of pressing it on the Trustees and on the government. It was not until 1878, well after Panizzi's retirement, that the final decision to transfer the natural history collections to South Kensington was taken and embodied in an Act of Parliament. The actual removal took place between 1880 and 1883. The exhibited natural history specimens were then removed from the King's Library and a selection of books, the basis of the so-called permanent exhibition, substituted for them.

The Museum's space problems were still further alleviated, for the moment, by the erection of the White Wing – so-called after the donor of the building-funds – in the south-east corner of the Museum site. This new building, opened in 1885, provided some gallery space, but more important it allowed office and student room space for the departments of Manuscripts, Oriental Manuscripts, British and Medieval Antiquities and Ethnography. No longer was it necessary for manuscripts to be sent into the main Reading Room for consultation.

The period which followed Panizzi's retirement was one of relatively peaceful consolidation and progress and scholarly work. The catalogue of the printed books in Western languages, which in its manuscript form had reached such gigantic proportions, was put into print between 1880 and 1905, the Subject Index of Modern Books coming into the library was initiated and good progress was made with the catalogues of manuscripts. With the Stowe manuscripts, bought in 1883, the Museum acquired many charters and such treasures as the eleventh-century Register of Hyde Abbey, a wardrobe book of Edward II and accounts of robes and jewels of Queen Elizabeth I. The vast collection of the Newcastle papers covering the period 1683 to 1826, given in 1886-9, was followed at intervals by those of other famous statesmen, including the Hardwickes, Fox, Canning, Liverpool, Peel, and Gladstone.

Systematic excavation in Egypt in the last quarter of the nineteenth century brought great masses of papyri to light. Of these the British Museum obtained its fair share, including some texts that had been completely lost, such as Aristotle on the Constitution of Athens, odes of Bacchylides, the mimes of Herodas and poems by Sappho. The first three of these were identified and edited for publication by Sir Frederic Kenyon who was later to be Director and Principal Librarian (the original title, Principal Librarian, had been enlarged about the turn of the century) from 1909 to 1931.

When Kenyon took office the Museum had recently taken the important step of out-housing its newspapers to a new building specially constructed at Colindale, one of the nearby suburbs of London. Sanction to make this move was obtained in 1902 by special Act of Parliament, and after 1905 all the British provincial newspapers published after 1800 were transferred. Originally no facilities were provided for reading the newspapers on the spot and for many years, until 1932, they were brought up to the Museum by weekly deliveries and consulted in the newspaper room. In 1932 the newspaper repository was enlarged and became the Newspaper Library, with its own special reading room and normal library services.

Kenyon inherited another building extension, the King Edward VII building, the foundation stone of which had been laid by the King in 1907.

This large building, on the north side of the Museum site, was planned as the first of a series of galleries to be built on the west, north and east sides of the existing building. This enterprise was never completed, and the properties on the west and east have now been scheduled against such development. The last state ceremony performed by King George V before the war of 1914–18 began, was to open the new building, which housed on its upper floor the exhibition gallery and students rooms of the Department of Prints and Drawings, on its mezzanine floor the workrooms of the Prints and Drawings, the printed Music collection and the map room, and on its main or ground floor an exhibition gallery for the British and Medieval Antiquities. Two floors below ground were used for book stacks and foreign newspapers.

No harm came to the Museum in the First World War; the smaller antiquities and the most precious printed books and manuscripts were first stored in base-ment rooms which had been converted into strong rooms, and later, when heavier bombs began to be used, they were evacuated to the new building of the National Library of Wales. Some especially important volumes were stored in the strong room of the house of Mr Dyson Perrins, the well-known collector, near Malvern, in Worcestershire.

The British Museum actually benefited materially, if indirectly, from the war, as a result of excavations made possible in Iraq. Shortly after the war, in 1919, the Museum undertook an archaeological expedition to a small site at Tell el Ubaid which revealed a third-millennium Sumerian temple and led on to the rich harvest of discoveries at Ur of the Chaldees relating to the rise of the Mesopotamian civilization in the period from the fourth millennium to the fourth century BC. The excavations at Ur were undertaken, under the joint sponsorship of the British Museum and the University of Pennsylvania, by a team lead by Leonard (afterwards Sir Leonard) Woolley, who had already assisted, with T. E. Lawrence, before the war, in the Museum excava-tions at Carchemish. They succeeded in unearthing the Sumerian royal graves, with their great wealth of objects in precious metals and precious stones.

94

81

76, 90,
97, 99

The growing congestion in the library which was again a characteristic of the period between the two World Wars, was alleviated by the piece-meal reconstruction of the 'iron-library', – the cast iron book stacks, built when the round Reading Room was constructed in the 1850s. This reconstruction, albeit only half completed, was to stand the Museum in good stead in the Second World War, when its modern steel and concrete stacks offered reassuring storage space for books evacuated from other more vulnerable parts of the library.

Gallery space was significantly increased by the generosity of Sir Joseph Duveen, later Lord Duveen, the great art-dealer, who provided a splendid new gallery for the more spacious display of the sculptures from the Parthenon. The design of the gallery was entrusted to an American architect, John Russell Pope, who had designed the Jefferson Memorial and the National Gallery of Art in Washington. His classical design, despite the criticism it has aroused, provides an effective milieu for the appreciation of these important pieces. The gallery was completed in 1938, but the onset of the war in 1939 delayed the installation of the sculptures, which, in the event, were not able to be arranged until 1962.

The 1930s were marked otherwise by some remarkable purchases, including the *Luttrell* and *Bedford Psalters*, the *Codex Sinaiticus* of the Greek Bible, the 184, 195 Chinese antiquities from the collection of George Eumorfopoulos and the controversial Ashley library of Thomas James Wise. In the purchase of these and many other valuable acquisitions the Museum was materially helped by the National Art Collections Fund and the Friends of the National Libraries, two bodies which continue to offer generous and timely help in important purchases.

Preparations for World War II were such that by the end of August 1939, all the objects of first importance that could be transported had been sent away out of London, or stored in an unused stretch of the London underground railway. The exceptions were the heavier stone sculptures which were left *in situ* protected by sandbags and blast walls. Later on, as the air-raids increased in intensity, the major part of the collections was stored under ninety feet of rock in fully controlled atmospheric conditions.

Direct hits on the Museum by high-explosive, fire and oil bombs, blast from nearby explosions and consequent exposure to the elements justified only too well the scattering of the collections. Nothing was lost or damaged of the collections that were dispersed. Of those that remained behind, the library, which remained in use throught the war, was the major casualty. Losses in printed books amounted to about 200,000 volumes with another 25,000 or 30,000 volumes of newspapers.

The building itself was grievously damaged and though the process of restoration and rehabilitation began immediately after the war ended and, as will be seen, considerable progress has been made, this complicated operation is still, in 1971, not completed. Priority was given to the restoration of the services of the Library, including the repair of the dome of the Reading Room, an extension of the students' room of the Department of Manuscripts and the rebuilding of that portion of the book stacks destroyed in 1941.

The Department of Coins and Medals which had been completely destroyed and without a home for fourteen years was rebuilt and opened again in 1959. The adjoining Greek and Roman Life room which had shared the fate of the Coin Room was also rebuilt and re-opened in 1960. The Department of British and Medieval Antiquities had to wait until the mid-sixties for the restoration of its four galleries devoted to the display of Prehistoric and Romano-British antiquities.

Whenever possible, the opportunity was taken during these rebuilding operations to provide new students' rooms, custom-built storage space, new offices and well-equipped workshops.

The Duveen Gallery, which should have been brought into use for the display of the sculptures from the Parthenon in 1939, remained semi-derelict for over twenty years after a direct hit by a small high-explosive bomb in 1940. Its rehabilitation and its opening in 1962 provided the opportunity to remodel the adjoining ground floor galleries, and to re-plan completely the exhibition of Greek and Roman antiquities. This remodelled exhibition was opened to

10

10 One of the newly opened and re-organized ground-floor rooms of the Department of Greek and Roman Antiquities

11 Winged *lamassu*, man-headed winged bulls, dominating the Khorsabad Entrance in the recently re-arranged Assyrian sculpture galleries

the public in 1969. A year later the adjoining sculpture galleries in the Department of Western Asiatic Antiquities made possible a strikingly re-designed exhibition of the fine Assyrian wall sculptures.

As a result of this same rebuilding operation, the Museum has been provided, for the first time in its history, with a well-equipped, though small, public lecture hall.

The recent acquisition by the Museum of the former Civil Service Commission building in Burlington Gardens for the accommodation and display of its very fine, but multitudinous ethnographical collections at last provides space to display and study these important objects in a worthy manner. These collections which had been administratively attached over the years to various unrelated departments, ending as part of the Department of Oriental Antiquities and Ethnography in 1933, were finally made into an independent department in 1946. Oriental Antiquities became at the same time a separate department, bringing together under one administration the antiquities, sculptures, ceramics, prints and paintings of the Far East. The Department of Egyptian and Assyrian Antiquities was divided into two departments in 1955, dealing respectively

11

LIVERPOOL JOHN MOORES UNIVERSITY
LEARNING SERVICES

with Egyptian and Western Asiatic Antiquities. In 1969 another new department was created by separating Prehistoric and Post-Roman Antiquities from the Department of British and Medieval Antiquities.

A word in conclusion about finance and the recent changes in the constitution of the Museum. The general maintenance, involving both upkeep and a measure of current acquisitions, has from the beginning been financed by public money voted by Parliament. The first year such a grant was made, 1762, the sum voted was £2,000: currently the annual grant is well over £2 million, with a further sum also over £2 million spent for Museum purposes by the former Ministry of Public Building and Works (now part of the Department of the Environment) and the Stationery Office. The Museum's funds for acquisitions have, however, been materially aided by two benefactions made since the war, which have dwarfed all previous donations. The first was the result of a gift followed by a legacy, from Mr T. P. Brooke Sewell, given for the purpose of augmenting the collections illustrating the arts of India and the Far East; the will of George Bernard Shaw was responsible for the second. Under it the British Museum became the legatee of one third of Shaw's residuary estate, which has happily been swollen by royalties from Shaw's plays, including *My Fair Lady*. These two munificent gifts have enabled the Museum to make many important purchases during the last fifteen years. Happily the Museum is still the recipient of many remarkable gifts. To instance only two: in 1959 the outstanding Ilbert collection of clocks and watches was acquired for the Museum by Mr Gilbert Edgar through the Worshipful Company of Clockmakers and in 1968 Mr Henry Davis deposited in the Museum his superb collection of bookbindings.

Changes of great significance have taken place in the last few years. The British Museum Act of 1963, replacing all the previous Acts of Parliament under which the Museum had been administered since its foundation, changed the composition of the Trustee body, as has been indicated above, widened the Museum's power of lending and made it possible for it to outhouse the collections so as to permit the new Natural Science and Reference Library, formed by incorporating the former Patent Office Library into the British Museum Library, to be housed temporarily outside the present Museum building. In 1972, by the British Library Act, the collections of printed books, maps and music, the manuscripts and the oriental printed books and manuscripts were separated from the antiquities and the prints and drawings, and together with the British National Bibliography (hitherto a non-profit company), the National Central Library and the National Lending Library went to form the new British Library under a new British Museum Board. This important development is linked with plans for a new and separate building for the Library, to be constructed on a site immediately to the south of the present building, leaving the present building, except for the King's Library, for the Department of Antiquities.

FRANK FRANCIS

THE DEPARTMENTS

CHAPTER ONE

Coins and Medals

The Department of Coins and Medals, which had previously been grouped with Manuscripts and then Antiquities, was formed into an independent department of the British Museum in 1861. Unlike the other departments of antiquities, its collections are defined not by cultural frontiers but by the nature of the objects, totalling half a million specimens, and including not only all kinds of coined money but other cognate objects (medals, counters, etc.), yet excluding primitive money and banknotes. The main divisions of the collec-tion, with a very brief mention of some of the outstanding sources, are as follows:

1. The coinages of ancient Greece and Rome. Among the most important sources were: the Cracherode bequest (1799); the Payne Knight bequest of Greek coins (1824); H. P. Borrell, Count de Salis, Edward Wigan, Duc de Blacas, James Woodhouse, all in the nineteenth century; and in the twentieth century, Richard Seager, John Mavrogordato, J. W. E. Pearce and notably A. H. Lloyd's Greek coins of Italy and Sicily (1946).

2. The medieval and modern coinages of Europe and of the world as a whole; the British material is especially complete. The Sloane and Cotton cabinets formed the basis in 1753, and the unceasing growth of the collection can be seen in many notable accessions from then until now – the Royal collection presented by King George IV (1823); the Bank of England collection (1877); the British historical medals of Edward Hawkins (1860); the Banks sisters, C. B. Roberts, Sir Augustus Franks, Dr F. Parkes Weber, J. Weightman, T. G. Barnett, Helen Farquar, L. A. Lawrence, R. C. Lockett; and the T. B. Clarke-Thornhill bequest (1935) specially important for continental coins. Much important material for British, as well as for Roman coins has come from finds of Treasure Trove.

3. The Oriental section including coinages of China and the Far East, of the Islamic world, and especially of India. Notable acquisitions were those of: William Marsden (1834); the India Office (1882); General Sir Alexander Cunningham, Director-General of the Archaeological Survey of India (1893); R. B. Whitehead (1922); and, among many others, Pandit Baghavanlal Indraji, Nelson Wright, Sir Richard Burn and General H. L. Haughton.

GREECE AND ROME

Greek coinage forms the prototype in one way or another for the whole develop-ment of coinage in the Western tradition, and is of the greatest intrinsic import-

12 Some of the earliest coins of the sixth century BC. *Left,* an electrum stater of Phanes, of Ephesus (?); *centre,* an electrum stater of Smyrna (?), *right,* a silver tetradrachm of Acanthus. All have incuse punches on the reverse

ance for its high aesthetic qualities, reflecting every stage in the evolution of Greek art.

These first coins (*c.* 650/600 BC) – whether invented by Greeks or Lydians – were made from small nuggets of electrum (a natural gold-silver alloy) and display a number of different simple heraldic designs on one side only, probably representing personal or civic badges. One of these has the type of a stag with an inscription 'I am the badge of Phanes', thus certainly a personal signet; the connection between the cutting of dies for coining and the cutting of gems as signets was, in any case, an intimate one on technical grounds alone. Another such electrum coin, possibly struck at Smyrna, shows a fierce and impressive lion's head. These early examples stand at the head of a tradition of coinage typical of the east Greek cities of Cyzicus, Phocaea and Mytilene, as well as of the Lydians and Persians. The same kind of single-sided coin, whose reverse side shows only the mark of a punch, was taken up in the sixth century for the minting of silver coins with civic emblems, the first mints being those of Aegina, Athens and Corinth. The Macedonian region was specially rich in silver-mines and there the mint of Acanthus produced an outstanding series of silver tetradrachms (four-drachma pieces) showing a group of a lion attacking a bull, powerfully rendered. The technique of the die-cutter soon extended to the reverse side with a second design, one of the earliest examples of which comes

from Athens on a tetradrachm minted *c*. 520 BC. The helmeted head of the   13
goddess Athena is balanced by the appearance on the reverse of her sacred bird
the owl, with a short inscription to indicate the name of the city. This, or a
similar formula, was to become the classic arrangement for most Greek coins.

By the late sixth century the minting of coins had become widespread not only
in Greece itself but also in the western part of the Greek world. In some of the
cities of southern Italy a somewhat peculiar technique of minting was invented
(perhaps by Pythagoras) where the reverse is conceived as a mirror-image in
intaglio of the obverse in relief; a typical example from Metapontum shows the   13
city's emblem, a corn-ear, rendered in this way.

In Sicily, at Syracuse and other important cities, the art of coinage developed
so strongly as to surpass that of all other regions of the Greek world, and it is
clear that this art was highly thought of by the Greeks themselves. So much so
that, for a time at the end of the fifth century, we find numerous artists' signatures on the coins of Sicily, preserving the names of Kimon, Exakestidas,
Myron, Euainetos and others and enabling us to distinguish individual styles.
The earlier coins, however, are never signed, and the name of the creator of one
of the early masterpieces of Sicilian coinage, the so-called 'Demareteion'   14

13 *Above,* an archaic style silver tetradrachm of Athens, *c.* 520 BC; *below,* a silver didrachm of
Metapontum, in southern Italy, *c.* 500 BC

14 Silver decadrachms of Syracuse. *Above,* the so-called 'Demareteion', *c.* 479 BC (or later); *below,* a later example of *c.* 400 BC. The reverse type, the head of Arethusa, is signed under the bust by the die-engraver, EYAINE = Euainetos

14

15

decadrachm of Syracuse, is quite unknown. The head, rendered with extreme sensitivity, is that of the fountain goddess Arethusa and on the other side is a four-horse chariot, one of the hall-marks of the Sicilian coinage reflecting the many Olympic victories won by Sicilians. A later version of this decadrachm design, from the end of the fifth century, shows the chariot in full career with the goddess of victory hovering above and, in a panel below, a panoply of arms; the Arethusa head, of rich and subtle style, is signed by Euainetos below. Another masterpiece, though of earlier date, *c.* 460 BC, is the tetradrachm of Naxos with the head of Dionysos retaining a trace of the 'archaic smile' and a boldly composed reverse showing a squatting satyr holding a wine-cup, executed with truly sculptural firmness and vigour and with cunning fore-shortenings.

During the fifth and fourth centuries, coin artists began to experiment with designs in depth, and this resulted particularly in renderings of the head in a frontal pose. Deriving inspiration perhaps from some Sicilian examples, an unknown artist at Amphipolis in the early fourth century produced an Apollo head which is a splendid and expressive example of this genre, contrasting with the austere geometric reverse showing a race-torch and the name of the city as a frame. Another splendid figure composition is the group of Herakles grappling with the Nemean lion on the reverse of a didrachm of Heracleia in Italy, a dynamic grouping which would look well in a temple metope and which recalls the dictum of François Lenormant, the nineteenth-century French numismatist, that the finest Greek coins seem almost like fragments of the Parthenon frieze. The obverse is a splendid head of Athena wearing a helmet decorated with a figure of Skylla hurling a rock.

A development in Greek coins which was to be of major significance was the advent of the human portrait in place of the head of a god or goddess. The first fine example we have is the head, not indeed of a Greek, but of the Persian satrap Tissaphernes, shown wearing the typical Persian head-dress, a fine and dignified yet individualized head. The reverse is copied from the owl of an Athenian coin, yet the inscription is not of Athens but of the king of Persia (*Bas* = Basileos). This unique specimen, so important for the history of the art of Greek coinage, was acquired by the Museum in 1947 with a number of the ordinary Athenian coins which had all been found together in southern Turkey. It was probably made by a Greek artist at Miletus in 411 BC. Portraiture, however, did not become a regular feature of Greek coins until after the time of Alexander, who in his lifetime organized a new and far-flung system of mints to produce his imperial currency bearing the head of Herakles. Portraits of Alexander appeared only after his death, when the coinage of Lysimachus

16

16

16

17

15 Silver tetradrachm of Naxos, Sicily, *c.* 461 BC

16 *Above, left,* silver tetradrachm of Amphipolis, *c.* 380 BC; *left,* silver didrachm of Heracleia, *c.* 370 BC; *above,* silver tetradrachm of Tissaphernes, *c.* 411 BC

17 Silver tetradrachms of, *above,* Lysimachus with the portrait of Alexander, *c.* 290 BC; *centre,* Antimachus, *c.* 180 BC, and, *below,* Mithradates VI of Pontus

18 Celtic gold staters: *top row,* the Bellovaci, *c.* 100 BC (obv. and rev.); the Aulerci Eburocives, first century BC (obv.); *centre row,* the Catuvellauni, first century BC (obv. and rev.); the Treviri, first century BC; *bottom row,* Cunobelinus, first century AD (obv. and rev.); the Coritani, first century AD (obv.)

established the classic type of the great Macedonian conqueror in the guise of a god, with the ram's horn of Ammon growing from his brow. Alexander's heroic and passionate nature are finely expressed in this coin, which was produced at the mint of Pergamon. The reverse shows Athena enthroned with victory poised on her hand.

The coins of the Hellenistic period provide us with a long series of excellent portrait heads of most of the individual rulers of the kingdoms, the Ptolemies in Egypt, the Seleucids in Asia, the kings of Pergamon, and even those of Sparta and of Syracuse. Arguably, however, it is from the most easterly of all the regions settled by Greeks, from Bactria (northern Afghanistan), that we have some of the best of all ancient portraits. Of these, none is finer than the head of Antimachus (early second century BC) shown wearing the *kausia*, a traditional Macedonian cap; the face quivers with life and is rendered with great psychological penetration; the reverse is a figure of Poseidon. The survival of an art of portraiture of this calibre on the coins compensates somewhat for the almost total loss of the history of the Bactrian Greeks. Again, a number of fine and distinctive portraits, often evidently by Greek artists, are to be seen on the coins of such kingdoms as Bithynia, Cappadocia, Armenia and Pontus. That of, for instance, Mithradates VI of Pontus, is a supreme example of the

17

17

19 *Left and centre*, Etruscan coins of *c.* 400–300 BC, they all have smooth blank reverses; *right*, Roman Republican gold coin (obv. and rev.), of the late third century BC

later art of the Pergamene school, well expressing the romantic yet ruthless personality of a ruler who for a time shook the Roman power in Asia Minor. The reverse of this coin shows a stag, probably as the emblem of Ephesus, one of Mithradates' bases.

Ultimately the Greek art of coinage blends into that of the Roman empire, but there should be mentioned here an extraordinary offshoot from Greek prototypes which occurred among the Celtic peoples of Gaul and northern Europe, including Britain. From the prototype of the gold stater of Philip II of Macedonia, showing a purely classical head of Apollo and a horse-chariot, there evolved on the Celtic coins a strange series of deformations, tending towards abstraction. The whole subject of the Celtic coinages and their morphology is a fascinating one, and the Museum has a specially rich collection of the coins minted in Britain, many of them from the collection of Sir John Evans.

In central Italy, the Etruscans anticipated the Romans in minting a coinage of gold and silver, inspired by Greek models, between the fifth and the third century BC. The coins are strange, having smooth blank reverses unlike Greek coins, and the designs include a lion's head, a human head, a gorgon, each with accompanying marks of value (50, 25, etc.). Many aspects of the earlier Etruscan coinage, its chronology and places of mintage, remain obscure. An indigenous style of currency consisting of large bronze pieces was also used by the later Etruscans at Volaterrae, as also by the Romans. One of the first Roman coins, of the early third century BC, is the large bronze bar (the *aes*

18

19

20

36

20 Obverse and reverse of a Roman bronze bar (*aes signatum*), 15 cm. long and weighing 1,746 gm.

21 *Left to right*, a gold stater of Flamininus, *c.* 196 BC; silver denarii of: the Roman Republic; Julius Caesar, *c.* 44 BC, and Brutus, 43/2 BC

signatum) cast with the form of a sow on one side and on the other an elephant, which seems to allude to the elephants brought to Italy by Pyrrhus. Regular coinage seems, however, to have begun with the use of heavy cast bronze pieces (the 'as') of a more money-like form, in combination with a silver coinage of purely Greek type derived from the Greek colonies in southern Italy. Before the end of the third century, the bronze currency had been reduced to a more manageable size. An exceptional issue of gold coins shows the head of Janus and, on the reverse, two warriors taking an oath over the body of a pig; the precise occasion of the issue cannot yet be determined with certainty.

The first portrait coin, minted by T. Quinctius Flamininus, the conqueror of Greece in 196 BC, was an exceptional one struck in Macedonia, and effectively a Greek coin, with the reverse type of Alexander the Great. In spite of the Roman tradition of preserving ancestral images, it was not until the first century BC that portraits are to be found on the coins. During the later

19

21

22 Imperial Roman gold aurei of: *left,* Claudius, AD 41/2; *centre,* Hadrian, AD 125; and *right,* Carausius, AD 287–93

Republic, when the denarius coinage began to reflect current events, we have portraits such as that of Julius Caesar, wearing his well-known laurel wreath, on a coin of the early months of 44 BC, and with priestly emblems on the reverse. In the next two years a mint in Greece produced portraits of the assassin Brutus, whose reverse, showing the cap of liberty and the daggers, proclaims unmistakeably the events of the Ides of March. Other coin portraits included those of the Pompeys and the triumvirs. With the final establishment of Augustus as supreme ruler, the effigy of the emperor and of other members of the imperial house became the normal type for the obverse of all coins, affording a rich store of iconographical detail which is of the highest historical interest.

The gold coinage of the early empire was typified by the contents of a hoard discovered in 1957 at Bredgar in Kent; it included coins from Julius Caesar up to Claudius, the reigning emperor, and clearly must have been buried soon after the Roman invasion of Britain in AD 43. The reverse of one of Claudius' coins shows a schematized picture of the Praetorian camp in Rome where the emperor had taken refuge in his first days. A later gold coin, of the time of Hadrian and issued between AD 125 and 128, shows on the reverse the legendary wolf suckling Romulus and Remus, a favourite type on Roman coins at all periods. But it was perhaps the bronze coinage which, under the empire, attained the greatest scope for elaborate compositions and artistic expression. A bronze medallion of Marcus Aurelius, struck while he was still Caesar in the time of Antoninus Pius (AD 158–9), gives not only a portrait which is rendered with the greatest sensitivity but also a reverse which is an excellent example of the complex pictorial and spatial compositions created by the Roman engravers; its subject seems to be Neptune, the sea-god, standing before the walls of Troy, his foot resting on the prow of a galley.

After the comparative peace of the Antonine age, the unstable third century produced a rapid succession of ephemeral emperors, some of whom set up

23 Bronze medallion of Marcus Aurelius, AD 158/9. The reverse shows Neptune, his foot on a galley's prow, before the walls of Troy

what were, in effect, separate empires. One of these, who is of special interest in Britain, and whose coins are specially well represented in the Museum's collection, was Carausius, whose dominion, centred on southern Britain and the Channel, lasted only from AD 287 to 293. One of his gold coins struck at the mint of London depicts him in regular imperial style, although he was a rebel against the legitimate emperor, and the reverse shows a figure of Jupiter holding the thunderbolt, and the mint mark of London ML (Moneta Londin‑iensis).

    The ultimate restoration of imperial unity under Diocletian and Constantine gave a fresh impulse to the standardization of the coinage, which was now minted on an absolutely uniform pattern at a large number of mints in every quarter of the empire, becoming in the process a more truly imperial coinage than it had ever been. The appearance of the coins now begins to acquire a stylized and hieratic character that is fully in accord with that of late Roman art and which seems to foreshadow the style of the Byzantine period. A gold medallion of Constantine the Great minted at Thessalonica shows the first Christian emperor wearing the *tunica palmata* and *toga picta*, and holding the globe and sceptre. Among the issues of his successors, there is a gold piece of Constantius II minted at Antioch whose reverse shows a chariot depicted in the strange perspective of the late‑antique, and in it the emperor who stands scattering largesse to the people. Another gold coin of the same emperor shows his portrait, wearing helmet and armour, with spear and shield, in a semi‑frontal pose which was to be increasingly adopted for the imperial effigy in the later Byzantine coinage. Perhaps most impressive, however, is a silver medallion, again of Constantius II, minted at Siscia to celebrate his twentieth anniversary as emperor; here we seem to have the quintessence of the later imperial style, in which the ruler attains an overwhelming and almost super‑human majesty of form.

22

24

24

24

24

24 Coins of the Late Empire; *above left,* a gold medallion of
Constantine I, AD 307–37; *below left and right,* coins of Con-
stantius II, a gold multiple solidus, a gold solidus and a silver
medallion

25 *Right,* a gold solidus of John Zimisces,
AD 969–76; *left,* a gold augustale of
Frederick II, AD 1220–50

MEDIEVAL AND MODERN EUROPE

After the fall of the Roman empire in the West, coinage of a sub-Roman
type forms a transition to the Middle Ages. In Britain, a new stage began with
King Offa of Mercia (757–796). His extraordinary and unique gold dinar
recalls relations between Christian Europe and the Islamic world, and consists
of a close copy of a dinar of the Caliph Al-Mansur, on one side of which is
superimposed the king's name. It is more important, however, that in Offa's
reign began the regular coinage of the silver penny, the typical early medieval
coin of all Europe: on the specimen shown, a finely executed portrait of the
king is complemented by a reverse whose design works the name of the moneyer
Eadhun into a semi-cruciform pattern. Offa's coinage has, artistically speaking,
few successors and many of the Saxon designs in subsequent reigns were purely
epigraphic, as were those of many coins of Charlemagne and other rules on
the Continent. A later penny, of Harold II, minted at Chichester, shows that
the art of portraiture was however by no means lost: though later the typical
English penny, the 'sterling' so widely copied in Europe, displayed a conventional facing effigy of the king entirely lacking individuality.

Meanwhile, in Constantinople, the classical tradition continued and
developed: a tenth-century solidus of John Zimisces (972–976) shows the
facing bust of the emperor being crowned by the Virgin, with the hand of
God above: on the reverse is the figure of Christ Pantokrator which evokes
the typical mosaics of Byzantine church architecture. Byzantine tradition in

26

26

26

25

26 Anglo-Saxon coins. *Left,* a gold dinar of Offa, AD 757–96; *centre,* a silver penny of Offa; *right,* a silver penny of Harold II, 1066

coinage became apparent in other parts of the Balkans such as Serbia, as well as at Venice. A consciously classical revival is to be seen in the gold 'august-ales' of the emperor Frederick II minted in southern Italy (1198–1250); here the ruler is depicted very much in the manner of the later Roman emperors wearing a laurel wreath, while on the reverse is the imperial eagle.   25

The development of commerce led, in the thirteenth century, to the institution of larger silver coins (the French 'gros') as well as the beginning of gold coinage, notably at Florence and at Venice. In England there was an isolated gold issue by Henry III in 1290, but here gold became regular only in the time of Edward III, from 1344 onwards. The style of the finest medieval gold coins   27 is typically French-Gothic and full of rich and crowded detail. In England the most important was the 'noble', showing the king armed, in a ship, a design supposed to proclaim English naval supremacy as a result of the battle of Sluys in 1340. The reverse is a cruciform composition of great sophistication, crowns and fleur-de-lis alternating with heraldic leopards. Similar reverses appear on the coins minted for the English kings in their French domains, with a variety of obverse types all in the French manner—the heraldic leopard; the 'chaise' showing the king enthroned; the 'guiennois' where the king in armour stands below a Gothic canopy, and the 'pavillion' of the Black Prince, whose graceful figure stands in an even more elaborate architectural setting. The two latter coins were from the mint of La Rochelle.

27 *Left*, a gold noble of Edward III, 1327–77 (obv. and rev.); *centre and right, below*, Anglo-Gallic gold of Edward III—a Leopard, Chaise and Guiennois; *right, above*, Anglo-Gallic gold of the Black Prince, 1330–76

28 Bronze medal of John Palaeologus, by Pisanello, 1438

29 Bronze medal of Henry VIII, by Schwartz

30 *Above*, a silver testone of Galeazzo Maria Sforza, 1468–76; (obv. and rev.); *below*, a silver shilling of Henry VII, 1485–1509 (obv. and rev.)

The fourteenth century was surely the high point of the Gothic style in coinage. In the following century however the Italian Renaissance saw the invention of the portrait medal. It was in 1438 that Pisanello created the first example of this genre, on the occasion of the visit to Italy of the Byzantine emperor, John Palaeologus. It is cast in bronze, and the realism of the portrait and of the equestrian group on the reverse is typical of the sculptural style in which Pisanello worked, and which thereby established the medal as a distinct art-form. The influence of this new art was soon to be felt in the coinage, and in the same century we have, for instance, masterly portrait coins of the dukes of Milan executed by Caradosso: our example shows Galeazzo Maria Sforza (1468–76) with a reverse of a fantastic helmet surmounting the Sforza arms. The new impulse reached England in the time of Henry VII (1485–1509); his portrait, on a testoon designed by Alexander of Bruchsal, is a masterpiece which sets a quite new style for the English coinage and gradually replaces the older Gothic designs. The invention of larger silver coins, notably the thaler and its equivalents in the later fifteenth century, afforded ever greater opportunities to the designer and encouraged the assimilation of the coin and the medal both in conception and technique.

Among the medals of the sixteenth century some outstanding pieces were made by Albrecht Dürer, one being the portrait of an unknown woman dated 1514, the original stone model of which is preserved at Chemnitz. Another German artist, Hans Schwartz, was responsible for one of the finest of all medallic portraits from the Tudor period, that of Henry VIII. Neither this nor the previous medal have any reverse. A very different style is to be seen in a gold medallion of Elizabeth I, made to commemorate the best-known event in English sixteenth-century history, the defeat of the Spanish Armada in 1588. The rich and florid detail of the queen's dress is as minutely rendered as in the paintings of the time and, indeed, a smaller and slightly different version of

28

30

30

29

31

31 *Above,* a gold Armada medal of Elizabeth I, 1588; *below,* a gold medal of Charles I, by Briot, 1633

this medal has been ascribed to Nicholas Hillyard, the miniature painter. These medallions, on the reverse of which is shown the impregnable island fortress, symbolized by a bay-tree struck by lightning yet unharmed, were made for presentation to naval officers and other notables.

In the following century, a gold medal was struck to commemorate the return of Charles I to London after his Scottish coronation in 1633. This was executed by the French artist Nicolas Briot, formerly chief engraver at the French mint; it displays the king on horseback, a more spirited equestrian

31

composition than that which appears on the silver coins of his reign, with the eye of Providence above and a plumed helmet lying among the flowers below. On the reverse is a fascinating panoramic view of old London, showing St Paul's cathedral, London bridge and the Traitors' Gate as they were before the Great Fire of 1666, and even such details as swans and boats on the Thames.

The most far-reaching innovation affecting the coinage was the application of new types of minting machinery, first experimented with in England in Elizabeth's time but only regularly established in the mid-seventeenth century. The older coins had been made by hand-hammering, the new were made in a mill press. The new milled coin is typified by the silver crown pattern pieces designed in 1656 by the greatest of English engravers, Thomas Simon; these show the portrait of the Protector Cromwell, in a rich yet restrained Baroque style that achieves a great degree of sculptural depth within a very shallow plane of actual relief. The portrait is well set off by the crowned shield on the reverse; the edge of the coin is marked with a Latin inscription. This coin, though

32

32 A silver pattern crown of Cromwell, by Simon, 1658; *below*, a silver thaler of Karl VI, by Thibaud, struck at Augsburg, 1740

approved, was never put into circulation, but in all its general characteristics it is typical of the style and quality of coinage henceforth both in England and elsewhere. The comparative economy of statement which can be seen in the Cromwell coin is in strong contrast to some of the more elaborate and quasi-medallic pieces issued elsewhere in Europe, as for instance in parts of Germany during the eighteenth century. A silver thaler of the mint of Augsburg struck in 1740 during the reign of the emperor Karl VI, has a reverse of an extremely pictorial character and an astonishing sense of space; in the distance are seen the towers of Augsburg while in the foreground the composition is focussed on the symbol of the Reichsapfel on an elaborate plinth, with figures of a male and a female river god posed beside it. This *tour de force* was the work of Jonas Thibaud whose initials I.T. are shown below the grandiose bust of the Emperor.

Contrasting with these examples from the main stream of European coinage there is a large gold piece struck at Venice in the time of the last of the Doges, Lodovico Manin (1789–97). It is a piece of ten zecchini, on the obverse of which we see the Doge kneeling to receive a standard from St Mark, while on the reverse is depicted Christ in glory surrounded by an oval mandorla set with stars. Though the style is extremely free and belongs to the eighteenth century, the types are an amazing example of the survival of coin designs, since these are virtually unchanged from their introduction on the first gold coins of Venice minted by Giovanni Dandolo in 1284.

Finally, the age of the neo-classic revival has left one of the finest of all coin designs of any period in history, that of the English sovereign. This is the St George and the dragon reverse conceived by Benedetto Pistrucci towards the end of the reign of George III. The vigour and delicacy of this masterly com-

32

33

34

33 Venetian gold 10-zecchini piece of Ludovico Manin, 1797

34 Gold £5-piece of George III, 1820, with Pistrucci's St George and the dragon reverse

position have never been equalled or surpassed in the whole range of coinage of the world. The specimen shown is a £5-piece dated 1820 which, though a regular coin, was not issued owing to the death of the king.

ORIENTAL COINAGES

In antiquity, the Greek tradition of coinage was essentially the one followed and adapted by many non-Greek peoples, often using their own language and script for the inscriptions. Thus we have distinctive coins of, for instance, the Achaemenids and Parthians in Iran, of the Phoenicians and of Carthage, the Iberians, the Jews, and even a unique coin of Egypt similar to the Athenian type but inscribed with demotic characters (fourth century BC). Other copies of Athenian coins were made by the Sabaean and Himyarite Arabs using a South Arabian script ancestral to modern Ethiopic.

Quite independently of the classical tradition began the indigenous currency of India, though not so early as the Vedic age, as used to be supposed. In fact, about the fifth to fourth century BC, it seems, bars of silver stamped with simple designs were made, and these developed, in the time of Ashoka and the Mauryas, into the more complex 'punch-marked' coins stamped with multiple devices. Similar devices adorned the copper coins of local tribes at a later date (second to first century BC). A decisive influence on the coins, as on the art, of India was exercised by the Greeks of the Hellenistic age: a unique bilingual tetradrachm of Demetrius II (early second century BC) has a purely Greek portrait and inscription to which is added a reverse with a figure of Zeus with the same inscription rendered in Kharoshthi. The square shape of a bilingual coin of Apollodotus I is typically Indian, as are the types of elephant and bull. Later, perhaps in the first century AD, a unique gold coin was minted at Pushkalavati (near Peshawar) with a female figure who is named as the divinity of that city

35

35

35

47

35 Early Indian coins. *Centre, above,* a punch-marked coin of the third century BC; *left,* a silver, bilingual, tetradrachm of Demetrius II, second century BC; *centre, below,* a silver, bilingual, drachm of Apollodotus I, second century BC; *right,* a gold coin of Pushkalavati, first century AD

and as Amba, consort of Siva, while on the reverse is the bull of Siva with the Greek legend *tauros*. The image of Siva with the bull is seen on the reverse of a double-aureus of the Kushan emperor Vima Kadphises (first-second century 36 AD), whose portrait is that of the divine king, with sacred radiance shown by the flames at his shoulder, emerging from the clouds of heaven. Other Kushan coins reflect Graeco-Roman influences, but in the later coins of the Gupta dynasty there is a profusion of pictorial compositions in purely Indian style, as for instance the lion-slaying king, of Candragupta II (AD 380-414) and the 36 god Karttikeya riding his peacock, of Kumaragupta (AD 414-55). The splendid gold coins of the Kushano-Sassanian rulers of Bactria show an interesting mixture of styles; thus a coin of Vaharan (third century AD) renders 36 both the standing figure of the king and also Siva with the bull in distinctly Iranian guise. The pure style of the Sassanian coins in Iran is well shown by the drachm of Sapur I (AD 241-72) where we see the Zoroastrian fire-altar with 37 attendant priests and the effigy of the king wearing a turretted crown surmounted by a globe.

The rise of Islam in the seventh century AD was a decisive event in the history of coinage. The earlier phases attest the interaction of the new civilization with

36 *Left*, a Kushan gold coin of Vima Kadphises, second century AD; *centre,* a Kushano-Sassanian gold coin of Vahran, third century AD; *right, above and below,* Gupta gold coins of Candragupta II, *c.* AD 400 and of Kumaragupta, *c.* AD 440

37 *Above,* a Sassanian silver coin of Sapur I, AD 241-72; *below,* an Islamic silver dirhem struck at Cordova, AD 771

38 *Left, above,* Indian gold coin of Jaunpur, 1475; *left, below,* gold coin of Lahore, 1607; *centre,* Mogul gold coin of Jahangir, 1605–27; *right,* Turkish silver *altmyslyk* of Mahmud II, 1808–39

that of Byzantium, and coins were sometimes made showing the Caliph in the guise of a Byzantine emperor; in Iran the Arabs adopted the existing Sassanian style. A thorough reform of the coinage by the Caliph Abd-al-Malik in AD 696 gave expression to the essentially iconoclastic and anti-representational taste of the Arabs, and all representational types were thereafter abolished from the coinage, which became devoted entirely to elaborate epigraphic designs, often of great intrinsic beauty, giving the place of mintage and date by the Hejira of Mohammad (AD 622), with quotations from the Koran: 'There is no god but Allah alone and he has no peer.' The imperial sweep and range of this new coinage is truly impressive, almost identical specimens being minted at a number of mints between Baghdad and Al-Andalus (Cordova in Spain). An example of the Ummayads of Spain shows the date AH 155 (AD 771). The aniconic, purely epigraphic style of the Islamic coinage was maintained with very few exceptions, and was copied even by certain Christian European rulers such as the Normans in Sicily and the Crusaders in Palestine who used the Arabic formulae to express Christian doctrine.

37

 The spread of Islam to Central Asia and to India opened up a vast new development of coinage of fundamentally the same kind. On a gold mohur of the kingdom of Jaunpur, minted for Husein Shah in AH 870 (AD 1475) the beautiful abstract pattern is an elaborated *tugra* or monogram of the ruler's name. The coinage of the Mogul empire in India conformed mostly to the traditional aniconic style, often elaborated with richly engraved patterns of lettering, as on a coin of Jahangir minted at Lahore in 1607. It is startling to see tradition suddenly abandoned when the same ruler struck a series of mohurs showing the signs of the Zodiac, and still more those which have

38

38

realistic portraits of himself holding a wine-cup, in allusion to his own very uncanonical tastes. A more traditional, though distinctive, line was pursued by the Ottomans in Turkey, on whose coins the dense epigraphy is relieved by devoting more space to a *tugra* with striking and graceful effect, as on a silver *altmyslyk* of Mahmud II (AD 1808–39).

38

The oldest of all the original traditions of coinage in Asia was, however, that of China, where the earliest coins are reckoned to be of the Chou dynasty (1122–255 BC), though the actual dates are often obscure. Chinese coinage in its primitive forms furnishes virtually the only example of a currency where actual objects previously used for barter were reproduced in bronze as money: thus we have the knife-money and spade-money (or *Pu*). Perhaps as early as the sixth century BC there began to be developed a form of round money with a central hole (the 'cash') and inscribed with characters – a type which survived longer than any other in the whole history of coinage, since it was still in use in the time of Kuang Hsü (AD 1875–1909).

39

G. K. JENKINS

39 Chinese coins ranging from the knife money of the ninth century BC (?) to the 10-cash piece of Kuang Hsü, AD 1875–1909

CHAPTER TWO

Egyptian Antiquities

At the time when the Museum was founded there was no lack of learned interest in ancient Egypt although the sources of information on the subject were limited. The main descriptions of the history, geography and religion came from classical authors such as Herodotus, Diodorus, Pliny and Plutarch. The only monuments which most Europeans would have seen were the obelisks and a few statues brought to Italy by the Roman emperors, some of which were discovered in Hadrian's Villa at Tivoli early in the eighteenth century. Travellers' accounts of modern Egypt helped to give an idea of the architecture and art of the ancients. Ludvig Norden was one of the first people to illustrate a journey through Egypt in 1737. In the same year Richard Pococke was also there making plans and drawings of ancient Egyptian temples. Both these travellers were founder members of the Egyptian Society in London whose purpose was to study Egyptian antiquities. Interest in deciphering hieroglyphs never waned. During the eighteenth century scholars were influenced by the work of Athanasius Kircher who had published his theories between 1652 and 1676. They were largely mistaken but provoked considerable discussion which gained in momentum until the actual decipherment in 1822. Until the hieroglyphs had been deciphered no all-round picture of ancient Egypt could be obtained. This is both the strength and the weakness of Egyptological studies, in that so much of what is known comes from the writings of the Egyptians themselves and not from external commentary.

Collecting antiquities began to become fashionable but collectors were not numerous, and Sir Hans Sloane, whose collection formed the nucleus of the British Museum, was one of an élite circle. He owned two hundred and fifty bronze and terracotta figures, ushabtis, scarabs and small pieces of sculpture. Travellers began to collect antiquities during the early part of the nineteenth century, and later scholars started to build up national collections for their own countries. The only control in Egypt was exercised by the Khedive who granted permits for excavation, but it was also necessary to enlist the help of local officials who quickly learnt to play off one searcher against another. There was no ban on the removal of antiquities until 1858 when Auguste Mariette set up the Antiquities Service, which became the only body allowed to excavate. In 1881, with his death, the policy changed and the Antiquities Service granted permits for excavation to many foreign expeditions. Illicit digging and chance finds brought many objects on to the market and it was

61

possible to form large collections. This situation lasted until after the Second World War, when private collecting in this country almost ceased. At the present, the only legitimate source of new material is from permitted excavation, following which the finds are divided between the Antiquities Service and the excavator.

Sir Hans Sloane's original collection was augmented during the next fifty years by gifts of mummies and coffins from the Lethieullier brothers and from the collections of the Earl of Bute, Edward Wortley Montagu and William Hamilton (who had supervised the transport of the Elgin marbles to London). Some sculptures had also been given in the 1760s by Matthew Duane, who was a numismatist and antiquary and became a Trustee of the Museum.

The great acquisition of large sculptures, which necessitated rebuilding the Museum in order to provide a gallery suitable for them, came as a result of the defeat of the French at the Battle of the Nile in 1801, and the acquisition of the Towneley marbles in 1807. The gallery then built has since been replaced by the present Egyptian Sculpture Gallery.

Napoleon had taken with him on his expedition to Egypt a team of scholars and artists whose task it was to record whatever they could of the flora, fauna and ancient remains of the country. The results of their labours filled twelve huge volumes and they also collected magnificent examples of ancient Egyptian art, all of which was assembled ready to be taken to France when the military were obliged to surrender Alexandria. The scholars stoutly defended their documents and drawings and were allowed to keep them, but many fine pieces of sculpture and the famous Rosetta Stone, which had not yet been deciphered, were ceded to this country under Article XVI of the Treaty of Alexandria. For twenty years scholars on both sides of the Channel tried to decipher the hieroglyphs, but it was not until 1822 that the Frenchman, Jean François Champollion, was successful. One of the three scripts, the Greek, was translated fairly soon after the discovery of the stone. It revealed that the text was a Decree of Ptolemy V Epiphanes exempting the priests in the temple of Ptah from paying certain taxes, confirming their revenues, and setting up a cult of the king in the temple at Memphis. The decree was written in Greek, the language of the rulers; ancient Egyptian hieroglyphs, the script used by the priests; and demotic, the type of ancient Egyptian spoken and written by the native population at that time. The clue to the decipherment was provided by the name of Ptolemy enclosed in a ring, or cartouche, which distinguished it from the other words in the inscription. A cartouche of Ptolemy and of Cleopatra occurred on another bilingual monument, the Bankes obelisk, and Champollion was able to give a sound value to each of the hieroglyphic signs contained in the cartouches and spell out the royal names. He then extended the decipherment from the reading of names to whole sentences through his study of Coptic, which was a much modified type of ancient Egyptian written in Greek characters with some special signs for sounds which the Greeks did not use.

65

41–42 *Opposite, above and below,* two late pre-dynastic ceremonial slate
[pal]ettes known as the Hunters' Palette and the Battlefield Palette respec[tiv]ely. On the latter the King of Upper Egypt is represented as a lion
[tea]ring at a victim. *Centre,* a small ivory figurine of a king wearing the
[heb]-festival robe, from Abydos, First Dynasty

[4]3, 44 *Above,* King Den of the First Dynasty, on an ivory label, smiting foreigners in an attitude common in Egyptian
[ar]t, as may be seen on the sandstone fragment showing Sanakhte of the Third Dynasty in similar pose

[4]5 Scenes of daily life on the walls of the mastaba of Wer-ir-en-ptah from Saqqara, Fourth–Fifth Dynasties

Some of the other sculptures which came to the Museum at this time were two obelisks from the Delta, the statue of Rui from Karnak and several sarcophagi.

The new gallery was completed in 1807 and the magnificent head of Ramesses II, called by the early travellers the Younger Memnon, was presented to the Museum by the British Consul in Egypt, Henry Salt, and J. L. Burck-hardt, a Swiss explorer who had become a Moslem and had made the pil-grimage to Mecca. The brawn as well as some of the brains behind the gift were provided by Giovanni Belzoni, who accomplished its removal from the Ramesseum. Twelve days of hauling and pushing the seven-ton burden on a platform mounted on rollers brought it to the river bank. Belzoni then went to collect other antiquities and four months later he loaded the head onto a boat and conveyed it to Cairo.

57

Belzoni began his working life as a strong man in a music-hall, and went to Egypt with the intention of selling the Khedive a machine for raising water. When his invention met with no success he accepted Henry Salt's invitation to collect antiquities for him, particularly the head of Memnon. In addition, he brought back six seated statues of the goddess Sekhmet from the temple of Mut in Asher and a statue of Seti Merneptah from Karnak, which did not reach the Museum until 1822.

Much of the monumental sculpture in the Egyptian Gallery was bought from Salt either in 1822 or at the sale after his death in 1835. A few pieces Salt excavated himself but the greater part had been the occasion of dramatic incidents for Belzoni, even his attempted assassination. From Karnak came the granite monolith carved in high relief with figures of Tuthmosis III, Mont and Hathor and the enormous royal head, possibly of Tuthmosis III or Amenophis II, in the centre of the Gallery together with the arm in front of it. From the mortuary temple of Amenophis III, marked now by the colossi of Memnon, came one of the black granite statues of the king (the other is from the Ramesseum), colossal heads of Amenophis III, and, from the tomb of Ramesses I or Seti I, two wooden figures of a king which may have guarded the entrance. The wooden figures of gods are probably from the same tomb. Also in the year of the sale of Henry Salt's collection (1835) Lord Prudhoe presented the two red granite lions which flank the entrance to the northern part of the Sculpture Gallery.

51

60

In 1836 a remarkable scholar, Samuel Birch, became an assistant in the Museum; his learning was vast, encompassing Chinese, cuneiform, ancient Egyptian scripts and numismatics.

The collections were enriched by purchases in 1839 of over fifty papyri and one hundred and seven stelae from the Swedish Consul in Egypt, Giovanni d'Anastasi. The documents, known as the Anastasi papyri, include advice to schoolboys to take up the profession of a scribe, for scribes were exempt from taxation and did not have to do any unpleasant manual labour. The Earl of Belmore's collection, amassed on his travels in Egypt, was bought by the Museum in 1842. It included sculpture, stelae and small objects. The stelae from this and the Salt and Anastasi collections are an important part of the Museum's monuments. They give the names and titles of the deceased, some of his family and sometimes biographical details. Their purpose was to ensure that prayers were said for the deceased, by being read from the stele itself.

Another large and important part of the collection is the papyri. Over eight hundred documents deal with every subject including religion, magic, history and medicine. They include stories and poems, personal letters, schoolboys' exercises, records of historical events, a treatise on mathematics and the delicately illustrated Books of the Dead. The ancient Egyptian name 54, 55, 71 for the Book of the Dead is 'Chapters of Coming Forth by Day'. They were spells to help the dead person on his journey through the underworld where he would meet many dangers and demons. Some spells were taken from the Old Kingdom Pyramid Texts which were designed to make possible the union of the king with the sun-god. Another strand of belief was the idea that the dead person had to justify his earthly life in front of the gods. His heart was weighed by Anubis against the Feather of Truth, with which it had to 54 balance. He then recited the Negative Confession in which he affirmed that he had not broken any of the moral laws.

Gifts from William Hamilton in 1838 included a statue of Ramesses II 59 found at Elephantine, and Lord Elgin gave the huge granite beetle in the Central Saloon. Then, in 1854, Queen Victoria presented an alabaster bust 69 of a Ptolemaic king.

The next half-century began with the purchase, in 1857, of more of Anastasi's collection and the Blacas collection in 1867. Blacas was Premier Gentilhomme de la Chambre of Louis XVIII and of Charles X. Mainly small objects, scarabs, figures of gods and amulets were acquired from his collection.

British excavation in Egypt, organized by the Egypt Exploration Fund, yielded its first fruits in 1885 from the efforts of a new recruit, William Matthew Flinders Petrie. During the next four years, Petrie, complaining all the while at the tribulations he endured from British, French and Egyptians alike, sent back a selection of his finds from Tanis (stelae of Ptolemy II), Naucratis (pottery and small finds), Nebesheh (a basalt coffin), Defenneh and Hawara. This last site in the Faiyum produced magnificent encaustic portraits on wood 66 of prosperous men and women of the Roman period; they were Greek-speaking settlers, merchants, bankers and the descendants of veterans from the Macedonian and Roman armies.

Sir E. A. Wallis Budge, who joined the staff of the Museum in 1883, 49 made his first journey to Egypt in order to buy antiquities on behalf of the Trustees in 1886. During the period until the outbreak of the First World War he made sixteen visits to Egypt and brought back the statuette of Tetishery, 50 'grandmother' of the Eighteenth Dynasty, coffins from el-Bersha, the Eleventh Dynasty stele of Tjetji, the papyrus of Ani and the *Wisdom of Amenemope*, 54 to name but a few of his most important purchases. Egypt Exploration Fund

46–48 Portraits from the Old, Middle and New Kingdoms. *Below, left*, Nenkheftka, a royal kinsman, of the Fifth Dynasty (*c.* 2400 BC), painted limestone from Deshesha; *below*, a grey granite statue of Sesostris III as a care-worn and aged king, Twelfth Dynasty (*c.* 1850 BC), from Deir el-Bahri; *left*, plaster mask, possibly a death-mask, of an old man, Eighteenth Dynasty (*c.* 1370 BC)

49, 50 Sir E. A. Wallis Budge in his study at the British Museum. In front of him is the papyrus of Ani (*Pl. 54*). The painted limestone statuette of Tetishery, *above*, was one of the many objects he brought back from Egypt

51 Colossal red granite head, probably of Tuthmosis III (Eighteenth Dynasty) found by Belzoni at Karnak

excavations were going on at the same time at Deir el-Bahri in the temple of
Mentuhotep, from which statues and reliefs were recovered including statues
48 of Sesostris III, Amenophis I and Paser. Edouard Naville also worked at
Bubastis and sent back sculptures from the temple of Osorkon II including a
62, 63 Hathor capital, reliefs showing the king, heads of Amenophis III, Osorkon,
and one of Ramesses II usurped by Osorkon. Percy Newberry was engaged
in copying the Middle Kingdom tombs at el-Bersha and Petrie moved on to
other sites including the cemetery at Abydos where important discoveries of
Early Dynastic tombs, small sculpture and inscribed material were made,
41 including the elegant ivory figure of a king or priest wearing an embroidered
44 robe. He also worked in Sinai, bringing back reliefs of an Early Dynastic king
and of Ramesses II, and in the tombs at Deshasha dating from the Old to
Middle Kingdoms.

After the end of World War I, excavation continued to provide material
for the Museum. The Egypt Exploration Society, the successor of the Fund,
worked at el-Amarna, the city founded by Akhenaten. Although the city
was very much destroyed most of its ground plan was uncovered and a large
74 quantity of small objects brought back, including a remarkable glass fish.
However, not very much of the particular sculpture associated with Akhenaten
was found by this expedition except for an unfinished head of Nefertiti and
heads of her daughters which have remained in Egypt. The Museum sent its
own expedition to Mostagedda and Matmar, sites occupied from the earliest
prehistoric times until the Coptic period.

Particularly generous benefactors in the interwar years were Sir A. Chester
Beatty and his wife who presented a collection of papyri covering a wide range
of subjects: *The Blinding of Truth by Falsehood, The Interpretation of Dreams,*
a hymn to the Aten, a hymn to the Nile and *The Instructions of Ammenemes I*
to his successor. Sir Robert Mond, who had been active in Egypt for many
years, bequeathed his collection, including eight painted portraits, in 1939.
In the same year Mr J. J. Acworth also bequeathed his collection which
68 included very fine bronzes, and Sir John Gayer Anderson gave a bronze cat
from among the *objets d'art* which decorated his house overlooking the mosque
of Ibn Tulun, one of the most beautiful houses in Cairo, now a museum.

The age of the great private collections was nearly over. In 1966 part of
Captain Spencer-Churchill's collection was acquired by the Museum and
this included a large porphyritic frog dating from predynastic times. The
National Art Collections Fund has frequently come to the aid of the Museum,
46 and in 1958 it helped to purchase a plaster mask which resembles those found
in a sculptor's workshop at el-Amarna. Less and less now appears in the sale
rooms, and the hope of adding to the collections rests almost entirely on
excavation and the generosity of the Egyptian and Sudanese Governments.
Since the Second World War the Egypt Exploration Society has been ex-
cavating on behalf of and in collaboration with the Antiquities Service at
Saqqara, the cemetery of Memphis, the capital of Egypt in the Old Kingdom.

During the last few years important finds have been made in the tombs of the earliest dynasties and the Museum has acquired a relief sculpture showing two figures of kings of the First Dynasty wearing the short cloak which was part of the costume worn for the jubilee ceremony at which the king affirmed his right to rule.

The first king of the First Dynasty was, according to tradition, Menes, who united the two previously separate kingdoms of the north and the south. He was the king of the south who conquered the Delta. Before the time of the First Dynasty human activity can be traced back to about 10,000 BC when the first flint-users began to inhabit the terraces above the river. Remains of the earliest settled communities, now identified by the name of the place (el-Badari) where they were first recognized, include tools and weapons made of flint and bone and red pottery with a distinctive black rim; another kind has an incised decoration filled with white paint. Naqada was another site where a slightly more developed people lived who carved slate palettes in the form of birds and animals, and who painted pictures of boats on their large red pots.

The art of the late pre-dynastic period (c. 3100 BC) is in sharp contrast with these primitive remains. Ceremonial slate-palettes, probably used in temple- rituals, were carved in an accomplished fashion with scenes of war, hunting and heraldic animals. The Battlefield palette illustrates certain features which remained constant in Egyptian art. They are the use of raised relief, the con- vention of representing the human body with frontal eye in a profile head and on frontal torso with profile legs, and the division of the area into registers, although in this early example no dividing line is drawn between the battle- scene and the prisoners above it.

40
42

Menes made Memphis his capital but it seems likely that he and his successors were buried in Upper Egypt at Abydos, perhaps with their ancestors. Some authorities, however, believe that the tombs of the First Dynasty lie in the desert above Memphis where a cemetery with monumental brick tombs of the First Dynasty has been found. Objects from both cemeteries at Abydos and at Saqqara are in the collection. The carved ivory figure from Abydos wears the same robe for the Sed-festival as the figures on the relief from Saqqara. At about this time the Egyptians devised a hieroglyphic script, perhaps influenced by the Sumerians with whom they must have had occasional connections. It was first used mainly to indicate ownership and to record events. An ivory label from this period shows Den, the fifth king of the First Dynasty, smiting the Easterners.

41

43

The Old Kingdom (c. 2686–2181 BC) saw the rise of monumental archi- tecture. This was the age of the pyramid-builders, the first of whom was Zoser, the second king of the Third Dynasty. His architect, Imhotep, built the Step Pyramid to be the tomb of his master. After Zoser, the kings of the Fourth Dynasty erected the three famous pyramids at Giza. The Great Pyramid, built for Cheops, is 481.4 ft high and covers an area of 13.1 acres. The one next to it belonged to Chephren, whose own face was the model for the face

52, 53 Daily life in the New Kingdom, wall-paintings from the tomb of Nebamun at Thebes

54 'Weighing of the Heart', papyrus Book of the Dead of Ani the scribe, c. 1250 BC

55 Book of the Dead of Pinudjem II, c. 1000 BC, from Thebes. Pinudjem offers incense to Osiris

56 Detail of part of the Great Harris Papyrus recording the trial of tomb-robbers, c. 1175 BC

57–60 Three pharaohs of the New Kingdom. *Opposite, right,* a black granite seated statue of Amenophis III found in his mortuary temple at Thebes by Belzoni, Eighteenth Dynasty, *c.* 1400 BC. *Left, above,* a grey granite statue of Horemheb as an offering bearer, from Thebes, Eighteenth Dynasty, *c.* 1340 BC. *Below, and opposite, below,* red granite busts of Ramesses II, the smaller from Elephantine and the other, *below,* the colossal Younger Memnon brought back from the Ramesseum by Belzoni

of the giant sphinx which guards his mortuary temple, and the third pyramid belonged to Mycerinus. Howard Vyse, who explored this pyramid brought back to the Museum what he thought to be the coffin of the king, but it has proved to belong to a much later period; it was, in fact, a pious restoration. All around the pyramids, arranged in neat lines, were the tombs of the courtiers who had served the king. They are known as 'mastabas' from the Arabic word for a bench. Statues of the owners were placed in the tombs, and the homely couple, Katep and Hetepheres, probably come from one of these.

75

A settled, ordered society continued under the kings of the Fifth Dynasty. They emphasized the worship of the sun-god and incorporated his name, Re, into their own, calling themselves 'Son of Re'. The centre of the sun-worship was at Abu Gurab and some of the kings were buried in pyramids nearby at Abusir. The Abusir papyri in the collection deal with the administration of the mortuary temple of Neferirkare after the death of the king.

The tombs of the nobles of the Sixth Dynasty were decorated with scenes of daily life on their estates, work in the fields, fishing, and music and dancing in the house. In the centre of one wall of the tomb was the 'false door' with the name of the owner written above it. Its purpose was to allow his relatives and the priests employed to carry on his cult to be able to communicate with him. Food was left there and the dead man was believed to come and go through the 'door' to partake of it. At the end of this Dynasty the country broke up, anarchy reigned, and the local rulers became independent.

45, 47

Central authority and the rule of kings was restored by the local lords of Thebes who formed the Eleventh Dynasty. They overcame their rivals, the rulers of Herakleopolis, and made possible the brilliant period of the Twelfth Dynasty. Sesostris I, the second king of the Twelfth Dynasty, moved his capital from Thebes to el-Lisht, which he called 'Seizer of the Two Lands', to emphasize his position as king over the whole country. Egypt was then prosperous and peaceful for the next two hundred years (c. 1991–1786 BC). Her impact on foreign lands was now more decisive than it had been in the Old Kingdom. Forts were established in the south, partly as trading-posts and partly as a defence against the Nubians. Along the eastern edge of the Delta a wall was built to keep out the 'Sandfarers' of the desert. Trade was re-opened with Byblos and irrigation work was undertaken in the Faiyum. The kings who ruled were called Ammenemes and Sesostris.

48

Sesostris III's portrait showing a careworn, serious man, contrasts with the blandness of portraits of his predecessors and successors. Such strong realism is not seen again until the Eighteenth Dynasty and the portraits of Akhenaten. Painted wooden models of daily life were found in tombs of this period. They show activities on the country estate: baking, brewing, ploughing and storing the grain. Tomb-walls were decorated as they had been in the Old Kingdom, with agricultural scenes and scenes showing the funeral procession. Belief in a life after death, mirroring and in some respects improving upon life on earth, accounts for the elaborate tombs and for mummification of the body. In tomb-portraits no one is depicted as old or ailing. A man might be fat, but that was a sign of prosperity and success. Women were eternally slender and beautiful, their skins pale, shaded from the fierce sun.

The Middle Kingdom broke up after the reign of Ammenemes IV and 73 there followed two hundred years of fragmentation and invasion from the east by the Hyksos. Their name means 'Rulers of Foreign Lands', not 'Shepherd Kings' as has been suggested. Again it was the rulers of Thebes who re-united the kingdom and this time the capital remained at Thebes. Egypt entered upon a period of expansion and foreign conquest led by a line of warrior kings called Tuthmosis and Amenophis, the most famous of whom is Tuthmosis III. 51 He extended Egypt's eastern boundary to the Euphrates and her southern one to the Fourth Cataract. Tribute and slaves poured in to Thebes, whose temples rose up to the glory of the gods, particularly Amun of Karnak. The tombs of the officials responsible for collecting the tribute often show Syrians and Nubians 52, 53, 72 bringing these gifts to the court.

The reign of Amenophis III marked the zenith. He enjoyed the fruits of the 60 empire and did not have to defend it; instead he devoted himself to peaceful activities such as building a palace and temples on the west bank at Thebes. Two seated figures of himself, the Colossi of Memnon, are all that remains visible of his funerary temple. His son, Amenophis IV (Akhenaten), took up a cult already gaining popularity under his father, that of the Aten, the sun's disc. He moved his capital away from Thebes to el-Amarna in Middle Egypt where he built an entirely new city. Dispatches, the Amarna Letters 89 found in the ruins of his Foreign Office, show that there was a confused situation in the Syrian coastal area and trouble with the Hittites.

The king's wife was the beautiful Nefertii, but he himself was of rather strange appearance, with an elongated skull and jowl and a body distorted by disease. Possibly in deference to the king, artists depicted his courtiers with similar proportions. Akhenaten was succeeded by his sons or half-brothers, Smenkhkare and Tutankhamun. The latter's tomb was discovered virtually intact in the Valley of the Kings at Luxor, and its extraordinarily rich furniture gives an idea of the splendours of court life at the time. Tutankhamun abandoned el-Amarna and brought the court back to Thebes where he and his successors, Ay and Horemheb, restored Amun to his former position. 58

A new dynasty, the Nineteenth (c. 1320–1200 BC), was founded by Ramesses I. His famous grandson, Ramesses II, the Great, reconquered much of the 57, 59 former empire, but met determined opposition from the Hittites who took him by surprise at the battle of Kadesh and nearly scored a quick victory. He recorded the story on the walls of five of his temples and copies of these inscriptions are written on two papyri in the Museum. Finally, after many years of fighting he concluded a treaty with the Hittites and married a Hittite princess. Ramesses' features are familiar from his numerous statues, and his fame is proclaimed on the many buildings which were erected or rebuilt in his name over the sixty-seven years of his reign.

61, 62 *Above*, Twenty-seventh Dynasty granite stele of Necho, from Sais. It was in Sir Hans Sloane's original collection. *Below*, red granite door-jamb from Bubastis showing Osorkon II and Queen Karoma, Twenty-second Dynasty, *c.* 850 BC

64 *Above*, a Hathor-headed capital from the temple built by Osorkon II at Bubastis; *below*, granite kneeling figure of ntuemhat holding a stele inscribed with a hymn to the setting sun, Twenty-sixth Dynasty, *c.* 600 BC

The Rosetta Stone, inscribed in hieroglyphs, demotic and Greek

66, 67 *Left*, the mummy of Artemidorus, a young man from Hawara in the Faiyum. His portrait is painted in encaustic on wood. Roman period, second century AD. *Right*, the mummy of an elderly lady with cartonnage mask and hands, *c.* 100 BC–AD 100

68–70 *Above*, bronze-mummy case for a cat with gold rings in its ears and nose. The Gayer Anderson cat, Roman, after 30 BC. *Right*, bust of an unknown Ptolemaic king. *Below*, Coptic wall-hanging, *c.* AD 500, decorated with figures, possibly Actaeon and Artemis

A new threat to Egypt arose during the reign of Ramesses' son Merneptah, from tribes displaced from their homes on the northern shores of the Mediter, ranean who were looking for somewhere to settle. The pressure from these 'Sea Peoples' increased during the reign of Ramesses III, the second king of the Twentieth Dynasty, who recorded his victories over them on the walls of his mortuary temple at Medinet Habu on the west bank at Thebes.

After the reign of Ramesses III, Egypt declined considerably. Her Asiatic empire was lost and the further eight kings who bore the illustrious name of Ramesses were unable to prevent the plundering of the royal tombs. The court proceedings at the trials of the thieves are recorded on papyri in the collection.

56

The High Priests of Amun took over much of the power of the kings in the Theban region and some even wrote their names in cartouches. The country split into its two halves and a new dynasty, the Twenty,first began to rule at Tanis, while the High Priest of Amun was the real ruler of the south. Two of the most famous of these High Priests are Herihor and Pinudjem whose copies of the Book of the Dead are in the Museum.

55

The Twenty,first Dynasty was succeeded by the descendants of Libyans who became the Twenty,second. A pair of bracelets which once belonged to Nemareth, son of Sheshonq I, the Shishak who sacked Jerusalem, are in the collections. A later king, Osorkon and his wife Karoma are represented on a relief from Bubastis. Egypt was in a weak and divided state and fell easy prey to the Kushite king Piankhi, who invaded and became the first king of the Twenty,fifth Dynasty. He set in motion an artistic revival which reached its climax in the Twenty,sixth Dynasty. He restored temples and paid particular attention to Karnak, for he was a devotee of Amun, whose worship had been taken to Napata during the New Kingdom. Queen Amenirdis had already been installed at Karnak as Divine Consort of Amun by Kashta, predecessor of Piankhi, and she was virtually ruler of the Theban area through the estates of the temple of Amun.

62

In Lower Egypt things were far from peaceful. The Assyrians invaded and twice occupied Memphis, in 671 and 667 BC, when they even reached Thebes. Ashurbanipal did not remain in Egypt and contented himself with large quantities of booty and princes as hostages. One of these prisoners, Necho, was allowed to return to Saïs. His son, Psammetichus, became the first ruler of the Twenty,sixth Dynasty, with his daughter, Nitocris, as Divine Consort of Amun. Together with her the most important person in Thebes was Montuemhat, Fourth Prophet of Amun. The art of this period is very much an attempt to revive the glories of the Old Kingdom without ignoring current tastes and feeling.

61

64

In 525 BC began the Persian occupation which lasted, with interruptions when native kings regained control of their country, until Alexander the Great conquered Egypt in 332 BC. The Macedonians and other Greek settlers and traders lived apart from the Egyptians in colonies such as Hawara, and the great capital city of Alexandria. The Ptolemies wanted to identify themselves with ancient Egypt and built additions to many temples showing themselves in the relief-sculptures performing the traditional rituals. They also introduced a hybrid god, Serapis, whom Greeks and Egyptians could worship. He was human in form and personified the new Egypt. In Roman times Isis was given to him as his wife and the child-god Horus became their son. Greek was the official language of the country and the administration and the army were run by Greek-speaking people from various parts of the Mediterranean world. Alexandria became a centre for learning and the arts, with the great library as its focal point.

In the third century BC, Egypt began a period of revival under the Macedonian rulers, but during the next century lost its position through enervating wars with Syria. Weak kings were unable to control internal disturbances and after a long period of decline Egypt fell to Augustus.

The Roman Emperors were as respectful to the Egyptian gods as the Ptolemies had been, building and repairing many temples and ensuring that their own royal portraits were present on the walls performing the same rituals as the ancient Egyptian pharaohs. Egypt was the personal property of the Emperor and no high official, apart from the prefect who ruled the country, was allowed to visit without special permission.

Christianity is believed to have been brought to Alexandria by St Mark, and there was a flourishing Greek-speaking Christian community in that city at the end of the second century AD. The Coptic script, invented in the first century AD to record the pronunciation of spells, was written with Greek letters and some additional signs to represent sounds not found in Greek. By the early fourth century both the Old and New Testaments had been translated. The word Coptic is applied to the art and architecture of Egypt between the second and the thirteenth centuries AD but its use should be confined to the Egyptian Coptic Church, unmistakably Christian buildings and objects, and to the writing and language. For it must be remembered that the adherents of Christianity increased only slowly and for a long time consisted only of hermits living in the desert, and certain town-dwellers.

During the reign of the Emperor Constantine, Christianity received a great impetus in Egypt as elsewhere, and it has thus been assumed that many of the surviving churches were founded at about this time. There is however, no positive evidence to date the earliest of these before the fifth century. The sculptural decoration of the early churches was Hellenistic in style, using acanthus leaves, vines, swags, cupids, river-gods and nymphs. The most obvious Egyptian motif is the cross in the form of the *ankh*-sign, and the representation of the Virgin suckling Christ may derive from figures of Isis and Horus. Gravestones are the earliest monuments which bear recognizable Christian symbols, the Cross and Chi-Rho signs. Ancient Coptic textiles have survived in great quantity, but rarely represent Biblical or Christian themes, though they frequently draw on Greek mythology. It may be assumed

70

that most of them came from burial grounds in Egypt, and many are the actual clothes or shrouds in which the people were buried. The main garment was a tunic with a decorated border and roundels. Whole figures, such as the Actaeon and Artemis on a piece of linen, may have decorated a cloak or shroud, and a woollen tapestry with cupids in a boat may be part of a wall-hanging depicting a scene from ancient mythology such as the Birth of Venus or the Triumph of Amphitritus.

70

In AD 641 the Arabs conquered Egypt and many of the Christians submitted to Islam. The Egyptian stonemasons and sculptors worked under the direction of Moslem architects and their style was slow to change. In spite of persecutions, Christianity did not die out: today there are still three million Copts in Egypt – the last descendants of the pharaonic Egyptians.

Away in Nubia, Piankhi's kingdom of Kush withdrew from Egyptian affairs after the end of the Twenty-fifth Dynasty and its brief conquest of Egypt. Psammetichus of the Twenty-sixth Dynasty turned the tables on the Kushites by sacking their capital of Napata in 591 BC and as a result they moved to Meroe. There they developed an independent civilization with its own language and script. At its peak the Meroitic kingdom stretched from the Wadi es-Sebua (between Aswan and the Second Cataract) to the province of Kordofan, and in time it spanned about nine hundred years until it was conquered in the mid-fourth century AD by the Ethiopians whose capital was at Axum. Roman armies had invaded in 23 BC but failed to annex the country.

At Meroe there was a large city with a temple of Amun and, outside, other temples dedicated to Isis, the lion-god and the sun. Four kilometres to the south-east of Meroe city lie the royal pyramid-fields. The first king to be buried at Meroe (and not at Kurru and Nuri, the burial-places of earlier rulers) was Arakakamani whose successor Amenislo (c. 297–284 BC) may have been the king who moved the lions of Amenophis III from Soleb to Barkal. The pyramids were built of stone with a chapel above ground and the burial-chamber below. The walls of these chapels were decorated with reliefs of ritual scenes showing the king or queen in the company of the gods as in ancient Egyptian reliefs. Although the iconography and arrangement of figures in Meroitic relief sculpture is evidently based on ancient Egyptian traditions, and follows fairly closely the designs on Ptolemaic temples, it should not be regarded as merely a crude copy. Meroitic art has its own individuality and draws on Persian and even Indian inspiration. The figures are much heavier than the slender idealized Egyptian representations, as can be seen in a relief from a second century chapel belonging to Queen Nahirqa.

Thus Egyptian artistic style came to an end in the south by becoming Africanized and in the north by being merged in the general Mediterranean culture. No longer was it the leader, the strongest force in the region, but part of another empire and another world.

A. WILKINSON

◄ 71, 72 *Above*, the 'Opening of the Mouth' of the mummy of Hunefer, from his papyrus Book of Dead, c. 1300 BC. *Below*, wall-painting of Syrians bringing tribute to Tuthmosis IV, from the tomb of Sebekhotep at Thebes, c. 1400 BC

75

73 Openwork gold plaque of Ammenemes IV with Atum, Middle Kingdom, *c.* 1790 BC. *Left and right,* two neck spacer beads in the form of cats with their kittens, inscribed for King Nub-kheper-Re Intef, Seventeenth Dynasty, *c.* 1 BC. *Centre,* heart scarab, green jasper set in gold, of King Sebekemsaf, Seventeenth Dynasty, *c.* 1600 BC

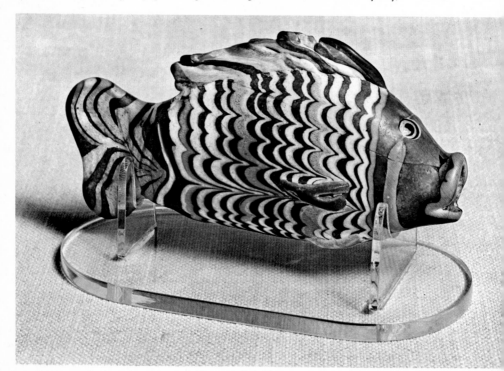

74 Glass vase in the form of a fish, from el-Amarna, *c.* 1400 BC

Painted limestone statuette of Katep and his wife, Hetepheres, from Giza, c. 2550 BC

CHAPTER THREE

Western Asiatic Antiquities

The Department of Western Asiatic Antiquities contains today collections illustrating the arts, culture and monuments of many peoples from one of the greatest centres of world civilization, from Stone Age times to the rise of Islam. What then is Western Asia? It comprises the area from the central plateau of Turkey, eastwards through Transcaucasia, Iraq and Iran to the Afghan frontier; and southwards from the Black Sea coast through modern Turkey, Syria, Lebanon, Israel, Arabia and the States of the Persian Gulf to Aden and the Indian Ocean. In the nineteenth and even early twentieth centuries, this area, if we exclude Iran, largely corresponded with a major part of the Turkish Empire; but now it is multi-national.

The origins of the collection of Western Asiatic antiquities in the British Museum (that is, of objects from ancient civilizations in that vast area) go back almost to the earliest period of the Museum, certainly to the eighteenth century. Some of these were inscribed Phoenician seals from the collection of Sir William Hamilton (1730–1803), though they were not recognized then as Phoenician, since the script and language were as yet unknown. In 1785 there arrived in England a young German scholar of erratic temperament, Rudolph Eric Raspe (d. 1794), whose reputation in his own country (where he had held the post of curator of the Markgraf's collection at Kassel) had left him somewhat under a cloud. This visitor showed that he possessed extra-ordinary and varied talent by producing first, under a pseudonym, one of the most successful works of wildest fantasy: *The Travels of Baron Munchausen* (1784), which immediately went through many editions; and second, one of the earliest serious works of critical archaeology, a catalogue of *Tassie's Gems* (Edinburgh, 1791, in English and French).

James Tassie (1735–99) having migrated in 1766 to London (being after-wards followed by his much younger nephew William, 1777–1860), had amassed an extraordinary, notable collection of casts and moulds of classical and pre-classical gems, cameos and Mesopotamian cylinder seals, from various collections. He became chiefly famous for inventing and marketing a successful method of reproducing impressions of such seals in a white enamel composition of vitreous paste. Tassie employed Raspe to write a catalogue of them and he lavishly illustrated it with some 15,800 gems and cylinder seals for com-parison, seventeen of which were in the British Museum's collections. Of these seventeen, eleven came from the Towneley Collection (1791) and six from that of Sir William Hamilton. Some of the engravings of these seals done for

Raspe by D. Allen are dated 1789. True, the cylinder seals, now known to be from Babylonia and Assyria, are mistakenly called by Raspe 'Persepolitan' (after the ancient Persian capital city of Persepolis, the ruins of which were known to western travellers since the fourteenth century). This was for the very good reason that in Raspe's time the only place where the cuneiform script was recognized as having been used, and where it could be seen inscribed, was Persepolis. The world was then as yet unaware of the script's real origin in ancient Babylonia and Assyria, the modern Iraq. Its true Mesopotamian origin was first demonstrated in 1801 by Joseph Hager (*A Dissertation on the newly discovered Babylonian Inscriptions*).

Thus we learn that by 1784 the nucleus of the Department's splendid collec' tion of cylinder seals, now totalling over 3,000, had already taken shape, though we do not know by what means or from what sources these pieces were obtained by Hamilton or Towneley.

The next name to be mentioned in the history of the formation of the Western Asiatic collection is that of Sir Robert Ker Porter, who was more important by reason of his influence than by his relatively trifling donations of antiquities collected in the East. The talented orphan son of a Scottish army surgeon, he was early sent to study art in London at Benjamin West's Academy where he rapidly made progress, acquired a general education, and acted as a 'war artist' in the Peninsula, sketching General Moore's retreat from Corunna. Then, finding employment with the Tsar of Russia as an 'historical artist', he married (after some vicissitudes of fortune) a Russian princess and was engaged, in 1818, by her relative, Olenin, the secretary of the Russian Academy of Sciences, and charged to travel to Persepolis to make for the first time true and accurate drawings of the Persepolis palace and its reliefs. Not only did he do so, but he also discovered and drew the previously unknown inscribed rock sculpture of Darius at Behistun, the trilingual text of which, first copied by Colonel Rawlinson in 1835–7, enabled Rawlinson and others to decipher the Babylon' ian cuneiform script in 1859. Ker Porter recorded a host of other valuable observations with the drawings and published them in his book *Travels in Georgia, Persia, Armenia, Ancient Babylonia*, (2 vols, London, 1822).

78

His journeying took him through Baghdad in 1819, where he was warmly received as a guest by another still more remarkable character, Claudius James Rich (1787–1821). Rich had been, since 1808, the East India Company's youthful but brilliant Resident in Baghdad, where he had arrived on his appointment from Bristol as a cadet of sixteen in 1803. A naturally gifted linguist and shrewd diplomat, Rich quickly made his mark. He solaced his inevitable isolation by developing an unusual interest in his surroundings and showed a marked bent for what we would now call archaeology, but which then, since no such name existed, was termed 'antiquarian studies'. The Western world, recovering from the shock and horrors of the French Revolution and the Napoleonic wars had been inspired not least by Napoleon and his scientific mission to Egypt, and perhaps by the careers of Lord Elgin and

77

Lord Byron, to take a more scholarly look at the ancient Near Eastern world, and to ask what remained, if anything, of Nineveh and Babylon. Rich himself identified the true site of Babylon in 1811 (*Mines de l'Orient*, Vienna, 1811), and visited the sites of both Kouyunjik and Nimrud, collected cuneiform in-scriptions (one of which his young German secretary Karl Bellino exquisitely copied), cylinder seals, coins and Oriental manuscripts. During Ker Porter's six-week visit, he and Rich became fast friends and Ker Porter drew many of Rich's antiquities for his own book. He also, accompanied by Bellino, visited Babylon and other nearby sites. Shortly afterwards, alas, Rich, while on a projected journey to Pasargadae and Persepolis, stopped in the plague-stricken city of Shiraz in Persia and, while assisting the sick and dying contracted the disease and died in the flower of his youth and talents, aged only thirty-four. After Rich's death, his widow, Mary, sold to the Trustees of the British Museum for £1,000 his collection of 900 oriental manuscripts, now part of the collections of the Department of Oriental Printed Books and Manuscripts, and his Mesopotamian antiquities. The list of the latter forms the earliest approach to a register of Western Asiatic antiquities in the Museum, since there was then little else from that area. It included fifty-six seals and the so-called Bellino cylinder, an eight-sided clay prism containing the annals of King Sennacherib of Assyria *c.* 700 BC, in cuneiform script. This was the text copied by Bellino.

It was perhaps also no accident but due to the influence of Rich that in this period the Museum acquired its only fragments of reliefs from the palace of Persepolis. These were presented by Sir Gore Ouseley (1825), and by Lord Aberdeen (1871), together with an inscription of Esarhaddon. These two had acquired the fragments while on their embassy to the Shah in Teheran.

There followed a pause of some twenty years in acquisitions, except for some seals from the Stewart Collection (1841), a fine basalt stele depicting the neo-Babylonian King Nabonidus and, according to Constance Alexander in her account of the Riches, *Baghdad in Bygone Days* (1928), some Assyrian sculptures of which no trace now survives. There were also some cuneiform cylinders from Hillah given by Sir Keith Jackson (1843).

A new meteor then burst on the Oriental sky. Again, it was a mere youth of genius, Austen Henry Layard, who, though he had never met Rich, admittedly owed something to him. Indeed, Layard was able to point effectively to the fact that before his own stupendous discoveries, the world's knowledge of Babylon and Assyria was confined to a single exhibition case at the Museum containing Rich's and Ker Porter's contributions. Encouraged by the powerful British Ambassador in Constantinople, Sir Stratford Canning, the youthful Layard was able to make a contribution to the world's knowledge that was unique. He was able to enormously enrich the Museum's collections with the harvest of his exertions in Turkish Mesopotamia where, in two campaigns of unbelievable energy with no training but the insight of genius, he skil-fully excavated four palaces and safely brought home scores of sculptures, thousands of tablets and other objects, with but little assistance from anyone.

107

80

80   76 The Goat in the Thicket, one of a pair from the great Death-Pit at Ur, *c.* 2750 BC ▶

77–79 Three of the pioneers of study in the field of Western Asiatic archaeology. *Left*, Claudius James Rich (1787–1821), the East India Company's Resident in Baghdad; *below, left*, Colonel Henry Creswicke Rawlinson (1810–95), British consul-general in Baghdad, the 'Father of Assyriology' and decipherer of the cuneiform script; *below*, Hormuzd Rassam (1826–1910); a pupil of Layard, he excavated many sites for the Trustees and the Balawat Gates (*Pl. 84*) were amongst his many discoveries

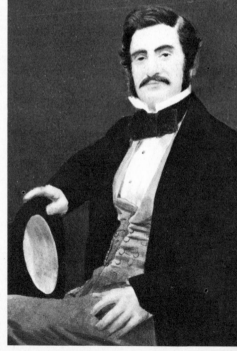

80 Sir Henry Austen Layard (1817–94) seen drawing antiquities in the bottom of an excavation pit at Nimrud. Such was his energy and brilliance that, with little training, he alone enlarged the Museum's collections a thousandfold, and prepared publications of his discoveries

81 A scene during the excavation at Carchemish (1912–14). Both young men here were to find fame in different ways – on the left is T. E. Lawrence and, to the right, C. L. (later Sir Leonard) Woolley

At the same time he prepared scholarly publications for the learned, and popular accounts for the ordinary men and women of the day which brought, and still bring home to the public, the impact of his realization of the extent and wealth and high artistic level of the Assyrians' civilization. The excitement that these discoveries, bearing on the evidence of the Old Testament, created in Bible-loving Victorian England was immense.

Others trod in his footsteps, and renewed or extended his excavations on behalf of the Trustees or others. There was H. Rassam, acting at Kouyunjik (Nineveh) and Nimrud (1853–4) for the Trustees; W. K. Loftus acting first for the Assyrian Excavation Fund at Susa and Warka (the Biblical Erech), Nimrud and Nineveh (1849–53), then at Nineveh again for the Trustees (1854–6); and Colonel Rawlinson at intervals. But this Mesopotamian activity practically ceased with the outbreak of the Crimean War, except for Consul Taylor's work in 1853–4 in identifying and beginning to explore the site of Ur of the Chaldees which he had discovered, followed by further work at Abu Shahrain (Eridu).

A late Punic (Neo-Punic) inscription from Maktar in 1833 was an early arrival. In 1850, Sir Thomas Reade, an ex-consul from Tunis, sold to the Museum eight Neo-Punic stelae including the second-century BC bilingual inscription, Phoenician and Berber (or Numidian), from the Thugga Mauso-leum. At about the same time too, activity was stirring in other directions in North Africa. In 1857 at Carthage and Utica, Dr Nathan Davis, a missionary, conducted some excavations or bought material, discovering fine Roman mosaics and many Punic inscriptions, mostly dedications of infants sacrificed in the sixth to fifth century BC at the Tophet to the Carthaginian Moloch, Baal Hammon. Arabia, too, was beckoning, but in general, the 1860s were a time of pause for efforts of Near Eastern exploration in other directions. In 1865 the Pal-estine Exploration Fund was founded and, though the Trustees unwisely rejec-ted in 1867 the offer to purchase the Moabite stone, a unique document found in Transjordan illustrating the wars of Ahab with Moab, the ancient culture of the Hebrews was soon to be represented (1870) in the Museum by two impor-tant inscriptions, one of them, probably from the tomb of Hezekiah's minister or scribe, Shebna, and, in 1903, a pair of Hebrew stone ossuaries, one bearing the name of 'Nicanor the Alexandrian, who made the gates,' i.e. the donor of a famous pair of bronze gates in the second Temple at Jerusalem, c. 10 BC.

In spite of the difficulties and dangers of Arabian exploration in those days, the Danish scholar, Lt Carsten Niebuhr, had penetrated the Yemen in 1762, and brought back copies of South Arabian pre-Islamic inscriptions. A Swiss traveller, Burckhardt, had discovered Petra and its wonders in 1812. Operating from the British controlled territory of Aden, Lt-Colonel R. L. Playfair and Colonel W. M. Coghlan were able to bring back in 1855 inscriptions on bronze, with others on stone, again in the ancient pre-Islamic script of South-west Arabia. These were added to in 1871 by Captain W. F. Prideaux and Major Hunter (1883). So too, the Syrian desert was now to yield up some of its history. Palmyra, whose magnificent ruins had been well known to travellers since 1678, but chiefly from 1751 when Wood and Dawkins first published the French edition of their *Ruins of Palmyra*, was represented in London from 1880 by fine funerary portraits (probably from Consul Henderson). Indeed, Her Britannic Majesty's army officers served the cause of Near Eastern archaeo-logy and exploration very handsomely in the nineteenth century. The foundation of the Palestine Exploration Fund led to the investigation of ancient Jerusalem by Colonel Warren (1869) and the mapping of Palestine (1872–78) by Colonel Conder and Lt Kitchener (afterwards Field-Marshal Lord Kitchener); all outstanding masterpieces of pioneering work in that country.

98

The general outcome of this growth of interest and collections was the forma-tion of a separate Oriental Antiquities Department in the British Museum, but the interest in Mesopotamia in the 1860s was concentrated on the field of decipherment of the cuneiform script. Here the leading rôle was that of Colonel Rawlinson, the decipherer, guide and doyen of the subject, working on the thousands of texts brought back by Layard and his successors. It was thanks to his influence that the Department of Oriental Antiquities, created in 1861 largely for Egyptian and Assyrian material alike, was already by then becoming the centre of cuneiform studies of the world.

The announcement, disclosed on 3 December 1872 of the discovery by Rawlinson's pupil and protégé, George Smith, Assistant in the Department, of one of these tablets containing the Babylonian version of the Legend of the Flood suddenly riveted popular interest once more on the site of Nineveh, whence it came. If he were sent out there by the British Museum, might he not seek and perhaps find the missing portions? The *Daily Telegraph* offered to contribute 1,000 guineas to the cost of such an expedition, subject to the condition that Smith himself should direct it. In 1873 George Smith went out on the Trustees' behalf without training, experience or linguistic equipment, and re-opened the excavations in March and, most remarkable of all, found what passed for the missing part, containing seventeen lines of column one, hitherto a blank. Public excitement knew no bounds. Smith on all accounts must go out again. He did, next year (1875), and after a conspicuously un-successful season, became involved in continuous conflict with the Turkish authorities and died aged thirty-six of dysentery on the return road to Aleppo, leaving a wife and five children. The public shock and grief were such that his family were granted a pension by the Queen.

78

88

Strangely enough, his death did not discourage the Trustees and the Treasury from further work in Mesopotamia; rather the contrary. One reason was the deteriorating political situation; Turkey, the 'sick man of Europe', appeared to be on the point of imminent collapse, and it was feared that the Russians would walk in to Mesopotamia and put an end to all foreign excavations. Accordingly, Rassam, who had recently retired from the Consular Service after a distressing period of imprisonment in Abyssinia at the hands of its unbalanced ruler, King Theodore, was re-engaged in 1877 as the Trustees'

82 The Black Obelisk of Shalmaneser III (859–824 BC), one of Layard's most interesting finds, is also known as the 'Jehu stele'. It recounts the king's military expeditions and exploits and, in the second register from the top, Jehu is seen making obeisance on his knees to the king

83, 84 *Right*, detail from the famous lion hunt relief scenes that decorated the North Palace of Sennacherib at Nineveh, *c.* 650 BC; *below*, a detail from the bronze Balawat Gates showing Assyrian chariotry and infantry. They were erected by Shalmaneser III to commemorate his victories between 858 and 848 BC

85, 86 A fantastic group of ivories was found in the north-west palace of Ashurnasirpal at Nimrud. Dating from the eighth century BC they are of Phoenician workmanship, often in Egyptianizing style. *Right,* the 'Woman at the Window', an ivory panel originally from a couch; *below,* a plaque in pseudo-Egyptian style with a name in a cartouche that may be that of Iaubidi, king of Hamath in 720 BC (*see also Pls. 92, 93*)

87–89 It was largely due to Layard's efforts that the British Museum became the centre of cuneiform studies, and still is. The tablet, *left*, is one of Layard's finds from the library of Ashurbanipal's library at Nineveh and tells part of the epic of Gilamesh and his search for immortality. The fragment, *below, left*, is the piece found by George Smith in 1872 giving part of the Babylonian version of the Legend of the Flood. *Below*, a cuneiform tablet from Egypt, one of the Amarna Letters written to Akhenaten (Amenophis IV) from Syria begging for help against invaders

excavator, a Turkish permit to excavate being obtained by Sir Henry Layard, his old friend, now British Ambassador at the Porte.

Rassam's brief was, properly speaking, simply to search for tablets. In 1878 he developed a mass attack, deploying excavations with incredible energy at at least eight sites of importance in Assyria and Babylonia or Armenia (Bala-wat, Assur, Kouyunjik, Abu-Habbah, Telloh, Tell Ibrahim, Van, Tell Igraine) more or less simultaneously; he found and sent home some thousands of finds, by no means all tablets. This harvest included two major monuments, the splendid sets of bronze gate-coverings from Balawat, twenty miles east of Mosul (1877), the parts of the bronze throne of the Urartian god Haldi, several Urartian bronze decorated shields, and other objects from Toprak Kale beside Lake Van, no less than the Sun-god tablet from Sippar and the Hittite bowl inscribed with Hittite hieroglyphs from Babylon. But it was of course impossible working single-handed in such frenzied activity to keep any reliable archaeological records of the digging conditions, or indeed any at all, nor apparently did the ageing Rassam appear to understand the overriding indispensability of such records. In his day, it must be admitted, few did, though his master, Layard, a genius before his time, had been as conscious of this need as Rassam was oblivious or indifferent. Not so much this as other errors led eventually, through accumulating tensions between the generations, to a distressing lawsuit in 1892 in which the aggressive young Ernest Budge (1857–1936) who became Keeper of the Department in 1894 (no longer called Oriental Antiquities but, since 1886, that of Egyptian and Assyrian Anti-quities), was sued by the now aged Rassam for slander and lost the case. The most unfortunate result from the standpoint of the Department, apart from lasting bitternesses, was that Budge did his best (not wholly unsuccessfully) to obliterate much of the record of all that Rassam had very positively achieved, which he affected wherever possible completely to disbelieve – such as the discovery of the bronze Assyrian gate-coverings at Balawat, which Budge was convinced came from Nimrud.

Fortunately Budge made other, greater and even more outstanding con-tributions to scholarship and to the Museum's history and collections. In the field of Western Asia, one may mention the priceless collection of 'Amarna Tablets', forming a lot of 82 tablets bought in Egypt in 1887, and many more hundreds of tablets from Assyria and Babylonia. Budge was one of the last of the great Victorian polymaths who was able to claim some mastery of both Egyptian hieroglyphs and Assyrian cuneiform, as well as of Syriac, Ethiopic and Hebrew: not least of his feats was his brilliant organization of the huge tablet collection and the inauguration of the system of Catalogues begun by Bezold on the Kouyunjik library, and followed by the publication of texts in the series known as Cuneiform Texts, which is still in progress. Dynamic, zestful, an excellent and humorous writer and raconteur, often combative and blindly quarrelsome, he was a wonderfully kind and loyal friend and teacher, but a fearsome opponent.

84

110

49

89

All this growth demanded not merely more staff, but also more space in the Department. The removal of the Natural History Departments from the Museum at Bloomsbury to more suitable accommodation at South Kensington, left the five rooms of the Upper Northern galleries, freed from fishes and mammalia, to be shared by the Egyptian and Assyrian antiquities and their offices in a much needed expansion. The building of the King Edward VII building in 1910 along the North side of the Museum gave the Department further space on the bridge leading to the new Prints and Drawings Department. Originally it was then proposed that the new space on the bridge would be used to house the exciting Hittite sculptures then being found in the Museum's excavations on the Upper Euphrates at Carchemish; but this is to anticipate.

81

The same period brought into the Museum the splendid gold and silver 'Treasure of the Oxus', mainly of the Achaemenid Persian period, by the generous bequest of Sir Wollaston Franks (1897).

91

Travellers passing by the overland route to Iraq or Iran, if starting from Alexandretta or Aleppo, would often take the natural road eastwards, crossing the Euphrates at the important ford then called Jerabis or Jerablus, dominated by a colossal artificial mound evidently marking the remains of an extremely important ancient city. In 1699, the Reverend Henry Maundrell, Chaplain to the East India and Levant Company factory at Aleppo passed that way and mentions it; in 1876 George Smith and Rassam commented on it. The French traveller Texier had discovered the capital of the Hittite empire in the north-eastern part of Anatolia at Boghazköy and in 1880 Professor Sayce had taken the first major step in deciphering their strange type of hieroglyphic picture-writing by recognizing an example of it on a large stamp seal of silver bearing a bilingual text as giving the name of Tarkondemos. This had been brought to the Museum, dismissed as a forgery and lost but, luckily, a cast made by Mr William Ready, who worked as a restorer and technician for the Department, had been preserved. It is still there. Examples of this writing had been observed on stone sculptures as far south as Hama in Syria in 1812, but their importance was ignored; they were then noticed in 1876 at Jerablus which was recognized by Smith as Carchemish, possibly the Hittites' southern capital. Some excavations were begun for the Museum in 1878 and 1881 by the local consul, and William St Chad Boscawen, an assistant on Birch's staff, was sent out. But he failed sadly in his duties. Nevertheless, some sculptures, such as the half column illustrating on the front the goddess Kubaba and heavily inscribed in hieroglyphs on the back, were sent to London in 1881. In 1906 German archaeologists began the excavation of Boghazköy. In 1909 the engineers of the Berlin-Baghdad Railway reached Carchemish and were thought to be about to cut through it before bridging the Euphrates. An expedition was urgently organized by the Director of the Museum, Sir Frederic Kenyon, supported anonymously by a wealthy patron and friend, W. A. Morrison, to explore the site more thoroughly and worthily.

113

The excavation of Carchemish was entrusted in 1911 to D. G. Hogarth, a veteran in the field of Greek and Asia Minor exploration and excavation, aided by R. Campbell Thompson of the Department of Egyptian and Assyrian Antiquities, who had gained some elementary experience in excavations at Kouyunjik in 1904 seven years before. Thompson, though addicted rather to hit-and-miss methods of digging, nevertheless found the main ceremonial roadway to the citadel, flanked with sculptures and Hittite hieroglyphic inscriptions; but his work was felt unsatisfying and the following seasons, 1912–14, were entrusted to two new, gifted younger men, C. L. Woolley and T. E. Lawrence, both destined to become celebrated in different ways. Thompson's discovery of the great roadway was extended by them in 1912–13 and proved richly, but rather unexpectedly, rewarding in monuments of the Late Hittite Period, or Iron Age. At the same time Thompson, at home, armed with the numerous Hittite hieroglyphic texts he had found, occupied himself with what proved eventually to be a remarkable advance in solving the problem of the decipherment of the Hittite hieroglyphic script.

81

The brilliant progress of these important excavations at this dominating and crucially significant site was abruptly interrupted by the outbreak of the First World War. After its conclusion the Treaty of Lausanne fixed the frontier between Syria and Turkey at Carchemish precisely on the line of the railway which ran between the ancient citadel and the lower town, leaving one in Turkey, the other in Syria, like a judgment of Solomon. As a result of the new situation only a few fragments of Hittite sculpture reached London from these excavations and no possibility has since existed for anyone to resume excavation on this politically sadly divided site. It was left to the French excavator, C. F. Schaeffer, at Ras Shamra-Ugarit near Lattakia in the 1950s to show from cuneiform tablets and Hittite texts found there, including letters addressed to Ugarit from Carchemish, that in the second millennium under the Hittite Empire, Carchemish was in fact as Hogarth had imagined, a potent Hittite capital, indeed the seat of the Hittite viceroy himself ruling over the Hittite vassal states of Syria.

The First World War brought, fortunately, little damage to the Department's treasure, some of which was evacuated. In other ways it brought advantages when, in the wake of the allied armies eventually victorious in Iraq, it was possible in 1919 for R. Campbell Thompson and H. R. Hall (another Assistant Keeper of the Department, primarily an Egyptologist, but a man of very wide interests) followed by C. L. Woolley in 1923–4, to undertake fruitful excavations at the small site of Tell el Ubaid, five miles from Ur. This resulted in the discovery of the remains of a lavishly decorated, middle third millennium Sumerian temple containing fine copper sculpture of hitherto unsuspected skill and beauty; it turned out to have been founded by A-ane-pada, a formerly legendary figure of Sumerian history. This was for Woolley an instructive introduction and a training for the more ambitious and serious undertaking of the excavations at Ur itself that he conducted for twelve years (1922–34) with a unique brilliance.

94

90 A detail of the War Side of the 'Standard of Ur'. It is ornamented on both sides (*see also Pl. 99*) with mosaic scenes made of shell and lapis lazuli set in bitumen, *c.* 2750 BC

91 Gold model of a Persian war-chariot from the 'Treasure of the Oxus'

This is hardly the place to give anything but the most summary account of the amazingly rich harvest of discoveries concerning the rise of Mesopotamian civilization from the end of the fourth millennium BC (Al Ubaid period) to the Persian period (fourth century BC) which the combined British Museum and University of Pennsylvania team led by Woolley achieved, enriching the museums of Baghdad, Philadelphia and the British Museum alike. To have planned this achievement was the last and greatest legacy of Budge and Hall. The same decade which witnessed with astonishment the discovery by British science of the Egyptian XVIIIth Dynasty Pharaoh Tutankhamun's virtually untouched tomb (1922), was also to witness the extremely dexterous unearthing, often by Woolley and Lady Woolley with their own hands, of the Sumerian Royal Graves of the Early Dynastic Period with their unbelievable wealth of gold, silver, copper, obsidian, shell and lapis lazuli objects, entombed together with mass burials of the king's and queen's royal attendants in c. 2500 BC. These finds, divided eventually between the three museums mentioned above, were all described by Woolley himself in a series of (partly posthumous) volumes. At the same time, a library of cuneiform texts, literary, administrative, religious, economic and historical, recovered from the houses and schools, is still being published; among them is much material helping the reconstitution of the lost literature of the Sumerians, the earliest in the world. Foremost in this work were Dr (afterwards Professor) C. J. Gadd, ultimately Keeper of the Department, (1948–55), Professor S. N. Kramer of the University of Pennsylvania and Dr H. H. Figulla, a Special Assistant in the Department (1938–66) and, latterly, Dr A. Shaffer of the Hebrew University, Jerusalem and Dr E. Sollberger of the British Museum. In this they were continuing the Department's century-old tradition of original work of cataloguing and publication in the highly specialized field of cuneiform.

Shortly after concluding his work in the field at Ur in 1936, the tireless Woolley was, in 1937, once more digging, this time on the North Syrian coast at Al Minah and Atchana; the latter turned out to be Alalakh, an important principality of the Bronze Age; here again a valuable collection of clay tablets inscribed in cuneiform was found. These were published by D. J. Wiseman in 1953 when Assistant Keeper in the Department; an important inscribed statue of the ruler of Alalakh, Idrimi, was published in 1949 by Sydney Smith, Keeper of the Department.

The Second World War brought grievous wounds to the Museum from direct bombing, but those inflicted upon the Department were relatively light. The Assyrian sculpture reliefs were all dismounted and sent to safety in the Aldwych Underground Tube Station; other antiquities were packed away first to selected country houses, then to a central deposit, while most of the staff dispersed to various forms of war work. The excavation of Atchana and Al Minah interrupted by the War was resumed in 1946–9, after which Woolley ceased work. After the spectacular Royal Graves of Ur anything else was bound to seem something of an anticlimax, however scientifically valuable or

76, 90, 97, 99

102

92, 93 Two Phoenician ivories from Nimrud (*see also* Pls. *85, 86*). *Above*, a negro boy has been caught in a thicket by a lioness who sinks her teeth into his throat; *below*, an openwork panel of a lion in a lily grove. He has an Egyptian sun-disk upon his head and wears an Egyptian broad collar

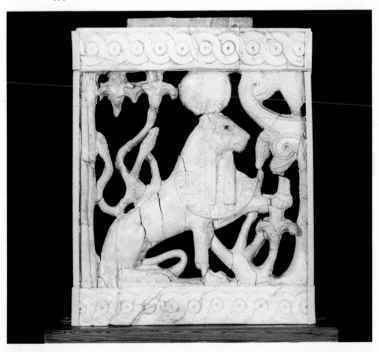

94–96 Sumerian metal- and stonework of the fourth to third millennium BC. *Above,* a copper panel from Tell el Ubaid, near Ur, showing Im-du-gud as a lion-headed eagle grasping a stag by the tail in each of his claws; *left,* a steatite vase from Khafaje, Central Iraq, decorated with an Indian humped bull; *below,* a limestone libation vase from Warka (Uruk) with a bearded god, possibly Gilgamesh, wrestling with two bulls

The reconstructed head-dress of one of the female
[att]endants buried in the Death-Pit at Ur

98 Bust of a Palmyrene lady, 'Aqmat, daughter of Hagago,
son of Zebida, son of Maan', second century AD

[T]he Peace Side of the 'Standard of Ur' (*see also* Pl. 90)

100–102 North Syrian and Sumerian sculpture. *Above, left,* white alabaster head, *c.* 3200 BC, from Tell Brak is one of earliest examples of North Syrian sculpture; *above,* a white magne[] statue of King Idrimi of Alalakh inscribed with a long b[] graphical inscription, fifteenth century BC; *left,* a diorite statue[] Gudea, governor of Lagash, *c.* 2100 BC

103, 104 The Hebrew stone ossuary of Nicanor inscribed for 'Nicanor the Alexandrian, who made the gates', – a pair of bronze gates given to the second Temple at Jerusalem in 10 BC

105, 106 Sassanian silver. *Left,* a bowl showing a Sassanian king attacked by lions, and, *right,* a bottle with a design of grape vines and a man carrying a basket of grapes. Both pieces are dated to the fourth century AD

107–110 *Above left,* a basalt stele showing Nabonidus, King of Babylon (556–539 BC) standing before the emblems of the Moon-god Sin; *above right,* Ashurbanipal, King of Assyria, represented as a basket-bearer at the rebuilding of the temple of the god, Marduk, 668 BC. *Below,* from Sippar, a stone lion's head, probably part of a throne, eighth to seventh century BC, and, *right,* a tablet recording the restoration of the temple of the Sun-god (Shamash) by Nabu-apal-iddina, King of Babylon, *c.* 870 BC

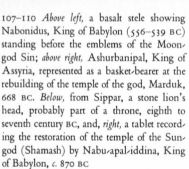

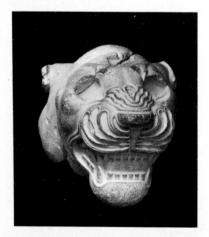

111, 112 *Above*, a bilingual inscription, Phoenician (left) and Numidian version (right), from the mausoleum of 'Ateban, [son] of Palu, from Thugga, third century BC; *below*, a lintel inscribed in monumental archaic Hebrew characters, 'The tomb [ch]amber in the side of the rock', from Siloam, *c.* 700 BC

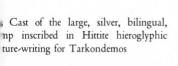

113 Cast of the large, silver, bilingual, [sta]mp inscribed in Hittite hieroglyphic [pic]ture-writing for Tarkondemos

114, 115 *Left,* calcite gravestone of a South Arabian named Aban, second century AD; *right,* a highly ~~mented~~ Punic stele

116–119 Impressions of stamp-seals covering a period of nearly four thousand years. *Far left,* a Sumerian seal with sheep, fourth millennium BC, *centre,* seals of Indus Valley type from Ur, *c.* 2500 BC; *above,* a Sassanian seal inscribed in Pahlavi around a royal figure, fifth century AD

exciting. Al Minah, on the other hand, was revealed as a most unusual discovery, a settlement of Greek traders, called Posidonium – a sort of miniature Hong, Kong trading with the Orient – on the coast of Syria, which flourished from the eighth to the fourth century BC.

After that point, 1949, Woolley went into retirement and gave up digging. In the post-war world when money was hard to get, it was thanks greatly to the new atmosphere of boundless public interest in archaeology aroused and stimulated by the brilliant performances of Sir Mortimer Wheeler and Glyn Daniel and others on the BBC television series, 'Animal, Vegetable and Mineral', that the government was induced to channel funds for excavations and similar research in the Near East, no longer to the British Museum, but to the appropriate British Schools or Institutes in the Near East, by way of the British Academy. In the countries of the Near East, also, much has changed. No longer are the excavators conducting the digs or the bodies supporting them able to withdraw and bring home all or a great proportion of their finds. The lion's share, if not all, is usually claimed by and remains in the country of its discovery, where today national museums, maintained by energetic government departments of antiquities, seek to build up their own collections to become important places of pilgrimage, both for scholars and tourists alike. Nevertheless, valuable additions to the British Museum collections have been received from the excavations of the British School in Iraq, under Sir Max Mallowan and David Oates, in the form especially of Phoenician ivory carvings from Nimrud.

85, 86, 92, 93, 416, 417

In the post-war years attention was first concentrated on restoring the Department of Egyptian and Assyrian Antiquities to some resemblance of pre-war normality. This phase concluded with a surprising but welcome development when in 1955 the Department was split into two to form the Department of Egyptian Antiquities and the Department of Western Asiatic Antiquities, as the Assyrian side was now more fittingly designated.

The last decade and a half since the division have been a period of consolidation devoted to a much widened scope of activity. Concurrently with the general resurgence of vitality exhibited by the Museum, a policy of modest but steady building of the weaker parts of the collections has been followed. Great stress has been laid on correct restoration and repair of objects (in many cases long ignored or neglected as hopeless cases), with the aid of the most scientific methods of modern conservation under the hands of an expert staff working in the closest liaison with the Research Laboratory. A new Students' Room was opened in 1959. The entire collection of clay cuneiform tablets, numbering about 120,000, has been checked and is in the process of being desalted, repaired and baked for preservation. Many loans have been made and others received. At the same time, an energetic publication programme of catalogues of the collections and editions of cuneiform texts has been pursued with the support of the Trustees, who, it must be stressed, have a record of publication of scholarly catalogues of their treasures which is not even remotely approached by any other comparable institution. It may now be fairly claimed that the Department has regained the position of being the real centre of cunei- form studies in this hemisphere which it occupied in the last century in the days of Smith, Rawlinson, Bezold and Pinches. Nor has the aspect of exhibition work been ignored, as all the galleries, noticeably the Assyrian sculpture galleries, at present owned by the Department have been, or are being, re- arranged. In particular, the Room of Writing has been added, showing all the history and varieties of cuneiform script on one side, and alphabetic writings on the other. The Palestine room was opened in 1974 and the Anatolian and Persian Rooms will be added shortly. The resources of the Western Asiatic Antiquities are indeed far from exhausted and should suffice to provide fresh material for study, contemplation and stimulation well into the twenty-first century.

R. D. BARNETT

CHAPTER FOUR

Ethnography

Although the Department of Ethnography did not become a separate entity until 1946, there have been collections of such material in the Museum from its foundation in 1753. These collections cover a wide field, which embraces the ethnography of all parts of the world outside Europe, and includes the archaeology of America (Neolithic onwards), Africa and Oceania, so that they really constitute a museum within the Museum. It is quite impossible within the limited space available to deal in detail with more than a very small representative selection of the Department's vast holdings.

The first specimens, which were part of the collection of Sir Hans Sloane, and classed as *Miscellanea*, included such things as the 'breastbone of a Pinguin' and a 'piece of rope used by ye common hangman'. The collection, however, had many important ethnographical specimens in it, among which may be mentioned Eskimo ivory carvings, American Indian carrying straps and tobacco pipes, and, of outstanding interest, a wooden drum collected in Virginia but of undoubted Ashanti type – the work no doubt of some unfortunate Negro slave who had taken his traditions with him.

Until 1861 all the antiquities were in one department, known as the Department of Antiquities, of which the ethnographical collections formed a very unimportant part. Between 1861 and 1866 the Coins and Medals, the Greek and Roman Antiquities and the Egyptian Department (which bore the name of Oriental Antiquities), were hived off into separate departments, the ethnographical collections remaining with British Antiquities until 1922. At this time a new department, Ceramics and Ethnography, was formed, which continued, with a change of name to Oriental Antiquities and Ethnography, until 1946, when a separate Department of Ethnography was created.

It cannot be said that there was any clear cut policy with regard to collecting during the late eighteenth and early nineteenth centuries but it was a time of great exploration, men were full of ideas about the noble savage, and the Department of Antiquities was nothing if not catholic in its taste. Collections made by the early explorers were among the earliest important acquisitions. Sir Joseph Banks was no doubt influential in some of these coming to the Museum. Most important perhaps were the collections of artifacts made on the voyages of Captain Cook in the Pacific between 1767 and 1780. It was by this means that the Department obtained some of its most outstanding specimens from Oceania and the north-west coast of America. T. E. Bowdich's mission to Ashanti in 1817, Captain (afterward Admiral) Parry's

129

120–123 Central American art. *Left and above,* a carved jadeite axe and a head, both Olmec from the Gulf Coast of Mexico; *below, left,* the Maya polychrome vase from Nebaj; *below right,* a basalt Aztec mask showing the flayed skin from the face of a victim sacrificed to the god Xipe

4-126 *Above,* an alabaster blood offering bowl from
~~~otihuacan in the shape of an ocelot; *below, left,*
~~~ue of the maize god, Maya, from Copan; *below,*
~~~t,* a Moche portrait vase from Peru

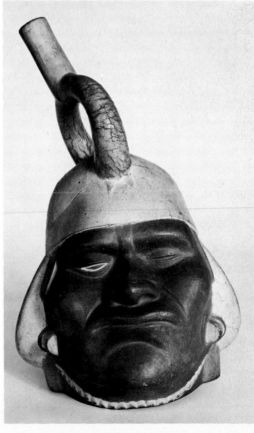

expedition to the Arctic in 1828 and many other voyages resulted in valuable ethnographical collections for the British Museum. Other collections came from private collectors such as W. Bullock's collection of Mexican sculpture, or from scientific expeditions such as that of Sir Robert Schomburgk to British Guiana between 1831 and 1835.

Thus, by the time the old Antiquities Department was divided in 1861, there was a very substantial corpus of ethnographical material in the Museum. With the appointment of Mr A. W. (afterwards Sir Wollaston) Franks to the Keepership, the expansion of the collections positively leapt ahead. Franks was a man of wide interests, primarily an archaeologist, but especially interested, partly owing to his friendship with Henry Christy, in ethnography. Anthropology was in its infancy. Darwin's *Origin of Species* was applied to the study of Man. There grew up a vogue for the study of the artifacts of primitive people as showing the various stages in the evolution of our modern material civilization. Quantities of specimens were collected with the idea of tracing evolution by seriation. This was particularly promising in the field of the decorative arts. Examples of this approach can be seen in the work of Henry Balfour and of A. C. Haddon. At the same time General Pitt Rivers was building up his collections of comparative ethnology, now at Oxford. The haphazard collection of practically everything made by primitive peoples became crystallized into a definite philosophy. A great many objects of all kinds, often many examples of the same kind with only minor variations, were now acquired deliberately. Looking at the collections of this time one has the impression that weapons predominated, possibly because so many benefactors were service people; really they are the least important. Any object which told anything about the life and background of the primitive peoples of the world became important to the Museum. Frequently an apparently meaningless design can be traced back to some religious or totemic emblem, as for example the scroll designs from the Massim area of New Guinea which have been shown to represent the frigate bird. This opens the road to speculation on the role of the frigate bird in Massim thought and religion.

In recent years the policy has been to collect everything possible before the native products disappear, ousted by the products of Birmingham, Detroit, Pittsburgh and the Ruhr. This policy, really crystallized in the days of Franks, is, and must be, the policy of the Department today. In such collections, made with these objects in view, fine art plays only a small part. Art *per se* is a part of culture, but only a part of it, and the Department of Ethnography is concerned with cultures as a whole, not any one aspect of them. Nevertheless there are some magnificent examples of the art of almost every branch of mankind in the Department.

It will be more convenient to consider important acquisitions by geographical areas rather than on a chronological basis. Dealing first with the Americas, including archaeology as well as ethnography, the most important additions ever made came from the Christy collection. Henry Christy, a member of a Lancashire textile family, became interested in ethnography and made frequent journeys abroad to collect. A journey to Mexico with E. B. Tylor, the founder of anthropological studies at Oxford, gave his interests a particular twist towards America (though his interest and collections covered every field). At his death he appointed four trustees to his collection with authority to donate it to some museum. Franks, who was one of the trustees, persuaded his fellow trustees to offer the collection, amounting to more than 10,000 pieces to the British Museum. In this collection were most of the Mexican turquoise mosaic masks and other regalia. They are made with an inlay of minute turquoise fragments over matrices of wood or, in the case of one piece, the mask of Tezcatlipoca, a human skull. These regalia are believed to be part of the gift made by the Aztec ruler Moctezuma to Cortés in the mistaken belief that he was a reincarnation of the god Quetzalcoatl. Cortés sent them to the Emperor Charles V, and they were ultimately dispersed throughout the Empire. Christy bought a number of these pieces wherever he could find them; a breast ornament in the form of a double-headed serpent, was purchased with money from the Christy fund in 1899, nearly forty years after his death; another piece, in Christy's collection at the time of his death, was, according to a Museum tradition, found in a shop in Florence where it was being used as a quarry for pieces of turquoise to make cheap jewellery.

145

Among other magnificent examples of American art in this collection is a ceremonial axe, carved in jadeite with the head of a ferocious being, half man, half jaguar. It comes from the Olmec, who lived on the Gulf coast of Mexico towards the end of the first millennium BC. We do not know its use, but similar sculptures suggest that the Olmec worshipped a race of demi-gods with these characteristics. Another Olmec piece, though not in the Christy collection, was bequeathed to the Museum in 1923. This is a fragment from a casket and represents a head with delicately carved drooping lips which are characteristic of all Olmec art. A very beautiful Aztec mask in the Christy collection has a rather grim subject, representing the priest of the god Xipe Totec, whose victims were flayed after sacrifice. The sacrificial priest donned the still bleeding skin and danced in it to symbolize the rebirth of the corn. The mask shows the skin stretched tightly over the priest's face; the reverse shows the priest dancing in his grisly costume.

120

121

123

The Department has a representative collection of pottery and figurines from all the Mexican, and many Central American pre-Columbian cultures, acquired from time to time by gift or purchase, and fair collections of sculpture. A wonderful example of the latter is a Cuauhxicalli, or blood offering bowl, of alabaster carved in the form of an ocelot. This comes from Teotihuacan, the dominant city in Mexico for about eight hundred years. It dates from perhaps AD 500 and shows the typical features of Teotihuacan sculpture, namely angularity and formalism, but, unlike most of the limited amount of sculpture from that site, it displays an almost incredibly mobile and vigorous quality. It is interesting to note that it was found by a labourer at the foot of the Pyramid

124

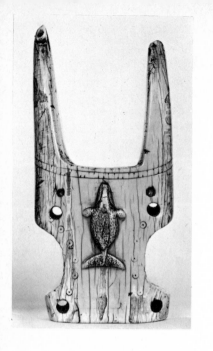

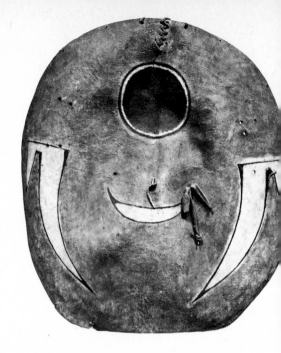

127–129 *Above, left,* an Eskimo ivory harpoon rest; *above, right,* a Plains Indian shield with abstract curvilinear desig *below,* wooden feather boxes from New Zealand, the lower from the Cook collection

130, 131 *Left,* a wooden figure of the war god Kukailimoku from Hawaii, and, *right,* wooden figure of a man, Arawak, Jamaica

of the Sun, and offered to the Museo Nacional. As they would not buy it, the labourer sold it to an English traveller, something which could not happen today. A fine piece of sculpture from the Totonacs of the Gulf Coast is a greenstone yoke, from the Christy collection. For many years these yokes were mysteries, but recently they have been shown to be ceremonial replicas in stone of protective belts worn in the ritual ball game played with a solid rubber ball.

The Department has always been strong in collections from the Maya of south-eastern Mexico, and Guatemala. Most important of all is the collection of Maya sculpture (both casts and originals), made by Dr A. P. Maudslay, who made a number of expeditions to Maya sites between 1881 and 1894. His work in the *Biologia Centrali-Americana* is a classic. When his collection was first offered to the Museum at the turn of the century, the Trustees declined it on grounds of lack of space. It was housed in the Victoria and Albert Museum until 1922, when it was finally transferred to Bloomsbury. In this collection 125 are a number of fine carvings from Copan, including the maize god, which came from Temple No. 22 and which dates from about AD 700. This shows the young god wearing a pendant in the form of a skull, which may indicate the death of the corn at harvest. The other important sculptures in this collection are the very fine series of lintels from Yaxchilan, one of which shows a penitent performing a blood-letting ritual before a priest. A large collection of post classic Maya material from British Honduras was given in 1899 by Thomas Gann, Medical Officer of Health in the colony, and in 1938 the Department received, as a bequest, his magnificent collection of jades, including a superb plaque in the style of Nebaj, which was found at Teotihuacan, and a number of very finely modelled stucco heads. Pottery from the whole of Central 122 America is well represented, the most important piece being the famous Nebaj vase which was in the Fenton collection, purchased in 1930.

From South America there is a fine sculptured figure of the Jaguar deity from San Agustin in Colombia, which was brought home by Vice-Admiral Dowding, and given to the Museum in 1899. The remaining South American collections are particularly strong in pottery, among which must be mentioned the collections from Nasca and the Moche valley in Peru. The most important pieces among the latter came from the collection of Mr Henry Van den Bergh, and were presented by the National Art-Collections Fund. These vessels date 126, 144 from about AD 600. They are mostly funerary, and often portrait heads.

Apart from vast quantities of stone implements there is little of note in the way of North American archaeology, except the Squier and Davis collection, purchased from the Blackmore Museum, of material from the Hopewell mound cultures of Ohio. Most interesting of these is a collection of tobacco pipes with bowls carved in faithful representations of birds, animals and reptiles, so well and so accurately that they could serve as a textbook to the fauna of the area. They may have been totemic in origin.

Turning to the ethnographical material from Arctic America, we find that the collections from the Eskimo are extremely rich, and abound in small ivory carvings of natural objects which carry the germ of the feeling of the magnificent modern Eskimo art. Most of it takes the form of ivory etchings on utilitarian objects such as bow drill handles, or the fine harpoon rest for an umyak, a   127 large skin boat used in whale hunting. This piece was bought in 1937 in the Caledonian market (one of London's street markets) and sold to the Museum. Most of the Eskimo collections, however, came from early voyages of explora/ tion. Parry's expedition of 1824; the Barrow collection, containing material collected in the search for the ill/fated Franklin Expedition, and another collection given by the Admiralty, both in 1855, form the basis for the Arctic American collection. They have been added to as opportunity offered by casual purchases ever since.

Except for the Indians of the north/west coast the North American collections are not outstanding in their art content, though a Plains Indian shield, with   128 abstract curvilinear designs in black and red, shows a marvellous sense of pattern. From the north/west coast, however, with its tradition of magnificent wood carving, the Department has excellent collections, of which carvings from Nootka Sound, collected during Cook's voyage and a number of important pieces from Vancouver's voyage, form one of the best collections in the Old World of this early material. From South America the earliest collection was made by Sir Robert Schomburgk in British Guiana between 1831 and 1835. This was the first really well documented collection, showing the life of a contemporary living people, to reach the British Museum. Since that date substantial collections of everyday articles have been received, chiefly from explorers of the headwaters of the Amazon.

Turning to Oceania, we shall see how the nucleus of Oceanic material collected on Cook's voyages was expanded very rapidly in the nineteenth century because of the intense naval and colonial activity of the period, result/ ing from the scramble for colonies by the principal European powers, and the missionary and scientific activity which accompanied it. Many of the im/ portant acquisitions mentioned from this area were collected by colonial civil servants, missionaries and naturalists. As a result, the British Museum has some of the finest examples of the art of Oceania before it was vitiated by European contact.

Mention must be made of the very fine carved wooden feather boxes from   129 the Cook collection, with their elaborate curvilinear carving undertaken with no better tools than stone chisels, shark's teeth or shells. Although the Museum did not receive it until 1891 the Polynesian collections, especially those from Hawaii, were much enriched by the collection made on Vancouver's voyage by J. J. Hewett, who was Surgeon's Mate on that expedition. In this collection was one of the Department's magnificent feather effigies representing the war god Kukailimoku. These objects, made by sewing the breast feathers of small birds on to a network foundation which was in turn stretched over a wicker framework, were carried on ceremonial occasions. Other feather work from the

132–135 West African art. *Above, left,* a Benin
mask; *above,* an 'Afro-Portuguese' ivory salt w
European ship carved on its lid; *left,* figure from
Lower Niger Bronze Industry showing a' h
returning with his kill, an antelope, slung ove
shoulders; *opposite,* a wooden portrait statue of I
Shamba Bolongongo of the Bakuba tribe,

Hawaiian islands includes a number of feather cloaks and capes; one formerly in the Beasley collection, to be mentioned below, was collected by the Russian Admiral Kotzebue. Others were given to Queen Victoria by King Kame⁄ hameha III of Hawaii, and deposited on permanent loan by her. Two stone figures from Easter Island, brought home by H.M.S. *Topaze*, were presented to the Museum, the larger by Queen Victoria, and the smaller by the Admiralty. These figures and others like them were quarried from the volcanic tufa of the extinct volcano of Rano Raraku. Some were set up on small platforms; many more remain in the crater where they were quarried. A very fine collection of gods from Eastern Polynesia, made by the London Missionary Society, was lent to the Museum in 1899 but was finally purchased for a nominal sum in 1910. Mention should be made of the figure of the creator god Tangaroa.

136   One notable Polynesian specimen is the Tahitian mourner's dress. How this was obtained is not clear from Museum records but, judging from Webber's drawings, it must almost certainly have been collected on Captain Cook's voyages. It was worn by the chief mourner who perambulated with a band of youths. Recently the costume had to be dismantled for conservation purposes and it was discovered that the whole assembly had been built up on an old black⁄board easel, and incorporated in the structure to support the head⁄dress was a very fine little Tahitian god. Evidently whoever made the original assembly considered the collection so rich in Tahitian gods that one could be spared for this mundane purpose!

Mention must also be made of two benefactors, Sir George Grey, Governor of New Zealand, who gave the Museum his excellent collection in 1854, and the late H. G. Beasley, a wealthy brewer, who started his collection as a boy and bequeathed it just after the War.

In addition to these large acquisitions which form the bulk of the collections there was an almost infinite number of gifts by Franks, who made innumerable purchases for the Museum out of his own pocket. One such gift of great interest is a Hawaiian seat. At first glance this gives the impression of a crawling man, but it can be stood on its feet, when it assumes the appearance of a juggler; this can be duplicated by other examples of Polynesian art in the Museum. The very good collections from Australia, New Guinea and the Melanesian islands, like those from Polynesia, were partly the result of naval and colonial activity in the nineteenth century. A list, by no means exhaustive, of some of these collections will show this. The first was a collection from New Guinea, made on the fourth cruise of H.M.S. *Rattlesnake*, given to the Museum in 1851; this was followed, among others, by collections from the Admiralty Islands by Sir Wyville Thompson and H. N. Moseley, both naturalists on the H.M.S. *Challenger* Expedition, 1872–6; from the Solomon Islands by H. B. Guppy, surgeon on H.M.S. *Lark*; from the New Hebrides by Captain Cross; from H. J. Veitch (New Guinea); from Torres Straits by A. C. Haddon; from New Ireland and New Guinea, formed by the District commissioner, H. H. Romilly, and presented by the Duke of Bedford.

In more recent years the Museum purchased the very fine collection from the Trobriand Islands made by the distinguished anthropologist Bronislaw Malinowski. Recently another was formed on an expedition to New Guinea sponsored by the Museum and undertaken by an assistant keeper in the Department, Mr B. A. L. Cranstone.

In all these collections art is incidental. Mention should, however, be made of the magnificent masks and figures from the Sepik river area of New Guinea, and the painted and carved shields from this same area and from Australia. Particularly interesting are the shields from the Eilanden river collected and presented by Lord Moyne shortly before the War, which show conventional patterns derived from the human form.

The rather limited Micronesian collections include a collection of vessels of various sizes and shapes in which the bird motifs are inlaid in white tridacna shell on the red painted ground of the wood. A quite interesting story is attached to these. An East Indiaman, the *Antelope*, was wrecked on one of the Palau Islands in 1783; the survivors were very kindly treated by the king of the islands; in Wilson's *Pellew Islands* there is an account of how they were fed from a bird-shaped bowl which held 'twenty-six quarts'. This magnificent bowl is now in the collections of the Department.

Just as the nineteenth century was the time of greatest expansion of the Oceanic collections, the twentieth has seen enormous expansion of the African. While there were a few important acquisitions from Africa in the nineteenth century such as collections made by Sir John Kirk in 1888 and H. H. Johnston in 1889, the real impetus to the growth of the African collections came from the Benin Expedition of 1897. Almost everybody on the Expedition brought home magnificent examples of ivory carvings and bronze casting. The greater part of the Benin collections came to the Museum in 1898, though not all from the same source. The pair of ivory leopards were given to Queen Victoria and later deposited on loan in the British Museum by King George V. Many important pieces, of course, remained in private hands, and the Department has endeavoured to complete its collections of this material whenever such pieces came up for sale. Among the bronzes was a wonderful collection of bronze plaques in high relief which formerly adorned the pillars of the Oba's palace. They depict soldiers, musicians and scenes from everyday life. Some particularly interesting examples show Portuguese soldiers in sixteenth-century costume. There are also fine castings in the round, including the famous Queen Mother's head, an early sixteenth-century work, in which the curved coral head-dress balances the slight prognathousness of the lips. Other castings in the round include arquebusiers, hornblowers, and a very fine cock who, however, suffers slightly from being tail-heavy. The ivories included delicately carved wristlets and many other objects. Among these must be mentioned a very fine double bell given by Mrs Webster Plass, an American lady who has benefited the African section of the Department with many magnificent examples of African art.

137

138

141

139

132

136 Dress of a chief mourner from Tahiti, probably presented to Captain Cook

137, 138 *Above,* a fine, carved and pain shield from Queenland; *below,* a bird-shap bowl, inlaid with shell and painted, from Palau Islands

139–141 *Above, left, and below*, examples of the art of Benin; the very fine bronze Queen Mother's head, and a pair of ivory leopards, their spots indicated by brass studs; *above, right*, the bronze head of a king from Ife, Nigeria

Not to be confused with the ivories from the Benin area is a class of ivories to which the appellation 'Afro-Portuguese' has been applied. They were obviously made by native craftsmen in the sixteenth century to the orders of the Portuguese, some by the guild of ivory carvers (Igbesamwan) in Benin, but mostly in Sherbro, in Sierra Leone. The technique and idiom of the carving is African but the subjects are often European, as, for example, is the very fine salt, the lid of which shows a European sailing ship complete with lookout in the crow's nest. This specimen came into the Museum in 1878, but the records give no information of the circumstances in which it was acquired.

134

If the Navy was not so forthcoming in material for the Department in the twentieth century, colonial administrators more than made up for the drying up of that source. From every British-administered territory there came collec- tions illustrating native life. It would be tedious to list all the benefactors, but among others there are P. Amaury Talbot (Southern Nigeria), and C. W. Hobley and Sir Claud Hollis (East Africa). It is interesting that collections made by people such as these were made not as a result of official instructions, as was the case of many continental colonial officials who had had definite instructions to make collections for their national museums, but were the result of purely voluntary activities. Perhaps the anthropological training given to some of them may have encouraged them in these 'extra- mural' pursuits.

To T. R. O. Mangin the Department owes a substantial part of its fine collection of bronze weights for weighing gold dust from Ashanti, though there are many other donors. These little weights, almost a sculpture gallery in miniature, were made in the form of men, animals or insects, as well as objects in everyday use, and in purely geometric form. They frequently symbolize Ashanti proverbs. A hornbill, for example, signifies patience, no bad thing perhaps for a gold trader. The actual proverb goes, 'The snake lieth in the grass, but God has given him the hornbill.' A porcupine stands for the Ashanti proverb, 'A man does not rub bottoms with a porcupine,' or, as we would say, 'It is hard to kick against the pricks.'

The area outside former British-administered territories from which the Department has the best collection of carvings and textiles is the former Belgian Congo, made between 1904 and 1910 by Emil Torday, and pur- chased from time to time by the Museum. Outstanding in this connection are three portrait figures in wood of three kings of the Bakuba tribe, the finest of which is that of King Shamba Bolongongo.

135

While still dealing with West Africa it is convenient to consider at this point the bronze head of a king from Ife in Southern Nigeria, which was purchased in 1939. The style differs substantially from that of Benin in being much more naturalistic, and it is considered to be earlier. The fine parallel lines emphasize the form of the face. It has been suggested that these are tribal cicatrization, but other heads in the possession of the Oni of Ife do not have this, so the argument is very weak.

140

Another style of bronze working from Nigeria is known as the Lower Niger Bronze Industry. As far as the author is aware no definite date has been applied to this industry. The Department's best example of this art style is a   133
figure of a hunter returning with his kill.

The collections of masks, fetishes and other objects of wood from West Africa are almost innumerable. While these collections were good before the War they have been enormously enriched since, first by the purchase of the Oldman collection, then by the generous gifts of Mrs Webster Plass, mentioned above, and finally by a very large gift from the Trustees of the Wellcome Historical Medical Museum. When the Wellcome Museum's warehouse was bombed during the War, the British Museum provided alternative storage space in the then empty Duveen galleries for the ethnographical material which had been accumulated during Sir Henry Wellcome's lifetime. When, after the War, the Wellcome trustees decided to disperse the collection, first choice was given to the British Museum. This added some twenty thousand specimens to the collections. All sections benefited from this gift, but none so much as the African section which obtained more than half the total number. Even today, some eighteen years later, this African material has not yet been fully in- corporated into the collections.

In addition to the big collections mentioned above, single objects have been given to the Department or purchased at appropriate times. One very fine Nigerian carving, or rather set of carvings, is a pair of doors and a lintel   143
from Ikere-Ekiti. It was carved by a famous Yoruba carver for the Palace of the Ogoga early in this century, and shows a ceremonial visit from the British administrator of the area. He is depicted sitting in a litter, complete with pith helmet, and looking on rather dyspeptically. This extremely interesting specimen was obtained from the Ogoga in 1924, by an unusual exchange. The Ogoga wanted a rather special throne, so the British Museum arranged to have one made to his specification in exchange for the doors and lintel.

The Department's collection of textiles from Africa is extensive. This is partly due to a gift in 1934 from Charles Beving who, like Christy, was a Lancashire textile manufacturer. In the years before the 1914–18 War he had travelled extensively in Africa and Asia, making a collection of locally-made cloths of all kinds with a view to obtaining ideas for his designers which would be acceptable in markets all over the world. This example of business enterprise has given the Museum a most comprehensive collection including many examples of the ingenious tie-dyeing process, whereby the cloth is tied or sewn in folds so that the dye only reaches part of the cloth and frequently produces very beautiful patterns.

The growth of the Asiatic collections followed the same pattern as that of the other sections of the Department, mainly a number of important collections from official donors but made in their private capacity, supplemented by smaller gifts and purchases. There are specimens from almost everywhere in Asia, mostly dating from the nineteenth century when they were collected, but there

142 Carved wooden figure of an ancestor from Easter Island

143 Carved, narrative, wooden door from the Palace of the Ogoga, Ikere-Ekiti, Nigeria

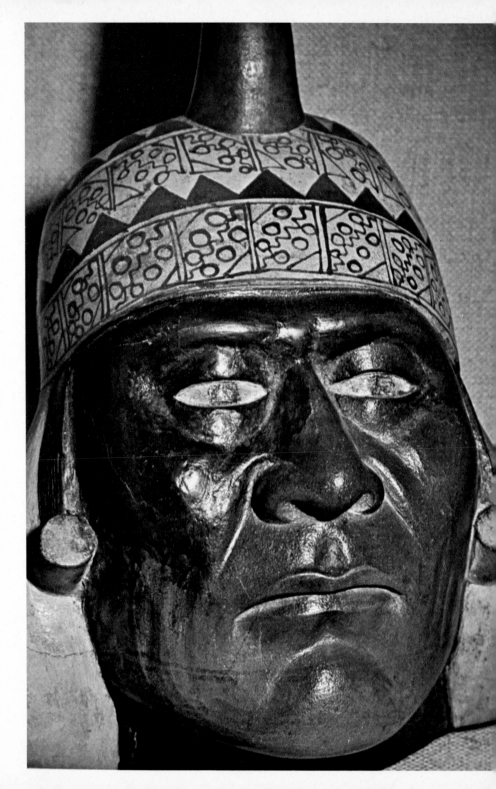

A Moche portrait vase from Peru

Mask of Tezcatlipoca made of turquoise mosaic built up on a human skull

are two areas from which the Department's holdings are particularly strong, namely Sarawak and Java. The first acquisition from Sarawak was a collection presented by Rajah Brooke of Sarawak in 1850. This was followed at various times by gifts and purchases from Dr Charles Hose's wonderful collection which included some very fine wood carvings, among which may be mentioned a number of house boards and masks. One specimen from Sarawak, which came into the Museum in 1931 and which has particular charm, is a wood carving from the Iban tribe, of a hornbill, gaily painted in red, blue and yellow. Objects of this kind were set up before houses, possibly as a kind of good luck charm, though the precise significance of them is uncertain.

148

Java is particularly well represented by the Raffles collection formed by Sir Stamford Raffles when he was Lieutenant Governor of the island from 1811 to 1816. It comprises a very fine *gamelan* (the instruments for a complete orchestra), masks and puppets for Javanese plays derived from Hindu legends. Especially fine are the hide puppets used in the shadow plays.

149

There are good collections from the Andaman and Nicobar Islands given by M. V. Portman in 1896 and E. H. Man in 1898, and from Sir Richard Temple between 1897 and 1905. It is from the Nicobar Islands that the very fine 'scaredevils' come – ferocious-looking monstrous animals and anthropoid figures used to ward off diseases and evil spirits.

147

Malay weapons and silver work of all kinds are well represented. Typical of this is a niello silver belt buckle from Negri Sembilan.

Mention must finally be made of the excellent collection of Palestinian textiles and costumes collected by Miss Shelagh Weir, an assistant keeper in the Department, who made two expeditions to the Near East, in 1967 and again in 1968. This may be the last opportunity of collecting in this field, but it is to be hoped that the Department will continue its policy of collecting everything it can while there is still time by sending its staff into the field whenever funds are available.

ADRIAN DIGBY

146–148 *Above,* hide puppet used in the Javanese shadow plays; *right,* a fearsome looking 'scare devil', from the Nicobar Islands; *below,* examples of finely carved house boards, from Sarawak

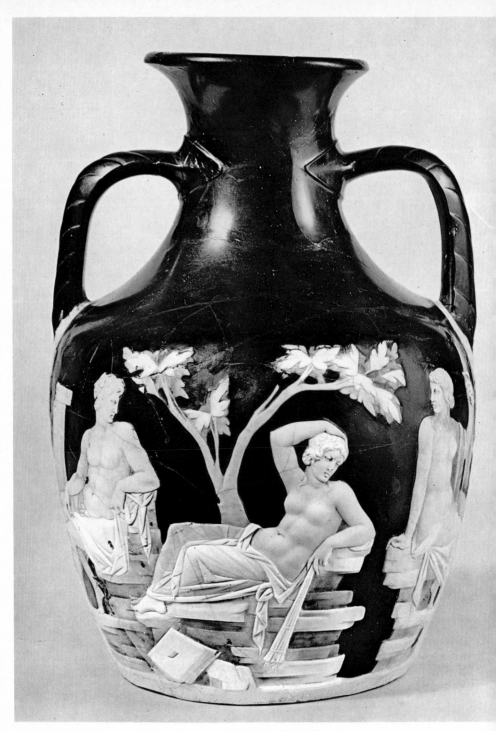

149 The Portland Vase, one of the best known antiquities in the British Museum

CHAPTER FIVE

Greek and Roman Antiquities

The British Museum possessed a few Classical antiquities from the foundation collection of Sir Hans Sloane, but none of any consequence until the acquisition in 1772 of the Hamilton collection. This fine assemblage, comprising Greek vases and other antiquities from southern Italy, was formed by Sir William Hamilton, Ambassador at the Court of Naples from 1764 to 1800 (and husband of Nelson's Emma).

The year 1805 saw the first substantial accession of Classical sculpture with the purchase of Charles Towneley's unrivalled collection of statues, bronzes and terracottas, mostly of Roman date. Two years later the Hamilton and Towneley collections, together with the Egyptian sculptures acquired in 1801, were installed in a new suite of rooms extending from the north-west corner of Montagu House, and known as the Gallery of Antiquities (later as the Towneley Gallery).

Greek sculpture came next. In 1815 the sculptures from the Temple of Apollo at Bassae, near Phigaleia in Arcadia, were acquired. This temple, built between 450 and 400 BC, had been forgotten in the Middle Ages and was not rediscovered till 1765. The sculptures were excavated in 1811 by a party of adventurers and shipped to Zante (then a British possession), where they were put up to auction and, thanks largely to the efforts of the Prince Regent, were bought for the nation.

168

A year later, in 1816, the British Government bought (for £35,000) the sculptures and other antiquities acquired by the Earl of Elgin in Greece in the early years of the nineteenth century. The cream of the collection (commonly known as the Elgin Marbles) consists of sculptures from the Parthenon in Athens. Elgin had originally intended only to make drawings and casts, but when it became apparent how seriously the monuments on the Acropolis were deteriorating, he sought, and obtained, a *firman* from the Sultan to remove sculptures and inscriptions.

167

In 1825 the Museum was enriched by Sir Richard Payne Knight's bequest, which included superb collections of classical bronzes. Temporary accommodation was at once built for the Phigaleia and Elgin collections, to be replaced in 1832 by permanent galleries.

By 1845 Montagu House and the attached Gallery of Antiquities had been pulled down, and in the new British Museum the Greek and Roman antiquities were allotted a substantial part of the area which they occupy today.

150 A large example of a marble, female, Cycladic idol, *c.* 2500–2000 BC

151 A unique Minoan bronze statuette showing a Cretan athlete somersaulting over the back of a charging bull, sixteenth century BC

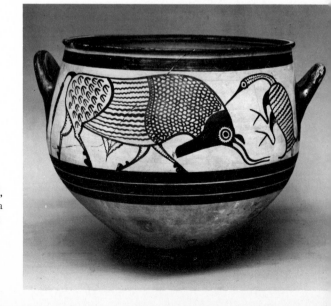

152 A Mycenaean vase from Enkomi, Cyprus, showing a bird removing a tick from the hide of a bull, *c.* 1250 BC

153–155 *Above, left,* a small stylized bronze horse, 800–700 BC, which has affinities with the Geometric style seen on the vase, *left,* made before 700 BC in Athens. *Above,* two Eastern Greek terracotta statuettes representing Aphrodite, that on the right is in the form of a scent-bottle, *c.* 550 BC

169   The next important acquisition consisted of sculptures from Xanthus in Lycia, excavated by Sir Charles Fellows in 1842–3, followed by the sculptures from the Mausoleum at Halicarnassus in Western Asia Minor which were excavated in 1856–7 by C. T. (later Sir Charles) Newton, a member of the staff of the Museum.

In 1861 the old Department of Antiquities was split into three, and Newton became the first Keeper of Greek and Roman Antiquities. The new Depart-ment was soon enriched by the arrival of sculptures and architectural ornaments from the great Temple of Artemis (Diana) at Ephesus. The site of this temple, built about 330–300 BC to replace an earlier one burnt down in 356 BC, had been completely forgotten and was rediscovered in 1869 by J. T. Wood after six years of patient searching.

The severe overcrowding from which the Greek and Roman Department was now suffering was relieved in 1880–3 by the transfer to South Kensington of the Natural History collections, and by the simultaneous erection of a new gallery for the sculptures from the Mausoleum (now Rooms 12–14 with their basements). The departmental gallery space was now very much as it is today.

The next substantial acquisitions came as a result of excavations undertaken in Cyprus in 1894–6 by the British Museum, with funds bequeathed by Miss E. T. Turner. As a result of these excavations the Department found itself possessed of a collection of Cypriote antiquities second to none, ranging from the Early Bronze Age to the time of the Roman Empire.

In 1904–5 the Museum sponsored a second expedition to Ephesus, which uncovered the remains of the earlier temple.

The great days of acquisition were now over, and the next landmark in the history of the Department was the erection of a new gallery for the more spacious display of the sculptures of the Parthenon. Undertaken at the expense of Lord Duveen of Millbank (and known as the Duveen Gallery) it was com-pleted in 1938, but the onset of war in 1939 prevented the installation of the sculptures.

The antiquities of the Greek and Roman Department survived the war intact. Many were removed to places of safety in the country, while much of the heavier sculpture was stored in a disused section of the London Under-ground Railway. The Department itself, however, suffered considerable bomb damage. The Greek and Roman Life Room and the Bronze Room were completely destroyed, and the new Duveen Gallery badly damaged.

After the War the collections were gradually re-assembled, and by 1961 most of the public galleries belonging to the Department were again open. The sculptures of the Parthenon were at first installed in their pre-war locations until the Duveen Gallery could be restored. At last, in 1962, they were trans-ferred to their new home.

This move left three ground-floor galleries empty, and the opportunity was taken for a complete re-organization of the Departmental collections in a manner more acceptable to present-day taste.

The ground-floor rooms (the old Sculpture Galleries) now contain a primary exhibition of sculpture and other antiquities, arranged chronologically.   10
The second stage of re-organization will comprise a primary exhibition of inscriptions and architectural members, and a secondary exhibition of inscrip-tions and sculptures, in the basements. The architectural room opened in 1974. As a third stage, the upper-floor galleries will be re-organized to contain primary exhibitions of Cypriote and Etruscan antiquities, an enlarged exhibi-tion of Greek and Roman Life, and secondary exhibitions of small antiquities.

The new arrangement on the ground floor displays the greatest treasures in the departmental collections; and, to grasp the scope of the department, we could do no better than to visit these new galleries.

The entrance is marked by a partial reconstruction of the façade of a royal tomb at Mycenae of about 1250 BC, the so-called Treasury of Atreus. The green marble columns incorporated in the reconstruction were given by Lord Sligo in 1905.

We pass into Room 1, devoted to Bronze Age antiquities from the Cycladic islands, of 3000 to 1600 BC. The principal attraction lies in the marble statuettes and vases made between 3000 and 2000 BC. One of the finest of these statuettes,   150 so-called Cycladic idols, was made between 2500 and 2000 BC and depicts a naked woman, perhaps a goddess, standing with her arms folded across her breast. The modelling is summary but remarkably effective. The head, tilted back, is oval in shape, with flat top; the nose stands out as a high ridge; eyes and mouth were originally indicated in paint, which has perished.

Room 2 is devoted to the Minoan civilization of Crete (3000–1100 BC) and the related Mycenaean civilization of Greece and the other islands (1600–1100 BC). The Minoan civilization, first uncovered by Sir Arthur Evans at Knossos in the early years of this century, is not here represented as wothily as one might hope, but certain outstanding pieces cannot fail to catch the eye. Among them is a bronze statuette, recently acquired from the Spencer-Churchill collection, of an athlete leaping over a charging bull. Made about 1600 BC, this statuette   151 is one of the very few representations in the round of the famous Cretan bull-sports to have survived.

Another Minoan masterpiece is a gold pendant from the so-called Aegina   156 Treasure. Acquired in 1892, it may well come (as was stated at the time) from the island of Aegina, but was made in Crete between 1700 and 1600 BC. The pendant, perhaps originally suspended from the head of a pin, shows a nature-god holding a water-bird in either hand. Although the influence of Egyptian art is strong, the god is a true Cretan, for he wears the typical tight belt, loin-cloth and frontal sheath.

The Mycenaean period is better represented than the Minoan, particularly by superb pottery from cemeteries at Ialysus in Rhodes and Enkomi in Cyprus. Space permits the illustration of only one Mycenaean vase but it demonstrates   152 particularly well the skill of the Mycenaean potter. Made about 1250 BC, it depicts on either side a bull, from whose hide a bird is removing a tick with its

156, 157 Examples of Greek jewellery, some 1300 years apart in date. *Above*, a gold pendant from the so-called Aegina Treasure; it is a Minoan piece of *c.* 1700 BC showing the 'Master of the Animals' (*cf. Pl. 166*). *Below*, a gold necklace of *c.* 380 BC from the Greek colony of Taras. Its detailed decoration must have been designed to provide maximum effect in sunlight

beak. The curious patterns on bull and bird were evidently inspired by embroidery stitches.

Room 3 is devoted to the long period between 1100 and 500 BC, and contains many of the finest small objects in the Departmental collections. We start with the Dark Ages, 1100–700 BC, represented by little but pottery in the so-called Geometric style, of which the best examples were made in Athens, such as the vase made shortly before 700 BC, especially for burial with the dead. In addition to the usual bands of geometrical patterns, it carries on the shoulder a row of panels with animals and birds and on the body a funeral scene. The matchstick figures in silhouette are characteristic of Geometric drawing. 10 155

About 800 BC the plastic arts, dormant since the Mycenaean period, began to revive. Typical of this is the large class of small bronze horses which were made between 800 and 700 BC. Their trim lines and simplified forms, not unlike their fellows painted on Geometric vases, endow them with great charm. 153

The Archaic period, between 700 and shortly after 500 BC, is best represented in Room 3 by small works of art, the large sculptures being all somewhat damaged. We note first two charming terracotta figures, perhaps representing the goddess Aphrodite, made about 550 BC, in the Eastern part of the Greek world. They are twins, except that the one on the right was made as a scent-bottle (the spout is on the top of her head), while the other was intended to be enjoyed for itself. The goddess stands rather stiffly, holding a dove to her breast, her mantle falling across her body in elaborate folds. In these miniature master-pieces we can surely see echoes of some long-lost statue. 154

Another masterpiece is a bronze figure of a banqueter, probably from Dodona in north Greece, of about 520 BC. Together with two companions, he originally decorated the rim of a large bronze bowl. He is altogether leaner and more alert than the sleepy goddesses, and probably belongs to the Pelopon-nesian school of bronze-workers. This beautifully executed and perfectly preserved statuette may well claim to be the finest small bronze to have come down to us from antiquity. 164

As examples of Archaic jewellery, no less accomplished than the bronzes, the Department possesses a large number of gold ornaments from Camirus in Rhodes, made between 700 and 600 BC, such as the set of rectangular gold plaques which were worn as breast-ornaments. A winged goddess is shown, holding in either hand a diminutive lion. She was really an Asiatic deity, but was associated by the Greeks, rather surprisingly, with Artemis. The principal forms on these plaques are embossed in low relief, while the details are rendered by the application of countless minute grains of gold, in the so-called granula-tion technique. 166

The Athenian pre-eminence in vase-painting had passed about 700 BC to Corinth, and examples of Corinthian vases are shown in this Room. Soon after 600 BC, however, the potters of Athens again led the field. A vase in the black-figure style, made in Athens about 540 BC, is signed by Exekias, the finest vase-painter of his day, as both potter and painter. The Greek hero 158

Achilles is shown killing the Amazon queen Penthesilea at Troy. Seldom have intricate detail and forceful style been more effectively combined.

We pass through the ante-room (Room 4) into Room 5, which covers the period 500 to 430 BC. The earliest, and finest, example of free-standing sculpture in this room is the so-called Strangford Apollo, a marble statue perhaps of Apollo, perhaps of a young man, made in one of the Greek islands about 490 BC. This statue marks the culmination of a long series of *Kouros* figures (statues of naked youths) which started about 600 BC. In this statue, formerly in the possession of Lord Strangford, face and body are shedding their archaic stiffness, and are beginning to come to life.

For the next stage in the development of the naked male figure we must turn aside to Room 15 and look at the Choiseul-Gouffier Apollo, a Roman marble copy of a lost Greek bronze statue of about 460 BC. He is probably in fact not an Apollo but a victorious athlete. The loosening-up process seen in the Strangford Apollo has now been carried a stage further. The face shows a considerable degree of expression, almost of serious thought; and the body has achieved an agreeable sense of balance by the transfer of the weight to one leg, and by the varied position of the arms.

The Chatsworth Head in Room 5, a bronze Greek original, comes from a statue like that from which the Choiseul-Gouffier Apollo was taken. It was found at Tamassos in Cyprus in 1836 and passed into the possession of the Duke of Devonshire; it came to the British Museum in 1958.

Relief-sculpture of about 480 BC is well represented by the Harpy Tomb, excavated at Xanthus in Lycia by Sir Charles Fellows. Four carved marble slabs were arranged in a square on the top of a tall shaft to make a tomb-chamber. The slab illustrated shows a young warrior offering a helmet to an older man, who is seated. On each side, facing outwards, is a human-headed bird, carrying a child. These creatures, after whom the tomb was named, are in fact Sirens, the spirits of the dead. The significance of the central scene is not clear.

In vase-painting, the technique of black-figure started to give way about 530 BC to red-figure, in which the scenes are rendered in the orange-coloured clay ground against a black background. A fine example of the new technique is an Athenian vase of 490 BC, a *crater*, a bowl in which wine was mixed with water for drinking. It shows two scenes of combat from the Trojan war: on one side Achilles and Hector; on the other, Achilles and Memnon. Like many of the best surviving Athenian vases, this was found in an Etruscan tomb.

An alternative method of decorating vases at this date was to paint the figures in monochrome or in colours against a white background. The disadvantage of this scheme was that the white colour was not sufficiently durable for everyday use and tended to flake off, carrying the decoration with it. Consequently such vases were used principally as tomb-offerings. A *pyxis*, a box for female toilet articles, made in Athens about 450 BC and decorated in brown and black shows scenes of women engaged in their household duties.

159

172

169

160

161

158 A black-figure vase signed by the vase-painter and potter Exekias. The scene shows Achilles slaying the Amazon queen Penthesilea

159 The Strangford Apollo was made about 490 BC on one of the Greek islands. It marks the turning point from the hitherto archaic stiffness of earlier *Kouros* figures to a more alive, vital, style

o An Athenian red-figure crater by the Berlin Painter, *c*. 490 BC. On the neck is a scene taken from the Trojan war; chilles, on the left, faces Hector in single combat

161 Scenes of women on a small Athenian *pyxis* engaged in their household duties, made *c.* 540 BC

168   The temple at Bassae was dedicated to Apollo in gratitude for deliverance from an outbreak of the plague. Its frieze (about 400 BC) has been re-erected in Room 6 as it was on the building (although considerably lower), running continuously round the four walls of the room. There are two themes: battles of Greeks with centaurs and battles of Greeks with Amazons.

167   We now enter Room 7, where the sculptures from the Nereid Monument, a royal tomb of about 400 BC at Xanthus in Lycia, are exhibited and from here we pass into the Duveen Gallery containing the sculptures of the Parthenon.

The Parthenon was a temple in the Doric style built on the Acropolis of Athens between 447 and 432 BC in honour of the goddess Athena. The prime mover was the statesman Pericles, and the sculptor Pheidias exercised overall artistic supervision. The sculptures consist of the *metopes* (square panels placed on the outside of the building); a continuous frieze running round the outside of the interior; and pedimental sculptures in the gables at either end. The subject of the east pediment was the birth of Athena from the head of Zeus in the presence of all the other gods. The style of the Parthenon sculptures exhibits a combination of truth to nature with grandeur of conception which has never been excelled.

Rooms 9 and 10 are devoted to the century between 430 and 330 BC. As we enter Room 9 we pass a colossal marble statue of a woman, taken from the Erechtheum, a temple on the Athenian Acropolis opposite the Parthenon, built about 420 BC, and also dedicated to Athena. Six such figures, known as Caryatids, supported the south porch of the temple. This one was acquired by Lord Elgin; the other five remain on the building.

171

Room 9 also contains some very fine jewellery, typified by a gold necklace from the rich Greek colony of Taras (modern Taranto) in South Italy. It is composed of interlocking rosettes and other ornaments, from which hang buds and female heads. The play of light and shade on the surface of the gold would have been extraordinarily effective when the necklace was worn by a Tarentine lady. It was made about 380 BC.

157

We have already mentioned the Mausoleum at Halicarnassus. Room 12 is devoted to the sculpture from this famous monument, which includes a frieze of Greeks fighting Amazons and colossal statues possibly of Mausolus and his wife Artemisia. Mausolus died in 353 BC and his widow, who succeeded him, outlived him by only two years. The tomb, which he had begun, was still

162 An ivory gaming box and two mirror handles from Enkomi in Cyprus, c. 1180 BC. The decoration of the pieces owes much to Mycenaean inspiration

unfinished when Artemisia died, but was quickly completed. The statue of Mausolus shows the beginning of that interest in portraying human personality which was to culminate in the Hellenistic period. That of Artemisia has unfortunately lost much of its face, but was surely equally expressive.

The Mausoleum was counted as one of the Seven Wonders of the ancient world. Another was the Temple of Artemis (Diana) at Ephesus from which a sculptured column-drum is also exhibited. Made about 340 BC, this lovely relief shows Hermes, messenger of the gods, leading Alcestis towards winged Death.

170   Room 13 is devoted principally to the Hellenistic period, from 330 to the end of the first century BC, when the Greek world was transformed by the conquests of Alexander the Great. A fine masterpiece is the statue of Demeter, the Roman Ceres. It was first seen at Cnidus in Asia Minor in 1812 by an expedition of the Society of Dilettanti. Some fifty years later C. T. Newton excavated the site and shipped the statue to England. The goddess is shown seated on a throne, mourning the death of her daughter Persephone. One of the finest fourth-century statues surviving, it was made about 330 BC, possibly by the Athenian sculptor Leochares, who executed the official portraits of Philip of Macedon and his son Alexander the Great.

More in the Hellenistic tradition is the allegorical relief made by Archelaus of Priene about 100 BC representing the Apotheosis (or deification) of Homer. The scene is set on a mountainside; at the top is Zeus, and slightly below him Mnemosyne (Memory), then come the nine Muses (daughters of Zeus and Mnemosyne) and Apollo. In the bottom row Homer is shown seated on a throne which is supported by two female figures representing the *Iliad* and the *Odyssey*. Behind him stand figures personifying the World and Time, and in front of him are an altar, a bull, and various literary personifications. The figures portrayed have their names written below them.

175   A charming bronze statuette shows Aphrodite (the goddess of love) putting on her necklace (now missing). This graceful and sensuous study of the female nude is a reduced copy made in the third century BC of a statue by the famous fourth-century sculptor Praxiteles, or by one of his followers. Although so small, it breathes something of the spirit of a lost masterpiece. Another out-

177   standing bronze in Room 13 is a small bust of a negress of about 100 BC. It is hollow-cast and originally served as a scent bottle, but the abrupt way in which it is cut off at the bottom suggests that it was copied from a full-length figure. The rather sad face is rendered with sympathy and understanding, the negroid features being indicated but not caricatured. The neck of the bottle is made to form a flower-like head-dress.

Among the finest examples of the minor arts of the Hellenistic period are the Tanagra figures of 325–200 BC. These statuettes of gaily-coloured terracotta, from the cemeteries of the city of Tanagra in Boeotia, first became known in the seventies of the last century and immediately won public acclaim. Although clearly influenced by the sculptures of Praxiteles, they yet present an unusually vivid picture of the ordinary men and (more frequently) women of their period.

163 Terracotta statuette of two women seated on a couch, from Myrina in Asia Minor, c. 100 BC

A typical statuette is the lady who stands naturally but gracefully, wearing a   176
tunic, a tightly-swathed cloak, and a hat resembling a Chinese coolie hat.

The cemeteries of the little town of Myrina, near Smyrna in Asia Minor,
have yielded statuettes as fine as those from Tanagra, but continuing into the
second and first centuries BC, and even later. Among the finest is the group,
of about 100 BC, depicting two women seated on a couch; probably an older   163
woman instructing a young bride in the secrets of the marriage-bed. The bride
is holding in her hand a love gift from her husband in the form of a toy hare.

The Hellenistic period is also rich in jewellery. To the arts of filigree, granula-
tion and enamelling was now added that of inlaying with coloured stones and
glass. An example of the jeweller's skill is a gold necklace composed of a   165
strap which looks at first sight to be plaited, but is in fact made of links of very
fine chain. From it hang on chains small pendants in the shape of jars and
where the chains cross are small discs, vividly enamelled.

Room 14 is devoted to Roman art. One of its finest exhibits is a magnificent
bronze portrait head of the Emperor Augustus (63 BC–AD 14), found at   173

143

164–166 *Below*, one of the finest of small Greek bronzes, *c.* 520 BC. Probably from Dodona, it represents a reclining banqueteer; *centre,* an elaborate Hellenistic gold necklace much in contrast to the Archaic rectangular gold plaques of a breast ornament, *below,* from Camirus on Rhodes. The figure on the plaques represents an Asiatic 'Mistress of the Animals' (*cf. Pl. 156*)

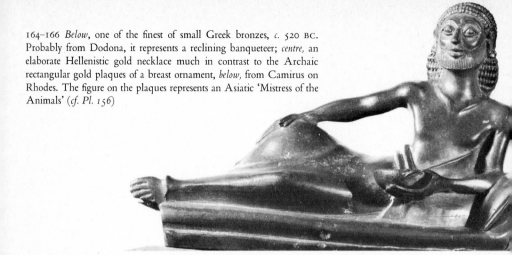

167–169 *Opp*
three Greek r
carved withi
century of
other. *Above,*
of the Parth
frieze (the I
marbles) of
432 BC; *cent*
detail of the ♦
from the temp
Apollo at Ba
c. 400 BC; *l*
carved slabs
the Harpy T
at Xanthus, *c.*
BC

170 The Demeter of Cnidus, a marble statue probably carved by Leochares, *c.* 330 BC

171 One of the six Caryatids from the south porch of the Erechtheum on the Athenian Acropolis, *c.* 420 BC

172, 173 A contrast of styles in two
large bronze heads. *Left,* the Chatsworth Apollo, a Greek original of *c.*
460 BC from Tamassos in Cyprus, and,
right, the emperor Augustus, 27 BC–AD
14, from Meroe in the Sudan

174 Found near Naples, this marble
bust of a young woman shown emerging from a flower is said to represent
Antonia, daughter of Mark Antony

175-177 Three rather charming ladies. *Above*, a bronze statuette of Aphrodite putting on her necklace. This is a third century bronze probably copying a lost original by Praxiteles or of his school. *Above, right*, a graceful Tanagra terracotta figurine of a lady swathed in her cloak and wearing a large sun-hat, *c.* 325-200 BC. *Right*, a hollow-caste, bronze, scent-bottle in the form of a bust of a negress. The modelling has been carried out with sympathy and understanding for the subject

178, 179 *Below,* a Cypriote polychrome amphora of
c. 600 BC, decorated with rosettes and a frieze of
sphinxes; *right,* an Etruscan seated terracotta figure of a
lady wearing a patterned cloak

180 A Roman parcel-gilt silver cup of *c.* 50 BC,
showing a scene from the adventures of Orestes and
Iphigenia

181 A Roman wall-painting of a marine landscape, c. 30 BC

Meroe in the Sudan, some four hundred miles beyond the Roman frontier. It belonged to a colossal statue of the Emperor and shows him in the prime of life: the protruding eyes and prominent ears, which are so marked a feature of this head, correspond well with what we know of Augustus's appearance. The eyes are made separately, of stone and glass. Their survival is a fortunate chance, for in most ancient bronze statues they have perished.

Another portrait, this time of marble, is also exhibited in Room 14. A   174
woman's head is shown emerging from a flower. She has been identified as Antonia, daughter of Mark Antony. Said to have been found near Naples, it was acquired in 1772 by Charles Towneley who mistakenly identified her as Clytie, a deserted love of the sun-god Helios. It is easy to understand from this portrait the almost unique reputation which Antonia possessed for beauty combined with virtue.

Another aspect of Roman art is the wall-painting of a marine landscape   181
from a villa at Boscoreale, near Pompeii, of about 30 BC. To the left is a high tomb; to the right, the first arch of a bridge on which a man stands, fishing with a rod and line. In the background is a broad stretch of water with two sailing-boats. The unemphatic style, with its soft colours and low contrast, probably originated in Alexandria.

Also from a Roman house, probably at Pompeii or Herculaneum is a floor mosaic of very fine tesserae. Made in the first century BC, it shows a spirited scene of a lion bound by cupids. Decorative floor mosaics go back at   182
least to the fifth century BC, when at first coloured pebbles were used, but they were gradually superseded by flat tesserae of stone or other materials.

Table silver was extremely common among well-to-do Romans. One of the finest examples which have come down to us is a recently acquired parcel-   180
gilt silver cup. Although it has lost its base and handles, what remains is in a remarkable degree of preservation. The scene, in low relief, is a little-known version of the adventures of Orestes and Iphigenia on the island of Sminthe. This cup, which has counterparts from Pompeii, was made about 50 BC.

The Portland Vase is probably the best known of all the antiquities in the   149
British Museum. First heard of in the Barberini Palace in Rome, it was bought by Sir William Hamilton towards the end of the eighteenth century. In 1785 he sold it to the Duchess of Portland; in 1810 the fourth Duke of Portland deposited it on loan in the British Museum, and in 1945 it was finally bought by the Museum. Meanwhile, in 1845, it had been smashed and immediately repaired, and it was repaired again in 1948. The vase is of blue glass, overlaid with white. It has been artificially shortened; originally it had the shape of a pointed amphora. The scene, cut into the white in gem-engraver's technique, shows two parts of the same story: the courtship of Thetis by Peleus in the presence of Eros, Aphrodite and other deities.

We pass now to the Cypriote and Etruscan collections, which will shortly be represented in primary exhibitions on the first floor. From the rich Cypriote collections space permits the illustration of but one piece, a typical polychrome

151

◄ 182 A Roman first century BC floor mosaic. Probably from Pompeii or Herculaneum, it shows a lion being bound by cupids

178   amphora of about 600 BC. The neck is decorated with rosettes and cable-patterns in black and red, while the body carries a frieze of sphinxes, also in black and red. Crude work indeed by Greek standards, but with much vigour and spontaneity to compensate for the crudity.

The Etruscan antiquities were acquired piecemeal from dealers throughout the nineteenth century. The Etruscans were a mysterious people (possibly from Asia Minor) who settled in Central Italy in the seventh century BC and evolved a highly sophisticated culture. They were celebrated for the manufacture

179   of terracottas and metalwork. Representative of these skills is a seventh-century terracotta figure of a seated woman from Cerveteri, the ancient Caere, wearing a patterned cloak, fastened on her right shoulder with an elaborate fibula.

R. A. HIGGINS

foreign currency, realized some of its religious assets. Amid great excitement the British public made a very large contribution towards the purchase price.

These are but some of the chief collections in the Department. The briefest look at its major manuscripts must begin with the *Lindisfarne Gospels*, the 204 earliest illuminated manuscript illustrated here, which was made about AD 698 in the monastery of Lindisfarne. At that time Northumbria was a province of the far-flung Irish culture. Lindisfarne, however, and its sister establishments at Jarrow and Monkwearmouth were also a springboard for the expansion of the influence of the Roman church, which had been on the increase in Northumbria ever since the Synod of Whitby in 664. The *Lindisfarne Gospels* illustrates this combination of Roman and Irish influences: on the one hand its excellent text is based on a good Italian manuscript, and the figures of the evangelists are weak attempts to reproduce Italian models, while on the other, it was written in a fine 'insular majuscule' (the script developed in the 'islands' of Ireland and Britain before the 'minuscule' or small letter alphabet was invented) with running scrolls, interlace, carpet-page and animal-headed decorations. These typically Celtic elements are stylized and the colours restrained in comparison with the exuberance of the Irish *Book of Kells*; throughout the Middle Ages the English genius was more for drawing.

In the eighth century, in southern England, which was more exposed than northern England to the authority of Rome, the *Psalter of St Augustine's, Canterbury*, was written in old-fashioned and extremely monumental uncials. In the same century Charlemagne re-united, as he thought, the Roman Empire. As order replaced chaos ignorance gave way to learning. Under Charlemagne the minuscule ('lower case') script called 'Carolingian' was invented. This truly revolutionary script quickly established its superior beauty, clarity and simplicity and almost entirely displaced all other Latin scripts. Its effects have been long-lasting, for today's main printing type-faces are based on the Carolingian minuscule by way of the fifteenth-century humanist script. Under Charlemagne, too, Alcuin, the cathedral librarian of York, was appointed Abbot of Tours. In this capacity Alcuin officiated at Charle-magne's coronation as Holy Roman Emperor on Christmas Day in the year 800, and presented him with a bible, whose text had been prepared and corrected under his personal supervision. The wide dissemination of Alcuin's revised text was assisted by the success of the 'scriptorium' or writing-school of Tours. The revised text was used in the large *Moutier-Grandval Bible* written 185 at Tours about 834–43. Its full-page miniatures show the survival of the style of the late Roman Empire both in the large heads and squat bodies and in the narrative or 'comic strip' manner of illustrating the text.

A different illustrative tradition surviving from the Roman Empire is that of the portrait-bust of the philosopher, which was adopted as the model for evangelist-portraits, as in the *Harley Golden Gospels*, painted in the Carolingian 205 court style. Here the miniature is independent of the text and the architectural 183 background is traceable to the theatrical backcloths of Pompeian paintings.

Omunt deu li puff sauur. En lepr feloyt oi sel uolaunt. Arbes duuses
ftuyz portaunr. Acens q estoyent auenaunz. De tere fyrt cretie erbes z flu
tes. De queus les mures fount luis cures. Bestes sure tere en ewe pyson
I sen ue efest saunduf noun. Car pirluy tut efest. Ceel z tere z tauurt q est
Cum ple penfoyt z le voulfit. Been tot fu feet ceo djit leferyt. Issen ue fyrt de
sa mesm. Fors houne z feutine ceo sorez certeyn. Tutes choses si fesoyt flurpte
 f tut ple felofyt pur houne seruyz

192 God the Father, the *Holkham Bible* (in French), English, 1327–35

193 Exodus from the Ark, the *Bedford Hours*, French, 1423

The Carolingian minuscule appeared in England in a regularized form, as in the *Benedictional of St Ethelwold* of about 962. The illumination of this magnificent manuscript shows the English feeling for line, but the colours are laid on with a rare extravagance. The benedictional, a collection of blessings that could be used only by a bishop, was a French invention, and is found only north of the Alps. An outstanding English literary manuscript written at the end of the tenth century is the unique copy of the Anglo-Saxon epic *Beowulf*. It shows the insular minuscule much influenced by the Carolingian. In the later tenth century St Ethelwold, St Dunstan and St Oswald were prime movers in the revival of religious life in England which inspired the extra-ordinarily faithful eleventh-century copy of the *Utrecht Psalter*, a fine Carolingian manuscript with half-page compositions combining in a satisfying way the literal illustrations of individual verses of each psalm.

In 1066 a Greek psalter was written in Constantinople in the monastery of the Studion by the monk Theodore. In its margins it also has literal illustrations of individual verses: one such illustration shows the iconoclasts destroying icons on the wall. The onslaught of the Normans, who in the years before and after 1066 made their presence felt throughout most of Western Europe, coincided with the emergence of the Romanesque style, which was a church art, and not the art of a particular court. The Gothic spires whose 'silent fingers point to heaven' are foreign to the Romanesque idea of the ritual and essentially static representation of God to man. This static quality is ideally adapted to book-illustration, and one of its greatest achievements is the Christ in Majesty of

188   the large *Bible of Stavelot Abbey* in Belgium, which was finished in the year 1097. This masterpiece conveys its ordered power and monumentality without suggesting solid flesh and blood beneath the drapery. Here the minor art of book-illustration most nearly achieved the status of a major art.

The Romanesque style reached its climax some sixty years after the dis-ruption caused by the Norman conquest. An example of the best English Romanesque art is the *Psalter of Henry of Blois*, Bishop of Winchester, executed about 1140–60 probably at Winchester. Henry was one of the new breed of ecclesiastical patrons who began to replace royal patrons of illuminated books. The psalter, or book of psalms, was, in the early Middle Ages, the chief book used for private devotions. It was replaced in the fourteenth and fifteenth centuries first by the breviary, a shortened form of the divine office for the canonical hours (often combined with a psalter), and secondly by the book of hours, a simplified form of the breviary. The breviary was used by the clergy in their private devotions, the book of hours by laymen and often by nuns.

About the year 1200 there developed an artistic atmosphere of intense excitement and keen experimentation. Now, instead of the ethereal and schematic bodies characteristic of Romanesque, we see bodies of well-propor-tioned corpulence as in the *Westminster Psalter*. About the same time the

186, 187   *Guthlac Roll* was drawn in outline. It takes its name from St Guthlac, a hermit who had once lived on the island of Crowland in Lincolnshire. These drawings do not show the classical monumentality of the *Westminster Psalter*, but they are transitional in combining Romanesque features with the lively gestures and drapery that give promise of the Gothic style to come.

Some years later, in June 1215 at Runnymede, King John accepted the terms of his enraged barons, which were embodied in the '*Articles of the Barons*'. Their terms, which at first were merely the settlement of their grievances, were confirmed in 1216 by Henry III, John's successor. From this point the agree-ment was known as Magna Carta, or the Great Charter, whose most famous clause is 'No free man shall be condemned except by the lawful judgment of his equals or by the law of the land.'

At about the same time the making of books passed decisively out of the hands of the monastic 'amateurs' into those of the secular 'professionals'. Artists experimented in representing individual emotions by means of different themes and ideas. The figures still have the Romanesque elongation, but there is an increasing tendency to naturalism and illusionism, that is, to escape from the limits of the two-dimensional page. The *Evesham Psalter*, written about 1250, is one of the masterpieces of English medieval art, and the Crucifixion shows skilful use of shaded drawings on a red, blue and gold ground. The contorted figures of Mary and John overlap the picture frame in an illusionistic manner and, by looking down at the abbot, involve the viewer in the Cruci-fixion. The Gothic artist aimed at drawing men up to God where the Roman-esque artist had aimed at representing God on earth. 189

In the *Evesham Psalter* we see the work of an English artist of true individuality. In France the first such identifiable artist is Maître Honoré, who executed his masterpiece, *La Somme le Roi*, towards the end of the thirteenth century. One 206 of the most important figures in the history of manuscript painting, he lived and worked in Paris, apparently at the head of an atelier, from at least 1288 to 1296, and counted Philip IV of France among his patrons. He was the first Frenchman to conceive full-page miniatures as independent pictures rather than as enlarged decoration. His figures are well-modelled and show expert characterization, but his scenes have little depth.

In England about 1300–80 there were produced the so-called 'East Anglian' manuscripts among which is the most copiously illustrated of all medieval psalters, the *Psalter* presented to Queen Mary Tudor in 1553. It was written and painted about 1310–20 with hundreds of tinted drawings and many full-colour miniatures of scenes from the life of Christ. Another 'East Anglian' manuscript is the *De Lisle Psalter*, a fragment of a psalter begun by one artist 190 about 1300–20 and completed by another between 1330 and 1339, when Robert de Lisle, Lord Lisle, gave it to his daughter, Audere. The first artist composed an imposing and monumental Virgin and Child and Crucifixion. The second artist shows the influence of the Parisian illuminator Jean Pucelle, who worked between about 1320 and about 1360. Pucelle's uninhibited virtuosity was able to assimilate and spread the ideas and techniques of Italian art, with its interest in perspective, architectural backgrounds and sculptural

194 A garden scene from the
Roman de la Rose. This copy,
made *c.* 1500, was written and
illuminated for Engelbert of
Nassau. It is probably the most
sumptuously decorated copy surviving of this popular romance

195 Sir Geoffrey I
trell in full dress arm
watched by his ad
ing wife and daugh
in-law. The *Lu*
Psalter, c. 1335–4(
best known for
scenes of everyday
that appear in the n
gins of the ms.

198 *Right*, a miniature depicting the
[Triu]mph of Love from a copy of the *Poems* of
[Petrar]ch, produced in Milan at the end of the
[fifteen]th century. Typically Milanese, it is much
[conce]rned with the problems of perspective and
[trans]parent solidity of form. Beneath is a detail
[of the] *Chronicles of Eusebius* of the same period.
[Writt]en by Bartolomeo Sanvito in roman and
[italic] hands, it exemplifies the humanist ms.
[Here] the written page with the miniature
[decor]ation was seen as a coherent whole.
[Left], a miniature from a late fifteenth-century
[Fle]mish *Book of Hours*, showing the martyrdom
[of St] Erasmus

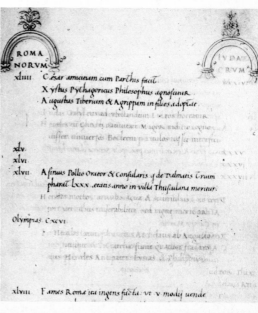

forms. He also invented, or at least popularized, the 'grisaille' or monochrome technique, which owed something to Italian influence. The pattern-book used for one of his manuscripts, the *Hours of Yolande of Flanders*, survived for half a century after his death and was used in two manuscripts made for the Duc de Berry, the great connoisseur and patron.

Not all English illumination of this period was in the 'East Anglian' style.

192   There was also a style of vernacular vigour exemplified in a *Bible Picture-Book* in French, formerly in the library of the Earl of Leicester at Holkham Hall in Norfolk. The illuminations are craggy, didactic and far removed from the elegance of Gothic art.

In the middle of the fourteenth century inspiration waned in England. Only the ingenious country scenes in the margin redeem the expensive but uninspired psalter made about 1335-40 for Sir Geoffrey Luttrell of Irnham

195   in Lincolnshire. He is portrayed in full dress armour, his wife and daughter-in-law looking on in admiration. For the next hundred years France led the field and the influence of Jean Pucelle continued in the extremely fine illustrations of the *Order of the Coronation of the Kings and Queens of France* which was commissioned by King Charles V and painted in 1365.

By the fourteenth century the Byzantine Empire had been much reduced by Turks, Western Europeans and Slavs. These last had established the Kingdom of Bulgaria, independent politically but culturally dependent. One of the two

191   monuments of medieval Bulgarian manuscript illumination is the *Gospels* made for Tsar John Alexander in 1355-6. At the beginning the Tsar and his family are represented in a flat, frontal and hieratic style; then the text is interrupted by sprightly scenes from the life of Christ.

During the period 1380-1430 artists were still using the medieval forms, but the spirit behind them was secular and highly sophisticated. The best work was centred on the courts of kings and wealthy noblemen like Jean, Duc de Berry, whose *Très Riches Heures* (now in Chantilly) has some claim to be regarded as the finest illuminated manuscript ever made. Many of the illuminations were painted by the three Limbourg brothers, whose work was known to the artist who about 1415 illustrated the *Breviary of John the Fearless*, Duke of Burgundy. The Duke found his breviary too bulky and divided it into two, the winter half and the summer half.

The influence of the Limbourg brothers is also obvious in a splendid example

193   of the finest Parisian work, the *Bedford Hours*, written and illuminated about 1423 for John, Duke of Bedford, the brother of Henry V and Regent of France from 1422 to 1435, who was married in 1423 to Anne, daughter of the Duke of Burgundy. On Christmas Eve 1430 the Duchess presented it to her nephew the young King Henry VI. The manuscript is richly decorated and illuminated throughout, and its thirty-eight large miniatures include representations of the Duke of Bedford kneeling before St George, the Duchess before St Anne, and the Legend of the Fleurs-de-Lis. The artist of the principal illumination is known as the 'Master of the Duke of Bedford'. His atelier seems

166

to have been the most flourishing and important in Paris in the early fifteenth century. His reputation is chiefly as a colourist, but he also made interesting experiments in landscape representation. This manuscript was once in the Harley library, but the second Earl's widow could not bear to part with it in 1753. It passed to her daughter, the Duchess of Portland, and through several hands until it was finally re-united with the Harley manuscripts in the Museum.

The same Duke of Bedford commissioned a *Book of Hours and Psalter* from the English workshop associated with Herman Scheerre, who came from the Rhineland. It contains the finest and most important surviving English illumination of the period. Some influence of Herman Scheerre can be seen in the *Hours* executed about 1420 and later owned by Elizabeth, Queen Consort of Henry VII. The pictures, though somewhat overcrowded, nevertheless show considerable technical proficiency.

By about 1430 the art of book illumination could develop no further within the limitations of the page. The mainstream of painting now turned to the panel, which offered more scope for the 'fight against the picture surface'. Nevertheless book illumination did continue for another hundred years, partly making miniature versions of panel-paintings, as in the work of Giulio Clovio, a Croat who came to Italy in 1516 and was often called 'the Raphael of miniaturists'. The original contributions to manuscript illumination came from Italy and Flanders, and the Italian humanists inspired a new layout combining pictures and several kinds of script. Flemish illumination was part of the brilliant culture that grew up at the court of Philip the Good, Duke of Burgundy (d. 1467) and his successors, and by 1500 the school of Ghent and Bruges was leading Europe. The masters of this school were Gerard Horenbout and Simon Bening, who achieved a harmony of format and contemporary technique which eluded the Italians. Gerard himself may have contributed some miniatures to the *Breviary of Queen Isabella of Spain*, made about 1490.

Bening and his colleagues portrayed characters 'warts and all', as we can see in the lumpish villagers of the *Golf Hours*. At the other extreme, the on-lookers in the extraordinarily gruesome martyrdom of St Erasmus in the *Hours* 197 made about 1480, probably for Lord William Hastings, are languid and elegant *fin de siècle* young men. The feeling in these pictures is completely secular, far from the earthly representations of eternity so characteristic of the twelfth century. Many large chronicles and romances were produced for patrons such as Edward IV. Perhaps the most sumptuously decorated copy in existence of the *Roman de la Rose*, that most popular of medieval romances, 194 was written and illuminated for Engelbert of Nassau, an enthusiastic bibliophile who was Lieutenant of the Realm in Flanders during the minority of Philip the Fair. By far the most popular chronicle was that of Jean Froissart, and what could be more dramatic than his account of the King of France's narrow escape from death? When he and five companions dressed up in animal skins, four died in agony as a flaming torch set their costumes alight, but the King was saved by sheltering under his aunt's skirts.

199 A fifteenth-century theological treatise still with its staple and chain that once secured it to its lectern

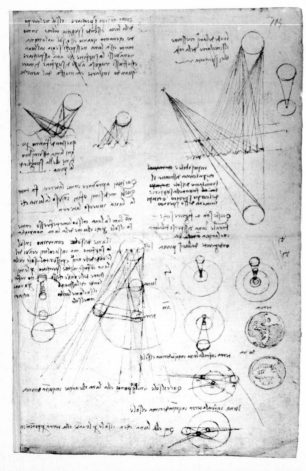

200 A page from a *Notebook* of Leonardo da Vinci. Begun in 1508, it is concerned with notes and diagrams on optics and astronomy

201 A sketch plan of the execution of Mary, Queen of Scots, either made by, or for, Robert Beale the Elizabethan diplomatist and antiquary

202, 203 Three famous Elizabethan signatures. *Below*, one of the six known signatures of William Shakespeare. It occurs on a mortgage deed for a house in Blackfriars, and is dated 11 March 1613. *Below, right*, a letter written by Roger Ascham (whose signature appears at the bottom) and signed in an ornate hand by Queen Elizabeth I. The letter recommends William Herle to the City of Hamburg and is dated 18 March, 1562

204 A 'carpet-page' from the *Lindisfarne Gospels*, Northumbrian, *c.* 700

The Flemish style was also dominant in England, where the French poems of Charles, Duke of Orléans were probably written and illuminated about 1500. Charles was taken prisoner at Agincourt in 1415 and was not released until 1440. The famous picture of the Tower of London shows Charles three times, once saying farewell as he enters the White Tower, once looking sadly out of a window, and once inside, perhaps writing his poems.

208

The court of Francis I, King of France, was a late stronghold of the now old-fashioned art of manuscript illumination. Some books were even printed on vellum and illuminated by hand. It was for Francis I that Albert Pigghe composed a fanciful French adaptation of Caesar's Gallic War, in which Francis has imaginary meetings with Julius Caesar in various royal hunting parks and discusses his campaigns. This work in three volumes was illuminated in 1519 by the Dutchman, Godofredus Batavus, using grisaille heightened with gold and occasionally picked out in colour.

Renaissance illumination in Italy took several different forms, one of which is the conservative format of the Dante, the masterpiece of fifteenth-century Sienese secular manuscript painting. Its layout, text with a miniature at the foot of every other page, continues a native Italian fourteenth-century tradition and is reminiscent of the didactic style of the psalters with marginal illustrations such as the Studion and Utrecht Psalters. Of the two artists who worked on the Dante, the first, who has not yet been convincingly identified, illuminated the Inferno and the Purgatorio in a sombre fourteenth-century style; the second, Giovanni di Paolo, illuminated the Paradiso in soft and glowing colours.

210

Another traditional style, which might be called the Italian version of the miniature with border, produced the 'aristocratic' Poems in Italian of Petrarch. The illumination of this manuscript, which was executed for a member of the Romei family of Ferrara, is closely related to the work of the artist Giovan Pietro Birago, who decorated the Sforza Hours for the widow of one of the Dukes of Milan. Milanese art at the end of the fifteenth century was much concerned with the art of perspective and the apparent solidity of forms.

196

Petrarch (1304–74), the poet and scholar, was the most influential precursor of fifteenth century humanism. His Livy was specially prepared for him and, indeed, is partly in his own handwriting. He also added copious notes in the margins and between the lines. It was for humanism that a new kind of manu-script was invented in which illumination and varied blocks of text were carefully arranged to make a coherent whole. The Chronicles of Eusebius show this new layout and, in particular, show both the roman and the italic hand of the learned scribe, Bartolomeo Sanvito, himself a connoisseur, who also wrote the text of several other humanist manuscripts, all finely illuminated in a classicizing style. Before the year 1513 he wrote the text of the Stuart de Rothesay Hours, which was illuminated for Cardinal Grimani about 1540 by Giulio Clovio. Here we see a brave but not altogether successful attempt to reproduce within the restrictive limits of a tiny book the crowded canvases and ceilings of Michelangelo and his contemporaries.

198

205 *Overleaf*, St Mark, the *Harley Golden Gospels*, ninth-century Carolingian (*see also Pl. 183*)

Renaissance Italy raised no more brilliant son than the incredible all-rounder Leonardo da Vinci, one of whose notebooks found its way to the British
200   Museum via the Earl of Arundel's library. This *Notebook*, which was begun in 1508, has notes in mirror-writing and diagrams on every conceivable subject, including optics and astronomy. More of his drawings of machines are to be found in the Department of Prints and Drawings.

The scientific knowledge of the Renaissance enabled improved maps to be made which, in turn, facilitated the expansion of European trade and influence. Among the Royal manuscripts is the *Book of Hydrography* made in 1542 by Jean Rotz, a Dieppe pilot in the service of Henry VIII. The maps are illustrated by colourful scenes of local activities. The map of the Coast of Brazil, for example, has scenes of savage life – warfare, dances, cannibalism, a stockaded settlement – as well as the loading up of a boat with the red dye-wood, or brazil-wood, which gave its name to the land of Brazil. The restless ambition of the Portuguese spurred them on to acquire a far-flung sea-borne empire in which Brazil was not the least member. A delightful record of this period lies in the portraits of colonial administrators like Martim Affonso de Sousa, inserted in the *Livro do Estado da India Oriental*. The exploration of the world begun by Portuguese mariners was taken up by other nations including the Dutch and the British. By the twentieth century few parts of the globe were left unexplored and to adventurous spirits the lure of the inhospitable Polar
207   regions was irresistible. The last entry in Scott's *Diary* is a grim reminder that the cruel Antarctic cold could take its toll.

It was also in Renaissance Italy that the 'roman' and 'italic' scripts were invented. Like the Carolingian minuscule from which they are descended, they achieved widespread use by reason of their superior beauty and simplicity,
198   as can be seen in the work of Bartolomeo Sanvito. In England the triumph of the italic hand was not immediate, but in the sixteenth century there were many accomplished calligraphers, of whom the most celebrated was Roger
203   Ascham. A letter in his handwriting was signed in a square official hand by Queen Elizabeth. Many of the documents that the Queen signed in her reign have survived, including the warrant for the execution of Mary, Queen of Scots, which Robert Beale had to read out to her. Beale was an Elizabethan diplomatist and antiquary who deputized for Walsingham and conducted negotiations with Mary between 1581 and 1584. He made, or had made for
201   him, a sketch of Mary's execution.

The reign of Elizabeth saw an efflorescence of dramatic literature, with Shakespeare outshining his rivals. In one respect, however, time has been less kind to him than to his fellow-playwrights, in that all that we have from his hand are six signatures. Three of them are on his will and one is on the mort-
202   gage deed of a house in Blackfriars that he and his partners bought in 1613. To this deed have been attached the wax seals of the contracting parties. The seal of an ordinary citizen was quite plain, but the seals used to authenticate the legal deeds of great men and kings are very splendid: the seal of Warwick the

        207 The last entry in the *Diary* of 'Scott of the Antarctic'

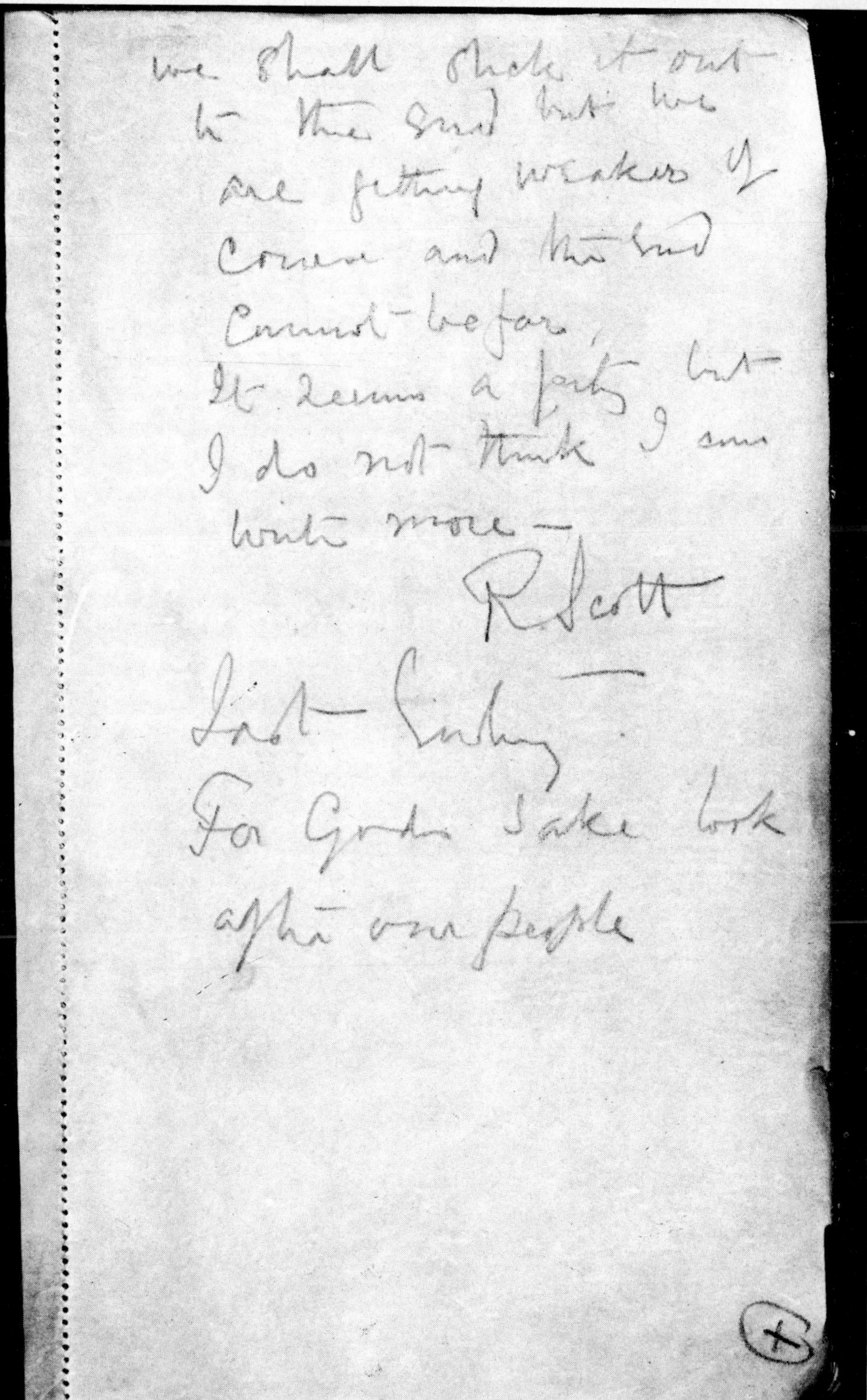

We shall stick it out
to the end but we
are getting weaker of
course and the end
cannot be far.

It seems a pity but
I do not think I can
write more —

R. Scott

Last entry —

For God's sake look
after our people

Es nouuelles ⸱ D'albion
Il vous en plaist escouter
Mon frere ⸱ ⸲ mon copaignio
Sachiez qua mon retoiner
Ay este sera sa mer
E ceu a joruise chiere

208–210 *Opposite*, a page from the *Poems* of Charles of Orléans showing the White Tower where he was imprisoned; *above*, Christine de Pisan presents a copy of her work to Isabel of Bavaria, wife of Charles VI; *below*, the departure of Hippolytus from Athens and his death at Troizen; a miniature by Giovanni di Paolo from the *Paradiso* of Dante's *La Divine Comedia*, *c.* 1440

Kingmaker, for instance, is a fine Gothic heraldic example of 1465. Because seals, though related in design to coins and medals, are attached to written documents, they are kept in the Department of Manuscripts. The instruments for impressing seals, the seal-dies, are in a different category and are kept in the Department of Medieval and Later Antiquities.

The majority of fine bindings are in the Department of Printed Books, but there are some manuscripts with fine bindings, such as the *Harley Golden Gospels*. This was sumptuously bound in red morocco gilt by Thomas Elliott in 1721 and illustrates the characteristic diamond-shaped 'middle-piece' of the Harley bindings. Another fine binding, made by the 'Naval Binder' in 1675, covers an abstract of Sir Thomas Osborne's accounts as Treasurer of the Navy for the years 1671 to 1673. It may have been made at official expense and retained as a perquisite of office. One volume of fifteenth-century theological treatises is bound in wooden boards covered in plain leather, with a staple and chain by which it was secured to a lectern. Neither the staple and chain, nor the curse against thieves often found on fly-leaves, has prevented manuscripts from making their way into the Museum, which will in the future continue to provide sanctuary for the treasures in its keeping as well as for others still to be acquired.

T. S. PATTIE

CHAPTER SEVEN

Medieval and Later Antiquities

The Department of Medieval and Later Antiquities came into being in 1969. In that year the Department of British and Medieval Antiquities, which had existed for over a hundred years, was divided into two and its prehistoric and Romano-British collections were hived off as a new Department, called Pre-historic and Romano-British Antiquities. 'British and Medieval' had always been a gross misnomer for the wildly heterogeneous material, from the 'eoliths' to Victoriana, grouped under that title. The designation 'Medieval and Later' now given to the Museum's post-Roman and essentially European collections indicates their scope more correctly, but requires amplification.

The word 'medieval' is taken in its broadest sense, to mean post-Roman and pre-Renaissance. When the Roman period may be said to end is a matter of opinion. In practice the Department covers those works of applied art which are not ranked as classical but which illustrate the marked phase of stylistic change and evolution that leads away from the classical and forward into the Middle Ages, known to art-historians as the Late Antique. An outstanding object in this category is the ambitious glass vessel with the unique property of changing its colour in transmitted light – from opaque green to translucent red and amethyst – known as the Lycurgus cup, and attributed to the fourth century AD. Within the Roman and the Late Antique periods the Department is also concerned expressly with antiquities which are either in themselves Christian – that is, which illustrate Christian subjects or have Christian symbols or inscriptions – or else have Christian contexts. While Christian antiquities of the Roman period found in Britain come under the Department of Prehistoric and Romano-British Antiquities, all others, whether from Europe or outside it, are the responsibility of the Medieval and Later Department. In this the Christian art of Abyssinia, Egypt (Coptic art), Cyprus, Syria, Asia Minor and Russia, and, much later, the seventeenth-century Christian ivories of the Portuguese colony of Goa, in India, all come under Medieval and Later Antiquities. Also included are Byzantine art and archaeology, together with its offshoot, Russian medieval art. The Department is not, of course, responsible for the art-historically all-important manuscripts of these periods or later, but is responsible for loose book-covers, styli, seal-matrices, book-bindings, stamps, diptychs and other ivories and metalwork which may have manuscript connections.

212

211, 213 The Late Antique Empire. *Above, left*, the silver, dome-shaped, toilet box containing silver bottles for perfumes and essences, from the Esquiline Treasure, fourth century AD. *Left*, the Lycurgus cup, an elaborately carved glass vessel of the fourth century AD which has the property of changing its colour in transmitted light. *Above*, an ivory panel from a sixth-century Byzantine diptych showing the Archangel Michael

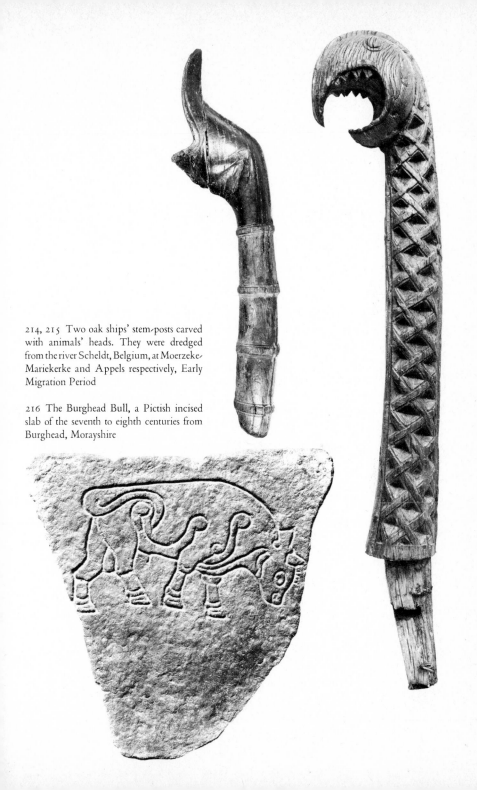

214, 215 Two oak ships' stem-posts carved with animals' heads. They were dredged from the river Scheldt, Belgium, at Moerzeke-Mariekerke and Appels respectively, Early Migration Period

216 The Burghead Bull, a Pictish incised slab of the seventh to eighth centuries from Burghead, Morayshire

Divisions between Departments are sometimes practical rather than logical. Since the Department has never had a sculpture gallery as such, Coptic sculptures and some Middle Eastern sculptures, those from Palmyra, for example, which might be called Late Antique or illustrate tendencies towards stylization that passed into medieval art, remain in the care of the Egyptian and Western Asiatic Departments, as do many Coptic portraits and other paintings. Many of the Coptic textiles, however, have now been transferred to the Medieval and Later Department.

Around the European fringes of the Roman Empire lived Celtic, Germanic and Slavonic peoples, some of whom were in due course to settle within its frontiers and rule its provinces. Their native traditions and achievements in material culture – the art and archaeology of the Migration period – have an important place in the collections, both because they contributed essential impulses and elements to the Middle Ages, and to modern times, and as data with which to reconstruct a part of European history. Germanic antiquities of the Continental mainland and Scandinavia are represented, but our own Anglo-Saxon antiquities of the pagan Germanic settlers in Britain, culminating

224   in the treasure of the Sutton Hoo ship-burial, are particularly extensive and important. The collection of metal-work illustrating the Anglo-Saxons, in their Christian phase, from about AD 650 to the Norman Conquest, is outstanding. The Department is also concerned with the antiquities of Celtic Britain in the Christian period (about AD 400–1200), chiefly metalwork but also stone and, more rarely, domestic material from habitation sites or monasteries such as Tintagel in Cornwall, illustrating the development of the culture and the styles that lead up to and correspond with the great Celtic Christian achievements.

A few very notable ivories and other pieces, of which the most important

229   is the Lothair Crystal, illustrate the Carolingian and Ottonian periods on the Continent, parallel with our Late Saxon material. When the full Middle Ages is reached (in this country, after 1066), the Department is concerned with Romanesque and Gothic art and archaeology and with the portable remains of medieval civilization generally.

In the Renaissance and later fields, the stamp of individual collectors and connoisseurs upon the collection becomes more marked and decisive. We enter the age of *objets d'art* and antiques, and it is to distinguished collectors that we owe the original formation, and often, by gift or bequest, the subsequent presence in the Museum, of the bulk of the collections of porcelain, pottery and glass, of clocks, watches and scientific instruments, Renaissance metalwork, seal dies, tokens and badges, silver and many other things which today would be beyond the Department's resources.

For many years the collections of European porcelain, pottery and glass were detached from the British and Medieval nucleus and belonged to the Department of Ceramics and Ethnography, only returning in 1945, when 'Ceramics', a Victoria and Albert Museum type of classification, was divided into oriental ceramics, which went to the Department of Oriental Antiquities, and European ceramics, which returned to the then British and Medieval Department.

It has been the understanding that, since the British and Medieval Depart-ment and the decorative art collections now developed into the Victoria and Albert Museum came into being at roughly the same time, such things as furniture, sculpture, stained glass, textiles and musical instruments should be collected at South Kensington. The Department has consequently little to offer in these fields, and does not seek equality with the Victoria and Albert Museum. Yet it is the function of the British Museum, as a museum of history, to represent each period by its material culture in a balanced way. Some examples of the best and of the routine in these categories should be included, and to this extent it is the Museum's policy to create a proper balance in the collections, as occasion offers, by acquiring examples in these categories.

The great expansion and development of the collections dates from the year 1866, when a Department of British and Medieval Antiquities and Ethno-graphy was set up, and Augustus Wollaston Franks was appointed its first Keeper. He was to be also one of its greatest benefactors.

There were, of course, important items in the Medieval and Later fields in the Museum before a special Department to deal with them and to foster these fields of study was formed. Some go back to the foundation collections in 1753. Among such pieces are the well-known large and fine late thirteenth century English astrolabe known as the Sloane astrolabe and a dozen pieces of Majolica, 239 Sèvres and Dresden china that had also belonged to Sir Hans Sloane. With the Cotton Library came the three wax discs, engraved with astrological signs and symbols, used by the Elizabethan alchemist, Dr John Dee. His gold disc, engraved with astrological data, and his magic mirror, were acquired recently. 252 Long after this, in 1783, the Trustees accepted two brand-new Chelsea vases, a very fine and elaborate pair with painted scenes, one illustrating the death of 253 Cleopatra. They now rank as important early documentary pieces in the history of the factory.

A major step in the history of the Department, as of the Manuscript and Oriental Manuscript Departments, was the building in 1884 of the White Wing, where the offices of the Department have since been. When in 1969 the Prehistoric and Romano-British collections and the staff concerned with them moved into new offices, the Medieval and Later collections were able to expand in the reserve areas and more accommodation (though not more gallery space) became available for the staff.

For the period immediately following the end of Roman occupation of Britain, the fifth–seventh centuries AD, we depend almost entirely upon excavated material. This comes mostly from nineteenth- and even eighteenth-century excavations of Anglo-Saxon cemeteries, generally most inadequately recorded. Such is the case with the material from one of the richest Anglo-Saxon cemetery-sites in England, King's Field, Faversham in Kent, where much

217, 218 *Above*, pagan Anglo-Saxon jewellery. Belt plates from Mucking, silver quoit-brooch from Sarre, gold bracteate with three eagles, long brooch and disc-brooch set with garnets, all from Dover. *Below*, glass bowl with red, trailed, decoration, late seventh/eighth century, from Amiens or Rheims

219, 220 *Above,* medieval jewellery: the 'Woman of Samaria' hat-badge, a sixteenth-century pendant with Hillyard miniatures, two pieces from the Fishpool hoard and the Dunstable Swan. *Below,* seventeenth- and eighteenth-century watches in decorated cases from the Ilbert Collection; the largest is a scent bottle enclosing a watch movement

fine jewellery and glass came to light as a result of the construction of railway cuttings in 1858–68 (the Gibbs Bequest). There is fine material of the later sixth and seventh centuries in the collection from rich graves in East Kent, and altogether the collection of knives, swords, brooches, buckles, pottery, glass vessels and other objects of the pagan Saxon period runs into several thousands of specimens. The heights that could be attained and the range of objects available at the top level of society in the early seventh century is best seen in the Sutton Hoo ship-burial. Found in 1939, in Suffolk, this royal grave, the only royal burial of its era to survive intact, contained rich and varied treasures which were presented to the nation by the landowner, Mrs E. M. Pretty. It may well be the burial of King Redwald of the East Angles (d. 625/6). The most popular element in this treasure is probably the superb, locally-made, gold jewellery and sword fittings set with garnets and, in the most impressive pieces, 224   the purse, shoulder clasps and pyramids, with glass mosaic – also the great gold buckle, which has no garnets. The reconstructed helmet and shield, pieces of the greatest rarity, are both of Swedish origin and part of a complicated chain of evidence which goes to show that the East Anglian royal house came originally from that country. Attention may also be drawn to the range of Byzantine silver in the ship-burial and to the reconstructions of chain-work, cauldrons, buckets, etc. Possibly the most remarkable object is the stone sceptre surmounted by a stag. The treasure was buried in a 90 ft long rowing boat, under a mound.

    The Sutton Hoo burial is one of the outstanding treasures of the Museum. Before it was discovered, the richest Anglo-Saxon grave known was that of the chieftain buried under a mound at Taplow in Buckinghamshire, excavated in 1882. The material from the Taplow barrow includes a fine set of four glass drinking vessels known as claw-beakers, gold buckles, an imported bronze bowl from Egypt, drinking horns, bone gaming pieces, the remains of a lyre, and gold braids from a rich cloak.

225   A notable piece from pagan Saxon times, the Castle Eden vase, given by the Hon. Mrs Slater-Booth in 1947, illustrates the high technical level attained by the glass industry. It is a baroque-looking glass drinking vessel of the late fifth or early sixth century, found intact, with a skeleton, in about the year 1775 under a hedge at Castle Eden in County Durham. It is a 'claw-beaker', light green in colour, conveniently held in the hand, not so tall as the Taplow claw-beakers, and with a rim that turns out slightly.

    A glass of somewhat later date, probably late seventh or eighth century AD, of exceptional interest and rarity, is a 'palm-cup', an open shallow bowl with rolled-out hollow, tubular rim. There are many air bubbles in it, and the unusual feature is the presence, suspended in the greenish, almost colourless 218   glass, of a spun spiral nebula-like pattern blood-red in colour. It illustrates a new tendency in glass manufacturing – polychromy and colouristic effects – developing just at the point of time when the practice of pagan burial with grave goods is ceasing and our supply of material consequently drying up.

Glass of the eighth century and later is extremely rare and survives only in small fragments.

The old finds of grave-goods of the pagan era are being increasingly aug-mented by those from modern excavations properly recorded and so of greater scientific value. A typical selection of some of these pieces comes from the   217
Anglo-Saxon cemetery at Dover excavated in the 1950s and purchased from the Corporation of the City of Dover. With them is a remarkable buckle with counter plate and matching belt-attachment from an important site now under excavation at Mucking, near Tilbury in Essex, illustrating a distinctive mid-fifth century ornamental style and repertoire, also seen on the fine silver quoit-brooch from Sarre in Kent.

To redress the balance of small finds of personal ornaments and effects from graves there are two decorated wooden stem-posts of early ships, pieces un-   214, 215
paralleled elsewhere. They have been dated by the C-14 method to the Early Migration period; that from Appels is fourth–fifth century, that from Moerzeke-Mariekerke somewhat earlier. Both were dredged up from the mud of the River Scheldt and purchased from dealers.

Some excavation is now done by the Department itself, on sites which promise to be of special interest to the collections. This possibility of productive new activity extends through thirteen hundred years or more of the medieval period down to modern times. These excavations include renewed work at Sutton Hoo and at the site of an Anglo-Saxon inhumation cemetery in Broadstairs; a thirteenth-century tile-kiln closely datable by documents to the period of 1237–44 at the royal Palace site at Clarendon in Wiltshire; and the Department has also to its credit, we believe, the first scientific excavations to be carried out on an industrial archaeology site, that of the eighteenth-century porcelain factory at Longton Hall in Staffordshire. (As early as 1921 Aubrey   251
Toppin, later Ulster King of Arms, had discovered and excavated the kiln site of the Bow factory.)

The rich Early Christian collections contrast sharply with our pagan Anglo-Saxon material. They illustrate the more civilized sub-classical world with which the barbarians were in contact. The Esquiline Treasure, a remarkable   211
treasure of silver ware from the Esquiline Hill in Rome, was found in 1793. Its most notable piece is the large parcel-gilt bridal casket with its portrait busts of bride and bridegroom in a roundel on the lid, mythological groups of Venus and sea-monsters, and the inscription with the Christian Chi-Rho monogram on the front edge of the lid *'Secunde et Projecta vivatis in Christo'*, which shows that the bride and bridegroom were members of prominent families in the Christian community. Secundus may have been a member of the great family of the Asterii. The dome-shaped casket, ornamented with figures of Muses, contains silver bottles for perfumes and essences. It is a remark-able collection of secular silver from a period when there was as yet no church plate. Besides these two pieces there are flasks, ewers, brooches, dishes, horse-trappings and four ornamental figures, representing the cities of Rome, Antioch,

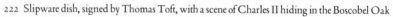

221 Roundel of fifteenth-century decorative tiles from a Bristol merchant's house
222 Slipware dish, signed by Thomas Toft, with a scene of Charles II hiding in the Boscobel Oak

223 A pair of Chelsea vases with painted scenes, one, on the right, illustrating the death of Cleopatra

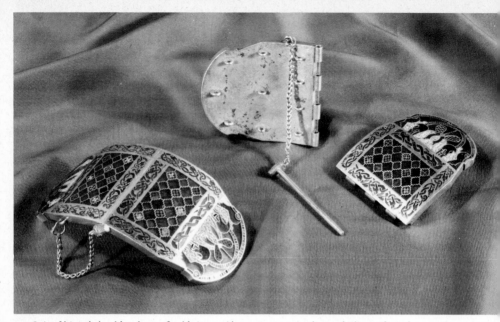

224 Pair of hinged shoulder-clasps of gold, inset with garnets, mosaic glass and filigree, from the seventh-century Sutton Hoo ship-burial

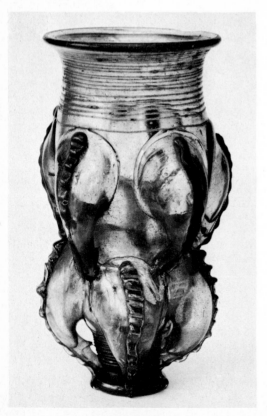

225, 226 *Left*, a sixth-century glass claw-beaker, the Castle Eden vase; *below*, the Angel Inn pitcher, Anglo-Saxon yellow glazed pottery of the ninth or tenth century

227 Part of a carved cross-shaft of the late Saxon (Christian) period from East Stour, Dorset, eighth or early ninth century

The Franks Casket, a whalebone box with carved scenes and runic inscriptions, Northumbrian *c.* 700 AD

Constantinople and Alexandria, which are thought to have decorated the ends of litter-poles. Important also are the treasures of silver of the early Christian period from Carthage, Cyprus and Lampsacus, on the Hellespont.

Early Christian sculptural art is represented by ivories, a sarcophagus and some stone fragments. Amongst the ivories four small casket panels which bear (apart from certain engraved gems) what is thought to be the earliest known representation of the Crucifixion (fourth–fifth century AD) should be noted. Wholly different in atmosphere and style is the superb panel of a diptych of the sixth century AD and probably made in Byzantium itself, depicting the

213 Archangel Michael. This figure, delicately carved in low relief, is an impressive and noble rendering of the Archangel with a staff crowned by a cross in one hand and an orb in the other. The Greek inscription, reading 'Receive these gifts, and having learnt the cause . . .', must have continued on the other half of the diptych which may have borne the figure of an Emperor to whom the angel was offering the orb as an emblem of sovereignty. There is a sunken panel at the back for wax for writing. Late Antique stone sculpture is represented by a characteristic sarcophagus depicting the story of Jonah, whose swallowing by the whale and subsequent regurgitation onto an island, where he is shown resting under a gourd tree, a popular theme in the art of the period, was held to symbolize the Resurrection, or immortality. The Lycurgus cup, already

212 mentioned, is one of the most remarkable ancient glass vessels to survive. It is a splendid piece and should be studied from the technical point of view to observe how the figures were made and the designs of vine, etc., under-cut and, of course, to see the effect of its change in colour from opaque pea green to translucent ruby red and amethyst in transmitted light. The cup was made from a thick glass blank which was probably moulded, given a polished finish, and then externally carved, under-cut and hollowed out to leave its elaborate surface decoration standing up in openwork and deep relief. It is unique in combining with this openwork, under-cut, 'cage-cup' sculptural technique a fully-presented figural episode from classical mythology: Lycurgus, King of the Thracian Edoni, who fell foul of Bacchus and his rout.

The remarkable stone sculpture of Anglo-Saxon England has no Conti-nental equivalent – it first appears in the seventh century following the establish-ment of the Christian Church, with the need for preaching crosses and carving in stone generally. Thousands of fragments of such carvings, mostly cross shafts, with some slabs, exist in parish churches and museums and in the landscape all over the country. The British Museum has some interesting pieces illustrating decorative themes and figure subjects, style and technique. The fragments from the seventh–eighth century monastery at Whitby, and the cross-shafts from

227 East Stour and Sheffield should be noted. The East Stour shaft, acquired in 1968, is carved on all four sides with foliate scrolls and with interlace. It had been for many years in the garden of a house in Wiltshire. Probably eighth to ninth century in date, it illustrates very well the decorative richness of its period and remarkable delicacy in the technique of carving.

A slab incised with the stylized outline of a bull-figure from Burghead in   216
Morayshire, given by James Sowerby in 1861, is the Museum's sole indisputable
example of Pictish art, known chiefly in sculpture.

Before we leave the pre-Norman Conquest phase of our history and the early
Romanesque of Europe, one or two objects of the highest distinction and
interest may be singled out.

The Franks Casket named after Sir A. W. Franks who gave it to the Museum,   228
is unique. It is a whalebone casket carved with scenes from northern mythology,
ancient history and the Christian story, surrounded by finely cut runic
inscriptions, probably made about AD 700 in Northumbria. In one instance,
where the subject is a historical one, the Siege of Jerusalem by Titus in AD 70,
presumably derived from a Mediterranean manuscript source, the accompanying inscription is in the Insular uncial script of contemporary manuscripts.
On the front of the casket is what we may regard as a deliberate confrontation
of the Virgin and Child in the Adoration of the Magi with a pagan scene
depicting the barbarous revenge of Wayland the Smith on King Nithad.
Other scenes on the casket include Romulus and Remus suckled by the wolf
in the forest. The casket, besides being a most rare and important document in
the history of Insular and of narrative art is also remarkable for the linguistic
interest of the inscriptions. It was found, with one end missing, by a French
professor, in use as a work-box in a house in Auzon, Haute Loire. The missing
end came to light later and is now in the Bargello in Florence. A cast of this
end is incorporated in the British Museum casket-reconstruction.

Another piece of great distinction has an even more romantic history. This is
the Lothair crystal, the leading surviving example of an art developed in the   229
Carolingian court, that of carving in intaglio in rock crystal. It was preserved
in the Abbey of Waulsort on the Meuse from the tenth century down to the
French Revolution. The crystal, which was probably carved in northern
France in the ninth century, is engraved in eight lively scenes with the story
of Susanna and the Elders. Its vicissitudes of fortune include being pawned
by a certain Count for a horse in the tenth century with a Canon of Rheims
who subsequently denied having received it. It was however found on his
person when the owner smoked him out by setting fire to the Cathedral; it
was in penance for this act of sacrilege that the Count founded the Abbey of
Waulsort where the crystal subsequently stayed until the Revolution. At this
time it was stolen, stripped of its jewels, and sold for 12 francs; the Museum
purchased it at Christie's in 1855 for £267.

Lastly, the Angel Inn pitcher is unique as an intact late Anglo-Saxon   226
vessel of the ninth or tenth century. It was acquired by Franks from a group
of similar pots (the others are destroyed or lost) found on the site of the Angel Inn
at Oxford, and given by him in 1887 along with his important collection of
English pottery. For many years it was catalogued as sixteenth century because
of the characteristic look of its yellow glaze. Pre-Conquest glaze was then
unheard of. As a complete example of ceramic table-ware of the period it is a

229–231 *Above*, the Lothair Crystal, a rock crystal with the story of Susanna and the Elders in intaglio, has a most romantic history since it was cut in ninth-century northern France. *Right*, an extremely fine Romanesque bronze crucifix figure of *c.* 1120. *Below*, some of the amusing twelfth-century walrus ivory chessmen from Uig on the Isle of Lewis, Outer Hebrides

34 *Right*, the
ley hoard of five
fourteenth-century
and the sixteenth-
y Welford cup.

left, bronze jug
Ashanti, West Af-
with an inscription
it to the reign of
d II (1366–88).

right, the Royal
Cup of the Kings
ace and England,

great rarity, and the use of glaze so early is remarkable. The Angel Inn pitcher was probably made in kilns at Stamford, in Lincolnshire.

Still in the field of early ceramics, the Department posseses an unrivalled collection of English medieval clay tiles, a standard type of decorative flooring in palaces, castles and merchants' houses as well as in cathedrals, abbeys and parish churches. The industry started up in the first half of the thirteenth century, when small tiles, dark green or pale yellow in colour, were used to build up geometric mosaics, probably a reflection of contemporary Italian floors in marble. The most common technique was to impress into red clay squares decorative devices; the impression left was then filled with white clay and the whole tile surface covered with transparent lead glaze, resulting in the typical dark brown and pale yellow colour scheme. Dark green was generally confined to tiles used for bordering or plain mosaic designs. The purchase in 1947 of the Duke of Rutland's collection of over seven thousand tiles more than doubled the Museum's collection. The Duke's collection included a complete floor measuring 20 ft by 12 ft from a merchant's house in Bristol and known as Canynges pavement, and a sizeable area of mosaic from a transept chapel in Byland Abbey, Yorkshire. The high point, both technically and artistically, attained by the tile-industry is represented by the splendid series from Chertsey Abbey, in Surrey. Here, large roundels 10 ins in diameter bearing figure subjects were framed with foliate borders to make up a series of 16-inch squares. The ambitious designs, which included scenes from the Romances of Tristan and Isolde and of Richard Coeur-de-Lion, and other subjects, were drawn by an artist of the first rank and translated into the medium of inlaid tile with a degree of technical skill never again achieved. Italian and ultimately Byzantine models in stone and marble were the sources of these types of elaborately designed roundels and floors. Wall-tiles were less common, but the Department has some fine examples of architectural and heraldic design from Great Malvern, and the potential range of the industry is illustrated by the rare series of tiles from Tring in sgraffito technique.

The Department possesses a fine collection of English medieval pottery, that is, post-Conquest pottery, mainly from London and the home counties. Apart from more or less complete vessels, the interests of students are being served, with help from provincial museums and from excavators, by the building up of a national reference collection of examples of pottery from known kilns of stratigraphically dated sherds, *i.e.* sealed in building layers which can be dated from documentary sources. Some excellent examples of the pottery of the Middle Ages are the polychrome jugs. Made in a thin white, tin-glazed fabric with painted scroll-designs and parrot-beak spouts, they probably come from the Bordeaux region and reflect the wine trade.

A source of gold and silver objects for the national collection is the law of Treasure Trove. A recent Treasure Trove acquisition is the Abberley, Worcestershire, hoard of five very fine diamond-point silver spoons of the fourteenth century, found walled up in a recess in the wall of the ruins of the

221

237

232

parish church. The latest find in this series is a small group of jewels, part 219
of a great hoard of 1,237 gold coins found at Fishpool (Blixworth), Nottingham-
shire, in 1966. The hoard was buried early in 1464. A rare, early sixteenth-
century silver font-shaped cup from Welford, Northamptonshire, found while 232
digging holes for fence-posts, was declared Treasure Trove in 1968.

The Museum administers the Treasure Trove system, on behalf of the
Treasury. The finder, if he has declared his find promptly and in its entirety,
receives the full market value as an ex-gratia payment. Finds of Treasure Trove
which do not fill important gaps in the National Collection are normally
offered to the local or regional museum, provided that it can pay the amount
awarded.

The Department has rich collections of medieval ivories and metalwork
including many unique pieces of great distinction. Most notable of all is the
Royal Gold Cup of the Kings of France and England, which can be recognized 234
in the inventories of Crown valuables made in the reigns of Henry VIII and
Elizabeth I. It is the only example of medieval secular gold plate at its most
sumptuous to have survived, although certainly not unique in its day. Originally
it had something of the squat shape of the later Welford Cup, but its stem has 232
twice been lengthened. Its distinctive feature is the use of translucent enamels,
chiefly deep blue, crimson, grass-green and *grisaille*, to illustrate an elaborate
iconography. The cup is embellished with a long series of exquisitely rendered
scenes from the life of St Agnes (on the lid and bowl) and around the foot are
the four symbols of the Evangelists. The piece is unmatched for richness and
splendour, in spite of the loss of the pearls and finial or knob on the lid which
originally completed the design. It is one of the best documented of medieval
objects. It was probably made at the order of Jean, Duc de Berry, in Paris in
about 1380 for presentation to the French King, Charles V, who was born
on St Agnes Day and made a cult of this saint. In the possession of Charles VI
of France from 1391, it was acquired by the Duke of Bedford in 1434, passing
from him into the possession of the Kings of England through Bedford's heir,
Henry VI. It came to light in a convent in the Burgos diocese in Spain, having
been presented in 1604 to the leader of the Spanish delegation on the conclusion
of peace between England and Spain in that year.

Of much the same date as the Royal Gold Cup is a remarkable small piece
which turned up in the course of an excavation conducted by the Manshead
Archaeological Society in 1965 on the site of the Dominican friary in the centre
of Dunstable, Bedfordshire. This is a gold and enamelled swan jewel, or badge, 219
probably made in France about 1400. It was held by a coroner's jury not to be
Treasure Trove and was put up for sale at Sotheby's and purchased by the
Metropolitan Museum, New York, for £4,800. An export licence was
subsequently refused and the jewel was then bought by the British Museum,
with the aid of grants from the Worshipful Company of Goldsmiths, the
National Art Collections Fund and the Pilgrim Trust. The Dunstable swan
jewel is the only example of an heraldic jewel to have survived in England,

235, 236 The Warwick Gitterne
guitar, a unique example of a med
wooden, musical instrument. The w
carving is particularly fine, as the
below shows

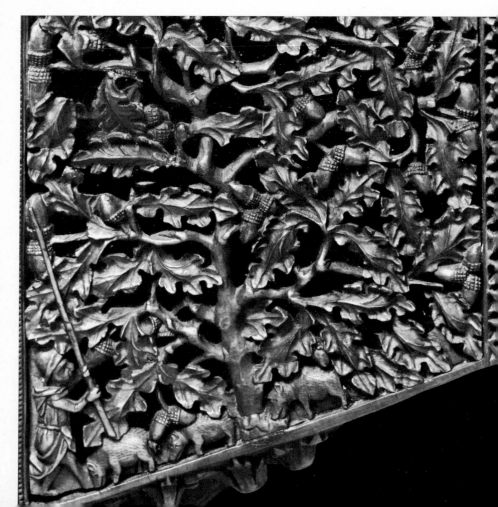

Glazed medieval jugs from London

238 Sixteenth-century 'wald-glass'

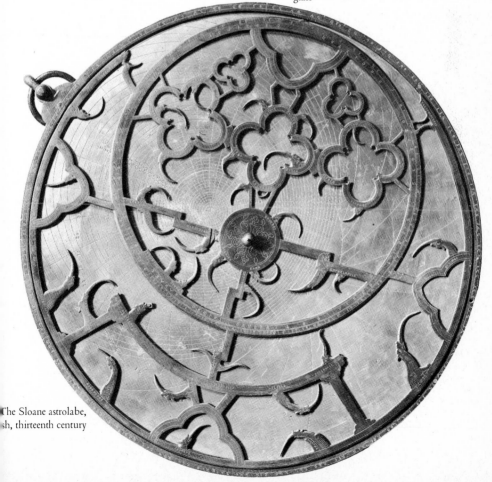

The Sloane astrolabe,
sh, thirteenth century

although they are known from documents and pictures. The badge is covered with white enamel attached to moulded blobs of gold to give the effect of feathers. It is flat and plain at the back where the pin was attached with a gold safety/chain to a gold coronet about its neck. Possibly it belonged to a noble who claimed descent from the legendary Knight of the Swan; or it may have been a livery badge from a highly placed noble retainer of the Lancastrian house.

235   Another unique find recently acquired is the Warwick Gitterne, or guitar, purchased for £40,000. It is an example of medieval late thirteenth/ or early fourteenth/century wood carving at its best. A detail from one side of the

236 deep sound box depicts a swineherd beating an oak tree with a pole to bring down acorns for his pigs. Elsewhere there are scenes of hunting, and grotesques, and panels of ivy and vine leaves and other rich foliage carved with great naturalism and deeply undercut. The gitterne at one time belonged to either Queen Elizabeth or her favourite, Robert Dudley, Earl of Leicester. Both coats of arms are engraved on a silver cover added to the peg box. It was adapted at this time or later for use as a bowed instrument or violin. As a medieval stringed instrument the gitterne is familiar from depictions in stone/carving, the Angel Choir at Lincoln and, in manuscripts, the Queen Mary *Psalter*.

The Department has a rich collection of ivory carvings and enamels of the Romanesque period, the eleventh and twelfth centuries. One of the most distinguished pieces is again a recent acquisition, a bronze crucifix figure of

230 Christ on the cross, with loincloth; often crucifix figures are of a somewhat routine nature, but this is a major work of art, and among the finest of its class.

231   A very popular exhibit is the group of chessmen in morse (walrus) ivory found in a cavity in a sandbank by the sea in the remote parish of Uig on the exposed north/west rim of the Isle of Lewis, in the Outer Hebrides. The place was evidently used to hide the stock of an itinerant trader, and was not a workshop. The chessmen include kings, queens, bishops, castles (in effect, mounted knights) and warders (on foot), together with pawns. Thought to date to around AD 1135–50 and to be the work of an Anglo/Norse carver, they are among the earliest surviving European chessmen, although board games were played much earlier.

233   A great rarity with a mysterious history is a massive bronze jug with lid, parrot/beak spout and a handle ending in an openwork floriated device. An inscription dates it to the reign of Richard II (1366–88). Heraldic stamps appear on the upper part of the jug. It is the finest medieval bronze jug known, and demonstrates the capabilities of the industry. The jug was found by the British Expedition of 1884 standing with other cult/objects on a table in the middle of a courtyard in the palace at Kumasi, former capital of the Kings of Ashanti (Ghana). The jug was probably a war/fetish and one account suggests that it was carried into battle as a standard. Its design influenced locally/made lidded bronze vessels. How it got to Ashanti remains a mystery.

Two other objects of special distinction may be singled out: one is a rare
240 fifteenth/century Flemish painted wooden shield of parade, the only one of its

kind to survive, used for pageantry and display. Of long and narrow form, with a slight carination down the centre-line, the halves of the shield to either side of the carination are painted with figures against a gold foil ground; a lady with open-toed shoes and carrying a pendant jewel on the end of a chain, on the left, and on the right, a knight in armour kneeling to her, his head bare, the words 'vous ou la mort' on a scroll above his head. His helmet and lance lie by his side. Behind him, hands stretched towards him, is a figure of Death, in the form of a skeleton. The painting is of the highest quality. The shield was given by the President of Trinity College, Dr John Wilson, in 1863 and was cleaned in 1938 at the National Gallery, when details such as the pendant jewel and helm and the inscription in white were recovered from beneath varnish and later overpainting. Lastly, in the Waddesdon Bequest is an out- standing medieval piece, the Thorn Reliquary (c. AD 1400). The scene in the   241 central arched recess of the reliquary shows Christ in Glory sitting on a rainbow; His feet on a globe, He is displaying the stigmata. In front of Christ is mounted a single large thorn, several inches in length, supposedly from the Crown of Thorns. Originally in Vienna, the reliquary came into the possession of Baron Ferdinand de Rothschild, with whose bequest it came to the Museum.

These are, of course, only a selection of highlights from the Medieval collections, which contain many objects of great rarity and quality.

For the Renaissance period, the quality of the collections owes much to two major bequests, the Waddesdon Bequest of 1898 and the Franks Bequest of 1897. The Waddesdon Bequest, by Baron Ferdinand de Rothschild, was one of smaller works of art largely formed by his father, Baron Anselm, and kept by him at his country home at Waddesdon Manor, near Aylesbury. It is a condition of the bequest that the objects in it are to be kept together in one room and are to be permanently displayed. The chief categories of this superb collection are bronzes, arms and armour, enamels, glass, silver plates, cups of hardstone with sumptuous jewelled mounts, and jewellery – numbering in all 265 objects of the highest class. To select only three items for mention, there is first the unique circular iron shield for ceremonial or pageant use, inscribed   242 and dated 1584, by Giorgio Ghisi of Mantua. The front is decorated all over with openwork motifs and subjects in silver damascened with gold. A beauti- fully designed and lively central combat scene is surrounded by figures in frames symbolizing Glory, Strength, Fame and Prudence. The frames carry exquisitely rendered minuscule scenes from the *Iliad* and classical mythology.

A second piece is the ovoid vase of mottled agate of Roman origin, carved   245 in deep relief with vine-branches and bunches of grapes; its two small handles rise from sculpted heads of Pan; the lid and base are Renaissance mounts of enamelled gold in the style of Benvenuto Cellini, possibly, as was at one time believed, from his hand.

Thirdly, from a remarkable collection of fifty-three rings and jewels, we may select as an English work the jewelled pendant of the early seventeenth century, known as the Lyte Jewel, which contains a miniature of King James I,

242–245 *Opposite, above*, a decorated, iron, ceremonial shie
Giorgio Ghisi of Mantua, 1584; *below*, the Stapleford Gold
c. 1610; the silver-gilt Bacon cup, 1574; and the Cellini vase

240, 241 *Above*, a Flemish wooden shield of
parade painted with figures of a lady, a knight
and Death; *right*, the gold, enamelled and
crystal, Thorn Reliquary. Both pieces fifteenth
century

considered to be by Nicholas Hillyard. It was given to Thomas Lyte, the antiquary and genealogist, by the King, and has come down in the family. The white and red enamelling is very fine and the border and initial of the openwork front are set with faceted tabular diamonds.

The Museum's ceramics and glass collections are of the first rank and abound in pieces of documentary interest. The expansion of these collections began during Franks's Keepership with the Felix Slade Bequest in 1868, which included many fine pieces of glass. An important year for ceramic acquisitions was 1887; the Henry Willett collection was acquired, and Franks himself gave the Museum 600 pieces of English pottery (including some fine Wedgwood) valued at that time at £4,500. In 1897 came the great Franks Bequest, which included his collection of porcelain. The Wedgwood collection of Isaac and Mrs Falke was acquired in 1909 and in 1919, the Harland Bequest of Whieldon pottery and Staffordshire slipware. The collections include several of the

222   finest celebration dishes by Thomas Toft. The large Frank Lloyd Bequest of Worcester porcelain came in 1921 and important pieces of Continental pottery and porcelain from Sir Bernard Eckstein in 1945. The most recent benefaction in this field has been the Macalister collection of Bow and other porcelain given in 1960.

The Department's collection of Bow porcelain is an important one and includes ten or more of the twenty-six known documentary pieces (i.e. dated

247, 248   by inscriptions). The Bowcock bowl is one. Acquired in 1956 as part-purchase, part-gift, from Mr I. E. Allman of Liverpool, it is a punch-bowl made at the Bow factory and inscribed JOHN and ANN BOWCOCK 1759. (John Bowcock was clerk to the factory and probably later its manager.) The bowl is in powdered blue with reserved panels of *chinoiseries*. It is described in the Bowcock papers, a collection of manuscript documents relating to the history of the factory, also in the possession of the Department.

246   In the Franks Bequest was a glass jug with metal mounts thought to be of Netherlandish origin and of the first half of the sixteenth century. It has broad vertical bands of opaque white glass with very narrow lines of clear glass between them and the silver-gilt mounts are hallmarked for London, 1548–9. The jug is similar to one described in Queen Elizabeth's inventories in 1559 and 1574. It is one of two surviving pieces of Continental glass in the 'façon de Venise' associated with Sir William Parr, uncle of Henry VIII's Queen, Catherine Parr; the other is the Parr jug in the London Museum, which can be shown to have reached England before the middle of the sixteenth century.

From the Felix Slade Bequest came an intact tall cylindrical goblet standing

238   on a flat circular pierced foot. It is of dark, greenish-blue, 'wald-glass' (forest glass) probably from the Rhineland and of the early sixteenth century, but in the tradition of late medieval glass-working. It is remarkable for having rows of vertically set 'prunts' (blobs of solid glass, in this case drawn out into spikes) both inside and outside – eight vertical rows of nine prunts externally and eight of seven prunts internally.

Described variously as 'one of the most important purchases ever made for the Museum by Franks' (in 1871), and as 'a technical wonder even to potters of the present day', is the life-size bust of Prince Rupert made by John Dwight, an early English maker of stoneware, at Fulham in about 1680. The Prince is shown with wig and lace cravat and wearing the Collar of the Garter with the Greater George. The bust reveals a complete technical mastery of the medium and Dwight's great modelling ability.

250

The fine collection of Wedgwood is almost entirely from the Isaac Falke and Franks collections. A black and white jasper-ware copy of the Portland Vase, marked 'No. 4' on the lip, is no doubt one of the first series of copies made by Josiah Wedgwood between 1786 and 1790. The collections also contain another copy of the Portland Vase, a light-blue Jasper-ware copy made c. 1800 (after Josiah's death) and given in 1802 by John Wedgwood, son of Josiah. There are amongst the Department's Wedgwood some notable portrait plaques, all from the Franks collection, dating from the period of Josiah's partnership with Thomas Bentley (1768–80) and made in the celebrated Etruria factory opened in 1769. An unusual item of a different sort from the Franks Bequest is a Meissen travelling set in perfect condition, packed in its leather travelling box and dating from c. 1725; it has gold printed designs on a white ground.

249

The collections include some fine plate, recently augmented by the Wilding Bequest (1970) of some thirty well selected, top class, pieces of Hugenot silver, mostly of the pre-Lamerie period. A notable example of plate is the Stapleford Gold Cup, dating from c. 1610. It is the earliest surviving example of English secular gold plate, and when acquired had been in the possession of the Church of Stapleford since the year of its donation, 1732. Secular vessels were still at this time being given for conversion to sacred use to make good the destruction of medieval plate by the Puritans of the Cromwellian era.

243

A category of considerable interest, and popular with visitors, is that of personal relics – objects associated with historical figures. They include such things as G. F. Handel's watch, a stone and silver-rimmed punch bowl, with an inscription on the rim, made by Robert Burns's father-in-law on the occasion of the poet's marriage; a gold badge for admission to the Vauxhall Pleasure Gardens which belonged to William Hogarth; Lord Palmerston's Garter, and finger-rings of Mary Queen of Scots, Lord Nelson, George III and Dean Swift. There is a Chelsea tea-service that belonged to W. E. Gladstone, himself a distinguished collector of English porcelain. It carries the gold anchor mark and was made c. 1765. Some of the relics are of more historical significance, such as three silver seals used by Sir Walter Raleigh as Governor of Virginia, a gold ring which is probably the personal ring of Richard Cœur-de-Lion and, much earlier and of great importance, the rings of King Aethelwulf of Wessex and Queen Aethelswith of Mercia, father and sister of Alfred the Great, these being exhibited with the later Anglo-Saxon collections. In the category of personal relics may be included the fine silver-gilt

246–248 *Left*, glass jug with silver mount hallmarked for London, 1548–9. *Below*, th Bowcock bowl, dated 1759, one of the fe pieces of dated Bow porcelain

249 A jasper-ware copy of the Portland Vase by Josiah Wedgwood, *c.* 1786–90 (*see also* Pl. *149*)

250 Life-size, stoneware, bust of Prince Rupert by John Dwight of Fulham, about 1680

251 Salt-glazed stoneware musicians. Connections with the Longton Hall kiln site are proved by wasters of the left arm and left leg of the male figure excavated there, but it is not known where the salt-glazed versions were produced as salt-glaze wares were not made at Longton Hall itself, only porcelain

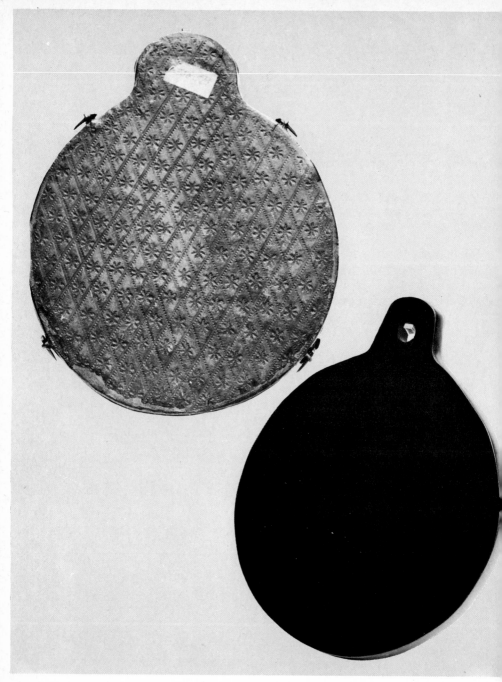

252 Dr Dee's magic mirror and its tooled leather case. The black obsidian mirror is, in fact, an Aztec antiquity

cup, its lid crowned by a boar figure, known as the Bacon cup. It was one of   244
three made in 1574 for Sir Nicholas Bacon (appointed Lord Keeper of the
Great Seal to Queen Elizabeth I in 1558) from the melted down Great Seal
of Mary and Philip II. It remained in the family and was presented in 1915
by Mrs Edmond Wodehouse. Personal relics were already to be found in the
foundation collections, the wax astrological discs of Dr Dee which were in
the Cottonian Library being an example. The most recent acquisition in
this field is the remarkable *speculum*, or mirror, of Dr Dee, a plain circular   252
slab of polished black obsidian, with a projecting perforated lug for suspension.
It is an American antiquity of distinction in its own right, made in Mexico
during the Aztec civilization of the fourteenth to sixteenth centuries AD and
brought to Europe soon after the conquest of Mexico by Cortéz in 1520/30.
Dr Dee acquired it for his magical pursuits and it eventually passed into the
possession of Horace Walpole, together with the tooled leather case made for it,
presumably by Dee.

Lastly, reference should be made to a section of the collections which has
recently become of outstanding importance – that of horology. The collection of
clocks and watches has recently attained the status of the best in the world for
the systematic study of horology, thanks to the acquisition of the entire collection
formed by the late Courtenay Ilbert of Chelsea. The saving of this unique
collection for the nation in 1958 was made possible by the generosity of
Mr Gilbert Edgar, C.B.E., later Master of the Worshipful Company of Clockmakers, who met the entire cost (£50,000) of the clock collection and contributed a further substantial sum towards the purchase of the watches. The Ilbert
collection comprised 277 clocks, 1,050 watches, 741 watch movements and   220
horological miscellanea (dials, hourglasses, watch papers, etc.). This great
acquisition added to the fine nucleus already possessed by the Museum as a
result of the Lady Fellows Bequest of 1874 and the Octavius Morgan Bequest
of 1888.

It is a matter of pride to the Department that with the Ilbert Collection a
finely equipped students' room has been provided, with a library of horological
books, a specialized workshop and expert staff. The horological collections
may be said to be not only the best in the world, but the best looked after and
the most conveniently studied. In the Horological Students Room is housed
also the collection of early scientific instruments, not great numerically, but
ranking according to some authorities as the sixth most important in the world.

R. L. S. BRUCEMITFORD

CHAPTER EIGHT

Oriental Antiquities

Apart from a small group of objects of great historical interest, mainly from the collection of the German doctor and historian of Japan, Engelbert Kaemp-fer, which entered the Museum with the Sloane Collection at its foundation in 1753, the basis of the Chinese and Japanese collections was laid by that remarkable man Sir Augustus Wollaston Franks (Keeper 1866–96). Among his very wide scholarly interests Far Eastern ceramics had a pre-eminent place. Recognized at home and abroad as the leading authority on this subject, he was consulted by all the major collectors and was also official adviser to the South Kensington Museum. He formed the pioneer collection on scientific principles to illustrate the history of the art and himself wrote the catalogue for its display in the Bethnal Green Museum, published in 1876 and revised in 1878. This systematic collection was bequeathed, with much else, to the British Museum on Franks's death in 1897. Meanwhile, he had consistently bought for the Museum additional pieces to supplement the collection. He never visited the Far East, but he went far outside the taste of his period in identifying and securing examples of dynasties earlier than the Manchu. No particulars remain of the sources from which he made his acquisitions, apart from a few which came from the dispersal of the decorative furnishing and china cabinets of old country houses such as Stowe, Blenheim and Burleigh.

The Franks collection of Japanese ceramics was very extensive, since it was formed at a time, in the 1860s and 1870s, when Japanese art was at the height of its reputation and enjoyed a vogue with artists, cognoscenti and a large general public. It was a healthy sign that contemporary art was included in this esteem, but well before the end of the century it had been recognized by the discerning that, largely because of Western influence and the attraction of an inflated, undiscriminating Western market, the level of achievement had entered a decline and the meretricious was gaining on the authentic tradition. Franks showed judgment and discrimination but, inevitably, acquired too many late pieces. However, his collection included the only piece of old Kutani ware then outside Japan, and a fine range of early Arita from the seventeenth century, with a dazzling series of the Kakiemon enamelled porcelains which had been imported into Britain when they were new, in the first half of the eighteenth century. Franks was also aware of the importance of the tradition in Japan of tea-ceremony pottery and he acquired a large series of bowls, caddies and water jars. The technical virtuosity and iconographical interest of carved *netsuke*, and of sword-guards (*tsuba*) also appealed to him, as to many

285

of the early collectors in this country of Japanese art. He also laid the foundation of the collection of lacquer, sword-blades and metalwork.

The principal British collector resident in Japan in the 1870s was William Anderson, a Professor of Surgery from St Thomas's Hospital in London, who had also received training as an artist. In addition to founding a school of surgery in Tokyo, Anderson formed an extensive collection of Japanese and Chinese paintings, which formed the basis of his monograph on Japanese paintings. The collection was acquired for the Department of Prints and Drawings at the Museum in 1881 at the instance of Colvin, and thus formed the nucleus of the collection of Far Eastern paintings, which was transferred to Oriental Antiquities on its foundation in 1933. There were great oppor-tunities in those early Meiji days for discriminating purchases; it is none the less remarkable that a busy professional man should have achieved so much in only seven years. While the collection lacks great masterpieces, there are works of all the major schools from the sixteenth century onwards, giving a clear conspectus of their history and a rich and still unexhausted field for research. Colvin also set the Museum on the way to its present rich and fine representation of Japanese wood-cut prints of the Ukiyoe school. He secured in 1902 the collection of Ernest Hart, a pioneer collector of Japanese art in the 1880s and a prominent London doctor. This was followed in 1906 by Arthur Morrison's much larger collection and by the purchase, in 1910, of the series of actor prints by Sharaku from Sir Ernest Satow, who had acquired these twenty-four prints by the rarest of artists on a stall in Japan, mounted in an album which had protected them from fading. The collection now contains every one of Sharaku's famous head and shoulder portraits of actors, and is probably the only place in the world where they can be seen together. Other acquisitions followed so that by 1915, when Laurence Binyon completed his catalogue, the collection was able to claim that it was already in the front rank.

It was Franks who ensured that the Museum would be the first in Europe to admit the East as a field suitable for archaeological and art-historical research. The acquisition of the Gowland prehistoric material from burial mounds in Japan and Korea was especially significant; it still remains an important source for these studies as it contains a series of undoubted authentic pieces from known sites, including examples of those now much imitated classes of *Haniwa* and *dotaku* – pottery images which surround the grave and bronze bells from the protohistoric period of Japan. Franks trained his successor, Hercules Read, in the same broad tradition of scholarship and liberal en-couragement of research. During his Keepership from 1896 to 1921 Read maintained this wide-ranging taste over the whole of his huge Department, but now with a team of able specialists in several of the subjects covered. He certainly encouraged the young Hobson in his ceramic studies and in seeking to carry back the Chinese collection into the Han and even the Chou dynasty; he also began the formation of a series of pottery and glass from the first thousand

254

この之由
遷致盈必損理斉固然美者皀美翻以
取尤冶容求好君子所仇結恩而絕宴

253, 254 *Above*, a detail from a Chinese scroll-painting on silk entitled the 'Admonitions of the Preceptress to the Ladies of the Palace'. It is attributed to Ku K'ai-chih (*c.* 344–*c.* 406 AD), but is more probably of the seventh or eighth centuries. *Right*, woodcut colour print with mica ground by Sharaku, 1793. It shows the actors Segawa Kikunojo III and Sawamura Sojuro III in character

255 Chinese ritual bronze vessel, a *tsun*, in the form of a pair of rams, Shang dynasty, twelfth to eleventh centuries BC

256 Chinese porcelain jar with cobalt blue decoration of peacocks and peonies under the glaze, Yüan dynasty, fourteenth century AD

257, 258 A ritual, black jade, *kuei* sceptre, Shang dynasty, twelfth to eleventh centuries BC, and a white jade ritual halberd blade, early Chou dynasty, tenth to ninth centuries BC

259–261 *Left*, Syrian glass pilgrim
flask with enamel decoration of the
late twelfth century (*see also Pl. 274*).
Below, left, an Isnik ware dish from
Turkey, *c.* 1530–40; *right*, Persian
shallow bowl, early twelfth century,
decorated with a hare carved in
black slip on a white ground

262, 263 *Left*, a brass ewer, inlaid with silver and copper, made at Mosul in 1232 by Shuja' ibn Man'a; *below*, a brass hand-warmer, pierced and inlaid with silver, and inscribed with the name of Badr al Din Baysari. Made in Syria between 1264 and 1279

264 Chinese gilt-bronze figure of the Bodhisattva Kuanyin, Sui dynasty, dated AD 595

years of the Islamic period. Read himself went all out to secure the great things
272 which came on to the market, such as the Lohan from I-chou, one of the best
of the series and the only one in Europe. He showed a special interest in the
art of Central Asia from the Indus to the Oxus, and from the Kushan period
to the post-Sassanian, including sculpture in stone and stucco from the
Gandhara region.

Read also seems to have been concerned with the acquisition of the greatest
253 Chinese painting in the Western world: the 'Admonitions of the Preceptress
to the Ladies of the Palace', attributed to the fourth-century painter Ku
K'ai-chih. Laurence Binyon was given the honour of the first publication of
this early silk scroll (which he successfully defended) in the *Burlington Magazine*
in 1903: this set him on his career as an ideal interpreter to the English-speaking
world of the visual concepts and criteria of connoisseurship of Far Eastern
painting. His penetrating and intuitive appreciation of the schools of China
and Japan found expression in his *Painting in the Far East*, 1908, subsequently
revised and enlarged three times until the last edition of 1934.

Read ensured that the British Museum should be jointly responsible with
the Government of India in the sponsorship of Sir Aurel Stein's first two
expeditions to Central Asia of 1903 and 1906–8. From the latter the Museum
received a half share of the finds of manuscripts and Buddhist paintings from
a sealed chamber of the early eleventh century at the great Buddhist monastic
centre of The Thousand Buddha Caves, near the city of Tun-huang on the
western border of China, an oasis on the great pilgrim and trade route to the
West. The Stein collection also contains remains of silk brocade, terracotta
and stucco figurines and all manner of small objects preserved in the en-
croaching sand over a period of more than a thousand years from the beginning
of our era.

When Read retired in 1921, it was recognized that no one man could be
expected to supervise the work of a department covering such a multitude of
interests. But the division then made had more regard to persons than to systematic planning. R. L. Hobson, who already had an international reputation
as a scholar of the history of ceramics, was given the charge of a department with
that name. To that was added the general supervision of the Ethnographical
collections, now formed into a sub-department. This odd arrangement had
the fortunate result that Hobson became responsible for the other collections
from the Far East, especially those from India and Ceylon, which, because
they were outside the ken of the classical Mediterranean world, were still
labelled 'ethnographical'. It may be said that the same attitude was shown in
Berlin where these collections remained in the Völkerkunde Museum up to
the outbreak of the Second World War. Hobson was thus able to keep the
Museum abreast of the growing knowledge of Chinese bronzes and jade which
were seen, moreover, to be closely connected with his own special study of
ceramics. Hence the pragmatic method of Museum administration did in
practice prepare the way for the formation of a Department of Oriental

Antiquities, though this was delayed for a further twelve years till 1933. It came just in time to provide for the acquisition of the major part of the Eumorfo-poulos collection of Chinese art, the most extensive and best chosen of all the 255 private collections of that golden age of the collector, from 1910 to 1935. Hobson was in almost daily touch with Eumorfopoulos, whose ceramic collection he was cataloguing in six great folio volumes, and he shared his 271 acute interest and enthusiasm for every form of Chinese art. At this time, 1921, the first Chinese ritual bronze was acquired for the Museum.

The other major event of 1921 was the foundation of the Oriental Ceramic Society with whose activities the Department has been so closely associated ever since. It brought together, for regular discussion of problem pieces and the latest discoveries, a closely knit group of keen collectors, meeting in one another's homes under the presidency of Eumorfopoulos and Hobson's professional guidance. It was at this time also that London began to dominate the Chinese art market, so that these collectors usually had the first refusal of anything outstanding which appeared. Hobson was always ready with his opinion and advice and, as a result, the Museum reaped a rich reward in terms of gifts and bequests, quite apart from its share of the Eumorfopoulos collection. Some of these bequests naturally matured after Hobson's retirement in 1938 and his death in 1941, but there is no doubt that his unique position at that crucial time still brings its benefits. A few only of the outstanding benefactors can be mentioned here: Oscar Raphael (long a voluntary worker in the Department) for his Chinese funeral jades and ritual bronzes, as well as much 258, 264 else; Harry Oppenheim, for the bequest of his entire Chinese art collection, especially noted for the ceramics, small bronzes and jades; Howard Paget, for his Ming enamelled porcelain; C.G. and Brenda Seligman, for their special collections of early Chinese glass and weapons and, ultimately, for the essential part of their carefully chosen collections of pre-Ming ceramics, ritual vessels and mirrors; and Mrs Walter Sedgwick, for the first pick of her splendid and very shrewdly chosen collection of T'ang to Ming ceramics and of early bronze and jade and T'ang silverware. In this way the Museum has inherited a large share of the British loans to the famous international exhibition of Chinese art organized by Sir Percival David at Burlington House in the winter of 1935/6, which was the crowning achievement of this group of collectors and their professional colleagues in the national museums.

Hobson's main pre-occupation was with ceramics, and he was able to see the representation of the pre-Ming periods begin to hold its own with the Franks collection of the later periods. He was himself, in fact, the leader in the progress of the study of Chinese ceramic history. He stayed on an extra year beyond the normal retiring age in order to complete the purchase of the Eumorfopoulos collection in 1938, and to put the share of the Museum on view. At a stroke the T'ang and Sung ceramics were placed in the front rank, and time has vindicated the skill of the collection's formation. It is difficult to particularize, where the standard is so high, but today the major part of the

265–267 *Left*, a stone figure of Garuda, the vehicle of Vishnu, from Orissa, thirteenth century. *Below*, marble drum slab from the facing of the great stupa at Amaravati. It depicts Maya's dream, its interpretation and the Birth and Presentation of the Buddha. Satavahana period, second century AD. *Right*, a life-size gilt bronze figure of Tara from Ceylon, tenth century AD

堪隱耆宿
脫石洞樹
雲亦不浮
似同去之
佐人漆木
石澗汾
遠人作
於天閒
山巧

石溪殘
白禿

Painting in ink and light colour of an autumn landscape by K'un Ts'an (active *c.* 1655–75), early Ch'ing dynasty, 1666

269 Korean lacquer sutra box decorated with silver wire and mother of pearl inlay, thirteenth century AD

270 Japanese gilt bronze meditating Buddha, Nara period, second half of the seventh century AD

271, 272 *Above*, Chinese plum blossom vase, Tz'u-chou type, Sung dynasty, eleventh to twelfth centuries AD. Opp. pottery figure of a Lohan from I-chou, Hopei, north China, tenth or eleventh centuries AD

spectacular T'ang three-colour wares on display are from this source, including the cavalcade of horses and camels with their drivers and attendants which furnished the tomb of Chancellor Liu T'ing-hsun, who died in AD 728. The offering dishes and storage jars form, with some support from the Oppen- heim collection, the finest display of this class in the West. The T'ang white wares are also distinguished, headed as they are by the unique phoenix-headed ewer of true porcelain from the Chichou kilns.

Up to this point we have limited our account of the growth of the collections almost entirely to the Far East: it is time to take stock of the situation in the rest of the large area covered by the Department at the time of Hobson's retirement in 1938. Franks had, at the outset of his museum career, ensured that Islamic metalwork should not be neglected when he secured in 1866 no fewer than twenty-one pieces of the collection formed by the Duc de Blacas, the subject of the first monograph on this subject published by Reinaud in 1828. It included the famous inlaid ewer of 1232 signed by the Mosul craftsman, Shuja' ibn Man'a. Even earlier, in 1855, the Museum had acquired another famous inlaid and signed piece, the astrolabe dated 1236 of 'Abd al-Karim of Cairo; this may well have been due to the young Franks who had joined the Museum in 1851. He can, however, hardly have had a hand in the purchase in 1848 of two inlaid twelfth-century Persian ewers from Khurasan which had then recently figured in the spacious monograph on inscriptions in Arabic script by the Roman scholar Michele Angelo Lanci (3 vols, 1845–6). Credit for this must go to Edward Hawkins the numismatist and Keeper of Antiquities at the Museum from 1826 to 1860. At this time objects of Islamic art were favoured by the medievalists, and it is no surprise to find a leading designer and architect of the mid-century, William Burges, bequeathing to the Museum on his death in 1881 several fine examples, including two Mamluk writing boxes. The finest writing box in the collection, signed Mahmud ibn Simqur and dated 1281, was secured by Franks in 1891 on the death of the owner, Rhode Hawkins, son of Edward Hawkins. Another friend of Franks's, John Henderson, who had arranged a small private museum in Bloomsbury, died in 1878 leaving his collection of Islamic metalwork, arms and pottery to the Department. The foundation was thus laid of the excellent collection of Isnik pottery which is one of the visual feasts the Department provides for the visitor. Persian pottery of the seventeenth and eighteenth centuries was also now well represented. In 1869 the Museum had received the Slade bequest of glass, including the enamelled glass mosque lamps which are so splendid when well shown, but so difficult to show. Franks improved all these collections during the rest of his Keepership so that, by the end, he left a very distinguished collection of the kinds of Islamic art (other than carpets and textiles which the Museum has always eschewed), which were then available, including even some ivories and rock-crystals.

None of these objects had been excavated, and it has been left largely for this century to try to illustrate the earlier period of Islamic life with material

262

263

260

259, 274

from the ground. Hobson secured examples of the decorative monochrome and overpainted (*mina'i*) pottery of the Saljuq period and the lustre wares of Kashan (including the earliest dated piece known) which are the particular glory of medieval Iran. He was also able, through the fortunes of war, to profit from German excavations at Samarra on the Tigris of a ninth-century palace city of the Abbasid caliphs. He insisted on the return to the excavators of the bulk of their finds, which were then still unpublished; but a good representative series of stucco, pottery and glass remained at the Museum as invaluable study material. These were supported by a few whole or made up pieces acquired in the market. Little was added to the Islamic metalwork at this time, but Mrs Spier gave a fine and rare standing cup of enamelled glass in 1924 and earlier some Fatimid lustre painted glasses from Egypt had come from Atfih.

Before Franks's time, South Asia had been represented by stray, if some-times distinguished, pieces. The dryad Yakshini figure from the fallen gateway of the great stupa at Sanchi, a great treasure for any Museum, came from a Mrs Tucker in 1843, while the widows of two famous men gave priceless tokens of their husbands' interest in antiquities; from Lady Raffles, in 1859, what remained after loss by shipwreck, of Sir Stamford's Javanese bronze images; and from Lady Brownrigg, in 1830, the superb tenth-century gilt bronze figure of Tara which Sir Robert, Governor of Ceylon, had found in the jungle as he toured the island near Trincomalee. When the largest collection of Indian sculpture in Britain in private hands came on the market in 1872, Franks showed himself as alert as ever. He attended the auction and, proving to be the only bidder, arranged with the owners that it should pass to the Museum as the gift of the family of James Bridge, who had acquired it *en bloc* from the heirs of General Charles Stuart in 1830. Stuart had served and lived in India from 1777 till his death in 1828. These were the days of enlightened interest in Indian culture, of the foundation of the Asiatic Society of Bengal (1784), and of Sir William Jones's translations from Sanskrit, printed in Calcutta while he was serving as a Judge of the High Court. Nonetheless, Stuart earned the name of Hindoo Stuart by his enthusiasm for Indian sculpture with which he filled his house. He seems to have gathered together fragments from ruined temples which were lying about in neglect. The collection received by the Museum in 1872 consisted of 115 sculptures, mostly of the Pala period in Bihar or from Orissa, but includes sculptures from Central India of ad-mirable quality.

Even more important to the Museum was Franks's success in arranging for the transfer to Bloomsbury of the collections of antiquities and sculptures originally acquired by the East India Company for their museum in the City of London. Fortunately the natural history collection of the British Museum had just been removed from Bloomsbury to the new building in Cromwell Road, South Kensington, so that it was possible to accommodate this collec-tion, in particular the great series of marble facing slabs and railing uprights

267

265

273 Portrait of a royal chamberlain by Mir Musavvir. Persian, Tabriz, Safavi period, *c.* 1540

275 Book-binding, one of a pair, painted in ▶ lacquer on a blue ground. Persian, Tabriz, Safavi period, *c.* 1540

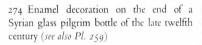

274 Enamel decoration on the end of a Syrian glass pilgrim bottle of the late twelfth century (*see also* Pl. *259*)

266   and frieze bars of the great stupa at Amaravati, which were given the position of honour and prominence that their quality and importance warranted, on the landing of the main staircase of the Museum.

When Hobson became the first Keeper of the Department of Oriental Antiquities and Ethnography in 1933, he was responsible not only for the South Asian and Far Eastern sculptures and metalwork and all else which Franks and Read had brought together from Asia, but also for the Chinese and Japanese paintings and woodcut prints which Laurence Binyon had had in his charge until his retirement in that year. This was in conformity with the traditional attitude in the East, adopted in the leading Western museums, by which instead of separating paintings from the other arts, there has been a common standard of scholarship in the appreciation and study of all the arts in the Far East, although painting was accepted as the major consideration. Now the Department was forced to realize that its holdings in paintings were not comparable in excellence or representation with those in ceramics or bronze. It has since been a primary duty to try to remedy this; but the search is long and exacting. Most progress has been made in the Chinese schools from the Yüan to the seventeenth century, which have been those preferred and studied in China since the end of the sixteenth century. To the Westerner, even now when the great breakthrough has occurred in our own painting to a freedom of choice and technique, it is not easy to move within the accepted

268   terms of the scholarly or 'individualist' schools, and to appreciate an art of the brush so intimately connected with calligraphy.

Japanese art did not regain its popularity until some years after the end of the Second World War, and less has been achieved in widening and deepening the holding of painting. On the other hand, there is now a good choice of screen painting which is the most appealing to the public and unmatched in its sense of the decorative use of broad line and colour on a plain paper or a gold ground. Only a beginning has been made in a showing of the great medieval art of Japan, bound up with the Buddhist faith and so impressive to those who visit the temples of Nara and Kyoto. However, in the past twenty years, the Department has secured one of the lost treasures of Horyuji, a Gigaku mask in lacquered wood of the eighth century and, even rarer, a gilt bronze

270   meditating Bodhisattva of the Nara period, of the second half of the seventh century, whose authenticity has been supported by spectrographic examination which showed the characteristic blow-holes and iron support to the core in casting, typical of this period. From the succeeding age of Heian, when aristocratic art in Japan reached its height of refined richness and delicacy, there is the lacquer document box painted in silver and gold with a design of insects and enhanced with mother of pearl. A devotional painting of the protective deity, Fuku Kenzaku Kannon, with two military attendants, in full colours on silk, dating from 1170 to 1180, is the first major painting of this period to enter any European collection. Two liturgical objects of the succeeding Kamakura period have been acquired, a carved and painted wooden canopy

for a temple statue, and a lacquer tray for the sutras with gilt copper mounts, both of the thirteenth century. The noble school of wood sculpture is now represented by four figures of the twelfth to thirteenth century, all acquired in the past twenty-five years. Much remains to be done in this field, but at least a good beginning has been made.

Korea is represented by a small but choice collection of Koryu celadon porcelain, by some bronze vessels with copper and silver inlay of the same period and a rare and beautiful large sutra box richly decorated with silver   269 wire and mother of pearl inlay, one of the best preserved of a small group of twelfth-century boxes. There are also some fine gilt bronze Buddhist figures from an earlier period, the eighth century, when Korea was the bridge between China and Japan.

By the beginning of the 1950s the great rain of benefactions from collectors had actually been received or could be clearly seen as promise. It was then possible to take stock and to decide what were going to be the major gaps in the collections requiring to be filled if they were to represent all the civilizations of Asia which were the concern of the Department. It soon became essential to do so, for there then appeared the most generous, modest, clear-sighted and reasonable benefactor that could be imagined in the person of P. T. Brooke Sewell, a retired British merchant banker living in Switzerland. He started with the idea of building up the collection of Indian jade, but very soon it became clear that he was thinking in bigger terms than this might have   276 suggested. It emerged that, while he was most interested to improve the holdings of Indian art, he would consider other defined areas in which the fund he was establishing might be used effectively to acquire groups of objects where they would notably improve the range and quality of exhibits. He was, above all, concerned to find things which would be likely to be worthy of exhibition, rather than study material. And so it came about that in the fifties and sixties the museum was enabled to compete in the market, despite steeply rising prices.

Naturally the greatest impact has been on the Indian collections, where it was most needed. There was much ground to make up, but opportunities have occurred and have been seized with avidity so that there is now no excuse for lack of appreciation of this great school of sculpture in stone, wood and bronze. The biggest gap had been in the representation of the schools of the Deccan and South India after the early period of Amaravati. Now, however,   280 the Department can boast of three Pallava pieces (eighth and ninth century);   277 a whole galaxy of the early Cola style (850–1014) in the hard granite or basalt of that area, and in bronze, which wonderfully combines delicacy of modelling and finish with plastic form. From the Deccan we can now show a unique bronze high relief appliqué figure of the third century; a tiny dancing youth of the eighth century, probably part of some bronze object, such as a lamp, and almost Etruscan in its stiff grace; two Western Ganga bronze figures of about 900 or soon after; a Siva as Kiratarjuna and a Jain image of Sarasvati,   281 goddess of wisdom.

276 The Sambas Treasure of gold and silver Buddhist images and a bronze, house-shaped, incense burner. Found in West Borneo but originally from East Java, tenth to eleventh centuries AD

Sandstone figure of Varaha, the boar incarnation of [Vishn]u, from Central India, eighth century AD

278 Granite statue of Siva as Dakshinamurti from South India, early Cola dynasty about AD 960

279 Schist dancing girl using a hand mirror, from Mysore, Horsala period, early twelfth century

283 Indian bronze figures. *Above, left,* Candikesvara, the seneschal of Siva. South Indian, Cola dynasty, first half of eleventh century AD; *right,* Sarasvati, the Jain goddess of Wisdom, from Mysore, Western Ganga period, tenth century *Below, left,* seated Buddha in the preaching mudra, from Dhanesar Khera, Gupta period, fourth to fifth century AD; Manasa, the serpent goddess, from Bengal, Pala period, about 750 BC

284 Ivory carved figure
a seated Bodhisattva, set
a polychrome, carv
wooden frame, forme
part of a shrine. Kashm
first half of the eigh
century

285 Japanese porcelain figure of a Beauty (but probably
a young man of fashion) with enamel decoration. Arita,
about 1673–83

Northern India has not been neglected, with the accession of a seated bronze
teaching Buddha of the Gupta period, a work of still vitality, and incidentally   282
of great rarity. A unique group of the newly identified Buddhist bronze images
from Kashmir of the eighth to tenth centuries combines the northern tradition
of Central Asia with the humanism of the Gupta tradition in a post‑Gandhara
style which corresponds in the north‑west to the early Pala style of the north‑east.
In Nepal we can see a gentler and more gracious style in the gilt bronzes of
the ninth to eleventh centuries, of which the seated Bodhisattva Maitreya is an
outstandingly beautiful example.

In wood, the Department had previously only the remarkable small group
from the Kashmir Swats cave in the Yusufzai country, found by Sir Harold
Dean in 1888. Now there is a good South India group from temple processional
cars, and a much older figure, probably of the twelfth century, of a male dancer
(33 ins high), very worn but still full of vitality. It is strange how little has sur‑
vived from the old art of ivory carving and it is a matter of satisfaction that two
carvings in this material in the full round, both probably from chair furniture,
have been acquired, one from Nepal and the other from Orissa.

Outside the Indian field, the Brooke Sewell Fund has made possible many
notable purchases. The Chinese bronzes include: the great bell of about 500 BC   287
from the Stoclet collection in Brussels, notable for its rich surface decoration
and plastic dragon handles; Shang ritual vessels and a four‑faced finial; inlaid
swords of the fourth–third centuries BC, and a large tripod vessel with gold,
silver and glass inlay of the same period. Lacquer was a favourite material for   286
objects of domestic use as early as the Chou dynasty as surviving pieces from
burials testify.

The opportunities to improve the Islamic collections have been fewer and,
when the exceptional piece is available, competition has been severe. Even so,   288
in one field at least, that of cut and engraved glass, progress has been well
marked. The acquisitions include one of only fourteen known examples of
the mysterious and beautiful 'Hedwig' glasses, long regarded as Egyptian   289
work of the twelfth century, but more probably Syrian and not much, if at all,
before 1200. The earlier, thick‑faceted and thinner engraved glass from Iran
is now well represented. Outside the scope of the Fund has been pottery, and
here the striking slip‑painted wares from the ninth‑ to tenth‑century Samanid
period in eastern Iran, unknown until the 1930s, have been well represented by
the more popular types with stylized or geometric patterns and also by those
which rely entirely on the use of calligraphy for decoration. The collection of   290
early Mesopotamian lustre ware has been much enriched, but it has proved
possible to secure only one piece of the later, more pictorial, Fatimid lustre from
Egypt. The range of the Islamic collection has also been increased by acquisitions
of carved wood panels in Tulunid style, of Persian jade cups and of medieval
gold and silver, including jewellery and domestic utensils.

The Persian miniature collection, founded in the nineteenth century by the
acquisition of some good albums of drawings and calligraphy, has been

286 Chinese lacquer toilet box, painted and inlaid with silver. Han dynasty, first century AD

287 Heavily decorated Chinese bronze bell (*pien chung*) with dragon handles, *c.* 500 BC

288 Pottery vase with a decorative benedictory inscription in moulded Kufic script under a blue glaze. Syria, Raqqa, about AD 1200

continued and increased so as to supplement the very distinguished collection contained in the illuminated manuscripts at present in the charge of the Department of Oriental Manuscripts. Through the bequest of Sir Bernard Eckstein (1948), several important fourteenth-century miniatures were received, including the only miniature in this country from the famous 'Demotte' *Shahnama* produced in Tabriz in about 1330. He also gave the only miniature in Britain from the 1222 manuscript of the Arabic version of Dioscorides *Materia Medica*, one of the key manuscripts of the Mesopotamian school before the Mongol conquest. The separate drawings and album pictures in the Department make it one of the most important places for the study of the painter's art in the Safavi period (1504–1725) in Iran.

275

273

For the future, it seems inevitable that reliance for the improvement of the collections and for the increase in our knowledge of the whole subject will come from a more intense study of the material, including that in the Museum on the one hand, and from participation in archaeological excavation on the other. A promising start has been made in the support given by the Museum, both with funds and with participation by its staff in the excavation of the ninth-to fifteenth-century trading port on the Persian Gulf at Siraf, which has been conducted for the five seasons 1966/7 to 1970/1 by the British Institute of Persian Studies in Teheran.

The future of the collections can thus be seen to lie in the hands of the scholars of the Department in exploiting the riches of the collection through display and publication and by working to improve them by concerted action with other specialists throughout the world.

BASIL GRAY

289 Smokey topaz coloured glass, wheel-cut with figures of a lion, a griffon, an eagle and a tree. Syrian, about AD 1200

290 Nishapur pottery bowl decorated with *thulth* calligraphy in black on a white slip ground. Persian, tenth century AD

CHAPTER NINE

Oriental Printed Books and Manuscripts

At present the Department of Oriental Printed Books and Manuscripts administers about 250,000 printed books and more than 35,0000 manuscripts, covering nearly all the languages of Asia and most of Northern Africa. Historically the collection spans a period of three millennia, ranging from

309   Chinese oracle bones found in the province of Honan to the ever-increasing production of modern printing presses set up in the new countries of Asia. The art of writing, basically only the attempt to preserve the experience gained by one generation for the benefit of the next, has over the centuries inspired a variety of highly ingenious solutions among different cultures. For instance

304   the Moso people of south-western China still use a purely pictographic script based on recognizable drawings of birds, animals, humans and everyday objects. The Bataks of Sumatra, practising a religion strongly dominated by magical concepts, scratch powerful spells on the leaves of folding books made of bark. At the other end of the scale we may come across a wealthy Javanese prince who could afford to have his letters written on thin sheets of pure gold. Since the written document extended one's sphere of influence, it soon became the favourite aid of the teacher, the missionary and the propagandist. In the case of the illuminated manuscript (or the illuminated book) the medium is doubled, script and picture further the same end. It is interesting to note that, although Judaism and Christianity were originally averse to the visual repre-

295   sentation of the living form, there are countless Hebrew, Syriac, Coptic,
297   Armenian and Ethiopian manuscripts in which picture and text have an equal share in the task of instruction. It was only the Arab calligrapher, not daring to tamper with the rigid iconoclastic traditions of his faith, who learned to pour all his genius into the perfection of the script. It would be wrong, therefore, to think of the Department in terms of a mere library. It is equally a miniature museum of Oriental book art and Oriental ways of thought.

During the first hundred years of the Museum's history, the Oriental material was administered by the two different Departments, Printed Books and Manuscripts. In 1867 the Trustees decided that the growing number and the value of the Oriental manuscript collection needed the attention of more specialists, and a separate Department was set up. In 1891 Oriental printed books were removed from the General Library and the Department of Oriental Printed Books and Manuscripts came into being. Though the history of the Department is thus relatively short, the history of its collections goes back well beyond a mere century. It is in parts intimately bound up with the names of

291 Angels at prayer, a miniature from an abridged Turkish translation of a Persian book of ▶
marvels, ʿAjāʾib ul-Makhlūkāt. Made in the sixteenth century for Prince Mustafa, son of Süleyman
the Magnificent, it illustrates a quotation from the Koran that angels pray like other created
beings

A page showing the Dance of Miriam and preparations for the Passover from the *Golden Haggādāh*, a fourteenth-cen.
Hebrew ms. written in Spain with miniatures in a French Gothic style

293 Adam and Eve and the Tree of Knowledge, a miniature from a North-French style *Hebrew Bible and Prayer Book*
of AD 1278

294, 295 *Below,* illuminated frontispiece of a thirteenth-
century Hebrew and Aramaic ms. of the *Book of Numbers,*
representing some of the tribes and their standards. *Right,*
Jonah sheltering under the gourd, a marginal illustration
from a thirteenth-century Hebrew *Māsōrāh* (marginal notes
on the correct traditional text of the Bible)

some famous eighteenth, and nineteenth,century collectors who long after the conquistadores, the colonizers and trading companies, turned their attention towards the East to seek a quite different kind of conquest.

Among the foundation collections Hebrew was better represented than any other language. This is not altogether surprising. Religion played a far greater part in the lives of most people than it does today. Hebrew manuscripts were equally important to Jews and to Christians and most eighteenth,century collectors went to great pains to purchase some of them for their libraries. But very few collectors had the resources of Robert and Edward Harley, the first and second Earls of Oxford, who were both keenly interested in manuscripts related to English history, Biblical and post,Biblical literature. The 130 Hebrew manuscripts of the Harleian collection formed a promising nucleus which contained such treasures as the *Code of Jacob ben Asher* and the *Code of Maimonides*, two lavishly illuminated fifteenth,century manuscripts; and a thirteenth, century copy of the *Guide for the Perplexed*. As far as printed books were con, cerned the situation was less promising. At the time of opening, the only printed Hebrew book in the Museum was a copy of the *editio princeps* of the Talmud from the Library of Henry VIII. Towards the end of the same year, however, the Museum received a gift of 180 valuable books from Solomon da Costa, an émigré Sephardi Jew from Amsterdam, as an expression of his gratitude for 'the many Favours which have been bestowed upon (him) by several Noble, Honourable, and Worthy Personages of the British Nation' (quotation from a letter accompanying the gift). The da Costa books had originally belonged to Charles II whom financial difficulties had forced to abandon them at the bindery. They still bear the king's cipher and the original red morocco binding. Until the middle of the nineteenth century the collection of both printed books and manuscripts increased steadily but unspectacularly. An outstanding exception was the acquisition of a magnificently illuminated

293 thirteenth,century *Hebrew Bible and Prayer Book* bought in Paris from the Reina collection of Milan. The manuscript has some 750 folios of text and 41 full,page miniatures dealing with Biblical subjects. The miniatures are in the early French,Gothic style, painted in delicate colours, depicting slim, almost emaciated figures. Most of them are framed by a thick circle of solid gold. In 1848 the printed collection was greatly strengthened by 4,420 volumes from the famous library of H. J. Michael in Hamburg. About twenty years later, by a stroke of good fortune and, it seems, some merciless bargaining on the part of the Trustees, the Museum secured the entire manuscript collection of the Italian scholar Joseph Almanzi for the ridiculously low sum of one thousand pounds. A bargain indeed when one considers that this collection included

292 the famous *Golden Haggādāh*, a fourteenth,century manuscript from Spain with a set of exquisite miniatures painted against a background of pure gold. About 1870, with the acquisition of a large number of rare Yemenite and Karaite manuscripts, the Department's collection had reached formidable proportions. The majority of these manuscripts had been supplied by M. W. Shapira, a

well-known bookseller from Jerusalem who a few years later committed suicide when fifteen leather strips he proposed to sell to the Museum for the then astronomical figure of one million pounds were pronounced a forgery by the experts. The leather strips, apparently from the ninth century BC and inscribed with the text of *Deuteronomy*, had been discovered under circumstances disquietingly similar to those which eventually led to the discovery of the real Dead Sea Scrolls. The last major acquisition was made in 1925 when the Department purchased the manuscript collection of Moses Gaster, Chief Rabbi of the Spanish and Portuguese Synagogue, which numbers well over 1,000 items. Today with about 40,000 printed books, including nearly 100 priceless incunabula and an almost complete set of sixteenth-century imprints, over 3,000 manuscripts and 10,000 Genizah fragments, the Department has few rivals.

The interest in Biblical studies which had led to the accumulation of Hebrew manuscripts in private libraries also prompted the collection of early Christian texts from Africa and from the Near East. Most foundation collections included a small number of Armenian and Syriac manuscripts. The real beginning, 296 however, in Syriac at least, was made in 1825 when the Museum purchased the collection of Claudius James Rich, one-time British Resident at Baghdad. Amongst other items Rich's collection included 59 carefully selected Syriac manuscripts, most of them from Mosul, which were particularly important within the category of Jacobite and Nestorian recensions of the Bible. Within the next fifty years the Museum increased the number to 581, mainly through successive purchases from the Convent of St Mary Deipara in the Nitrian desert where the monks kept a partly forgotten and grossly neglected collection of precious manuscripts in an old oil-cellar. Some of the Syriac manuscripts are illuminated, thus throwing interesting sidelights on early Christian icono-graphy. For the historian, however, the most outstanding item of the whole collection is probably a copy of the Old Testament from the year AD 464, one of the oldest dated Biblical manuscripts known to exist.

Early Christianity in Africa is well represented by about 1,300 Coptic manuscripts including such scholarly treasures as the *Pistis Sophia*, a gnostic work from the fifth century. Original gnostic manuscripts are rare since only very few of them escaped destruction. Another item which has not received as much publicity in the past as it deserves is a fine collection of Ethiopian manu-scripts, said to be the best in Europe. Apart from the 74 volumes presented by the Church Missionary Society in 1847, the majority was acquired in 1867 by a representative of the Trustees who accompanied Napier's punitive expedition to the city of Magdala. Ethiopian manuscripts are mostly written in Ge'ez, the 313 ecclesiastical language of Ethiopia, in oddly irregular, ornate-looking characters. They are often lavishly illuminated with boldly drawn figures painted in strong 297 contrasting colours. The iconographical details follow the Byzantine code. Until quite recently art historians tended to dismiss them as 'primitive', but it is exactly this naive simplicity which gives them a definite charm of their own.

296 Miniature of St John dictating his gospel to Prochorus, with the beginning of the Gospel, in Armenian, opposite. The ms. was written in AD 1280 and the miniatures and ornamentation added in AD 1618

297 St George killing the dragon, from a seventeenth-century Ethiopian ms. of the *Four Gospels*

اريكه جوانان نترحلوقريب صدوپنجاه نفرخو دراست بعدكه ركزارساخته پراپسپان ني زين سوارشده وآب زدند
وماننده شيران برسايهاي ازموح وكرداب ايند شيدند وبربادزد وجون شكان بيا يازردرمراجعت غزم اردوي معلي بود
جون زديك شبل سپيده داغانيان فيل رابازنامي كرد درجنگ جوسه جانب ارده بود شكستن بل سبردا
آن فيل ني اعتدال خود رابرپشن سائنده قواعدل درهم شكست درين وقت ازاردوي معلي قبي راهاكرد
كه قوايم فيلك ربازاخودرساخت وكرغنيم كرزورآورده بود بمزمت يافت وجوانان فتح وي ادبشجاعت
داده بسلامت آمد

The elephant Gird-
hit by a cannonball
en used by the Afg-
ns to break up the
dge of boats at Bhoj-
. A miniature by the
ed artist Dharmdās
m the first volume of
Akbarnāmeh, a his-
y of the reign of
bar, written at the
ghal court of Delhi
AD 1603

Although Christianity had reached Ethiopia in the fourth century via the Syrian Church very few early manuscripts survived the sixteenth century when Muslim invaders brought almost complete destruction to the country, and the Department is fortunate in having recently purchased a fifteenth-century *Book of Prayers of the Virgin* illuminated in an early style.

Three centuries after the beginning of Islam the Arabs had already achieved superb mastery of the art of calligraphy and book illumination. Though Arabic works reached Europe relatively late, today the Department's collection of 5,000 manuscripts is one of the finest in the world, surpassed, in fact, only by the libraries of Istanbul and Cairo. A good many manuscripts had belonged to the Rich collection. Others were acquired by the fortunes of war when the French, who had collected them in Egypt together with such famous antiquities as the Rosetta Stone, lost the Battle of the Nile to Nelson. The earliest dated Arabic manuscript in the Department is a passport on papyrus granted by the Governor of Egypt to a certain Copt in the year AD 750. The most outstanding

291, 301

items, however, are some very fine early copies of the *Koran*. One of them, consisting of seven splendidly illuminated volumes is the only surviving

316

work of the famous calligrapher Ibn al-Wahīd. The frontal pages of these manuscripts are often magnificently illuminated, sometimes with interlacing patterns of gold, blue and other colours, sometimes with brilliant arabesques which look as fresh as if they had just been painted. Pride in their ancestry had given a strong sense of history to the Arabs. One of the results was a vast literature of biographies and historical works. A fine example of this branch is the autograph of Ibn Khallikān's *Wafayāt al A'yān*, probably the most famous collection of biographies in Islamic literature. In the long centuries which elapsed between the fall of the Roman Empire and the coming of the Renaissance all knowledge of Greek science was in the hands of Jewish and Arab doctors. The Department has many important works on medicine and on the use of

314

drugs. Noteworthy amongst these manuscripts are those illustrated with miniature paintings.

Once Islam had unified the nomadic tribes of the Arabian desert, the single-mindedness of their faith soon turned their minds towards military conquest. In a relatively short time Muslim domination established itself from the Malay peninsula to southern Spain. But success brought problems. Islam was no longer the religion of one people. It was learning to live side by side with a number of highly sophisticated cultures whose own inheritance was often totally out of tune with the austere religion of their conquerors. In literature and the art of book production compromises had to be reached. Manuscripts illustrated with figures not only appeared, they became an essential part of court life; especially in Persia and India. They were, however, in most cases restricted to works of a fictional character and, as a further precaution, often kept in the women's quarters. If they passed through the hands of a specially pious owner he might ease his conscience by disfiguring the priceless miniatures. If he was too great a connoisseur of art to resort to so barbaric an action, he would at least draw a fine line across the neck of each figure as a token gesture of disapproval.

Among the foundation collections Persian manuscripts had not been a prominent feature, but in the course of the nineteenth century the Department acquired, by donation and purchase, most of its 3,000 priceless manuscripts. A decisive factor had again been the Rich collection with over 800 items. As scholarly interest in Persian studies increased, many an East India Company (later India Office) official became a keen collector. It would be futile to attempt, in so short a space, a description of the exquisite dream-like beauty, the meticulous technical perfection of Persian miniatures; nor indeed of the whole scope of the Department's collection. Calligraphy had been an Arab legacy, but the great impetus in the field of book illustration came after the fall of Baghdad in 1258 when the Mongol invaders brought new cultural trends from Asia, including Chinese artists and illustrated books. The Department has many fine examples from this early period. The illuminations are extremely beautiful and delicate though probably to the untrained observer very little will look specifically Persian. All the human figures have distinctly Mongoloid features and the landscape is reminiscent of that seen in Chinese painting. Later generations of Persian (and Indian) artists have modified the human features but the Chinese landscape lingered. The most favoured themes are violently realistic battle scenes, episodes from the lives of king and heroes and splendid court occasions. The utmost care is given to details such as armour, dress, jewellery, musical instruments and carpet designs. The Department possesses in addition a large number of poetical works, many of them charmingly illustrated by languid love scenes. 315

In India Islamic manuscript illumination reached a peak of perfection in the sixteenth and seventeenth centuries during the rule of the Mughal Emperors. The Department's collection is especially rich in this branch. A typical example is the recently purchased volume of the *Akbarnāmeh*. During the reign of Akbar, Mughal paintings begin to assimilate some of the native Indian Rājput style; their colours become stronger, more flat, and usually the artists produce fine effects of light and shade. As a whole this kind of book illustration exhibits distinct tendencies towards portrait art, not only when depicting individual kings and nobles but also in the case of illustrated chronicles. 298

The Harleian collection had included 34 Turkish manuscripts. Some were old copies of early poetry, one was an illuminated translation of an otherwise unknown Persian *Mirabilia mundi*. But again it was Rich's collection of 124 carefully selected volumes (Rich had once used a year's sick-leave to travel with his wife overland from Baghdad to Vienna to search for manuscripts) which gave the first touch of importance to the Museum's collection. At present the Department can count about 1,500 Turkish manuscripts, an impressive number if one considers how few large collections exist outside Turkey. As a whole the Turks were closer to the iconoclastic spirit of Islam than were their Persian or Indian neighbours. Illustrated manuscripts are rare, those which

300 Narrative picture page from a nineteenth-century Burmese album depicting the adventures of Prince Inaung. Originating in Java in the twelfth century it became widely popular in south-east Asia

do exist lack the delicacy of Persian miniatures, yet they are in no way less appealing. The figures are more boldly drawn, the colours stronger though of a rather limited range.

The beautifully illuminated volume of the *Akbarnāmeh* has already introduced us to India, but only Islamic India, and Islam is a relative latecomer on the subcontinent. Islam is in fact only one aspect of a rich cultural heritage that has left modern India the (sometimes irksome) legacy of fourteen well-developed main languages and a vast literature in the two classical languages, Sanskrit and Pali.

Writing existed in India as early as 2500 BC. Since then documents have been composed in a variety of languages and scripts on any possible material ranging from clay, stone, gold, silver, copper, ivory to bark, wood, palm-leaves and (after the coming of the Muslims who had learned the art from Chinese prisoners in Samarkand) paper. The Department has a fairly representative

291

◀ 299 *Opposite,* eighteenth-century Sanskrit roll-manuscript, five inches wide and sixty-five feet long, of the *Bhagavata-purāṇam,* the legendary story of Lord Viṣnu. It is written on very thin paper in the minute *devanāgāri* script and lavishly illustrated

collection, though from 1798 onward, the lion's share of manuscripts from India went to the newly-founded library of the East India Company. The Sloane collection had included 6 Sanskrit and 20 Tamil manuscripts, the latter being the largest single item in any Oriental language. But we can hardly credit Sloane with an interest in South Indian languages. Being above all a collector of 'natural objects' and 'curiosities', it was probably the physical appearance of these palm-leaf manuscripts which attracted his attention. Among the most outstanding items of the Indian collection are a copy of the *Yogayājñavalkya*, which may be as early as the ninth century, and a treatise on astronomy dated 1286. There is also a fine collection of Jain manuscripts, especially enriched by the 143 volumes Dr H. Jacobi brought back from Rajasthan. Noteworthy too are about 66 copper plates recording royal gifts of land, many of them dating from about the middle of the first Christian millennium. Since the actual grant is normally preceded by an account of the gracious king's ancestors, these documents supply valuable information on Indian history. Altogether the collection now numbers about 3,000 manuscripts in
299, 308 Sanskrit and in various modern Indian languages. The Department's real strength, however, lies in the vast amount of printed material which comprises 24,000 books written in Sanskrit, Pali and Prakrit; 40,000 items in North Indian and about 35,000 items in South Indian languages. The Pali collection of printed books is specially rich in Burmese and Ceylonese publications.

Buddhism had originated in India in the fifth century BC. At the start of the Christian era it was beginning to spread all over south-east Asia, China and, eventually, Japan. Many Buddhist monasteries became famous centres of learning where the sacred texts could be copied and preserved in carefully appointed libraries. Ceylon in particular acquired a reputation for the production and distribution of outstanding palm-leaf manuscripts which were regularly sent to Buddhist centres in China, Burma or Siam. At present the
305–307 Department owns about 2,500 Ceylonese manuscripts comprising 5,000 separate texts. A large proportion was donated by Hugh Nevill at the beginning of the century. The collection covers a variety of subjects and is probably one of the best outside Ceylon. Buddhism in the Himalayan countries is represented by some fine manuscripts from Nepal and from Tibet.

A branch of the collection which has not received much attention in the past is about 600 manuscripts from various parts of south-east Asia. They show an
300, 302, intriguing mixture of Indian, Chinese and local elements and are often most
303 charmingly illustrated.

At the beginning of the twentieth century, just before the age of the great travellers and aristocratic collectors finally came to an end, the Department received some of its most valuable and unique material as a result of Sir Aurel Stein's adventurous expeditions to Central Asia. The Chinese province of Sinkiang had not always been a rainless inhospitable desert. In ancient times, when the famous trade route linked China with the West, the scattered oases of the Tarim Basin had been a meeting-ground of many different races, languages and cultures. By a combination of resources, determination and good fortune Stein discovered countless paper fragments (paper having been invented in China in AD 105) and strips of wood inscribed not only in Chinese but also in unfamiliar languages, some of them no longer used or understood. They included documents in Sanskrit, Tibetan, Khotanese, Kuchean, Sogdian, Uighur, Tangut and Chinese. Perhaps his most exciting discovery, however, was in a walled-up chamber adjoining the Caves of the Thousand Buddhas at Tunhuang on the edge of the Gobi Desert. Here he found a vast library of Chinese manuscript rolls and block prints, many of them Buddhist texts translated from the Sanskrit. The climate which had driven away the traders by depriving them of essential water supplies had favoured the documents they had left behind. The paper rolls seemed hardly damaged by age. Stein's negotiations with the priest in charge of the sanctuary proved fruitful. He purchased more than 7,000 paper rolls and sent them back to the British Museum. Among them are 380 pieces bearing dates between AD 406 and 995. The most celebrated single item is a well-preserved copy of the *Diamond Sutra*, printed from wooden blocks, with a date corresponding to 11 May, AD 868. This scroll has been acclaimed as 'the world's oldest printed book', and it is indeed the earliest printed text complete with date known to exist. Six sheets of text and one sheet with woodcut illustrations have been neatly pasted together to form a paper roll sixteen feet long. The woodcut picture shows a highly advanced technique, far superior to anything produced in Europe before the time of Gutenberg.

310

In addition to these Buddhist texts, Stein found a large number of official records written on wooden tablets in the ancient *Kharoṣṭhī* characters of north-west India.

In the course of his second expedition Stein stumbled across a forgotten postbag in a watchtower of the Great Wall of China. It contained nine letters written in Sogdian. The letters, mostly business communications from about the fourth century AD (full of complaints about difficulties in getting the mail through!) are the oldest written documents in this once widespread Iranian language. The proper names mentioned in them reveal that the writers were still of the Zoroastrian faith. Later on the Sogdians became Buddhists and some of the Sogdian manuscripts Stein discovered in the course of further excavations are translations of lost Buddhist texts. There is also one attempt in the field of *belles-lettres* giving an episode from the life of the Persian hero Rustram not mentioned in Firdausī's *Shāhnāmeh*. The discovery of the Sogdian collection caused a minor sensation, since up to that time scholars had believed that all documents written in this language had perished.

Another interesting item for which the Department is indebted to Stein is a collection of documents in Uighur and Old Turkish written in runic and *Brahmi* script. Runic (Kök Turkish) manuscripts are extremely rare; only very few of them exist outside the British Museum. The oldest, found at the fort of Miran and almost certainly written before AD 770, is part of a return for receipts

301 The opening of the chapter of Victory, S
xlviii of the *Koran*, written in Morocco in AD 15

302, 303 Two leaves from a contemporary palr
manuscript relating the story of Prince Bagus
bara (the Prince Inaung of *Pl. 300*) and a princ
Java. One leaf shows the funeral of the prir
father

304 Nineteenth-century magical invocations
prayers in the pictographic script of the Moso
khi) people of south-west China

305–307 *Opposite,* eighteenth-century Singalese
leaf manuscripts and their wooden cover
Kandy. Theravaddha Buddhism does not
monks to paint, hence Singalese texts are
illuminated, but the wooden covers, being the
of lay-painters (sittarā), are frequently deco
with floral designs

308 *Opposite,* eighteenth-century miniature in R
style by the artist Sitaldās giving a visual represen
of *Devagāndhari-rāginī*, a musical mode co-ordi
with erotic sentiment

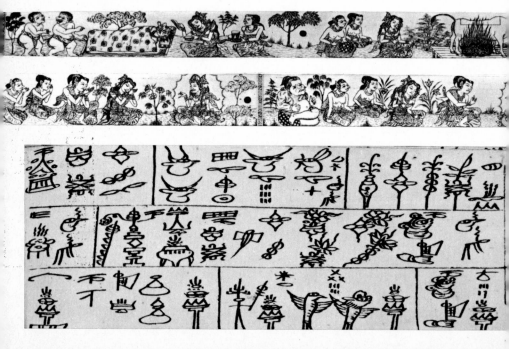

311 *Opposite above*, Japanese landscape from an album of cc
woodcuts based on paintings by Taigado, AD 1803

312 *Opposite below*, chapter vii of the *Saddharma-puṇḍrika* (*
Sutra*), printed in Japan in the thirteenth century from wood bl

309 Chinese oracle bone of about 1000 BC

310 The Sanskrit Buddhist work *Vajacchedikā prajña pāramita* in Chinese translation, found at Tunhuang. Printed in
AD 868, it is the earliest dated specimen of block printing. The illustration shows the Buddha addressing Subhuti,
an aged disciple

妙法蓮華經常不輕菩薩品第二十

爾時佛告得大勢菩薩摩訶薩汝今當知若
比丘比丘尼優婆塞優婆夷持法華經者若
有惡口罵詈誹謗獲大罪報如前所說其所
得切德如向所說眼耳鼻舌身意清淨得大
勢乃往古昔過無量無邊不可思議阿僧祇
劫有佛名威音王如來應供正遍知明行足
善逝世間解無上士調御丈夫天人師佛世
尊劫名離衰國名大成其威音王佛於彼世
中為天人阿脩羅說法為求聲聞者說應四
諦法度生老病死究竟涅槃為求辟支佛者

七

into the quartermaster's store for weapons and armour, and their issue to people with Turkish names and Turkish or Chinese titles.

Apart from Stein's Buddhist library the Department owns a number of interesting Chinese manuscripts recording historical and political events. Especially valuable in this respect is a collection of papers and documents dealing with the Taiping rebellion (1850–64), some of them a gift of General Gordon. Since the Manchu authorities took great care to destroy all publications of this kind in China, they are truly unique. Otherwise the real strength of the Chinese and Japanese collection lies in the large number of rare and early block-prints.

Printing, like paper, was a Chinese invention. At an early stage seals were used to reproduce short inscriptions and (later) images. This in itself was not unique. Other people had done the same in other parts of the world. The first breakthrough towards true typography came when Buddhist monks developed the original simple system of mere stamping into the printing of whole scriptures from wooden blocks. Together with Buddhism printing spread across Korea to Japan. It is not known when exactly wooden blocks were used for the first time, probably around the seventh century AD, but the earliest surviving examples are Buddhist charms printed by order of the pious Japanese Empress Shōtoku in AD 770. Between 1041 and 1048 movable types made of earthenware were used, in an experimental way, in China. In 1403, when Gutenberg was still a small boy, the Korean Government type foundry was already casting metal types. When the Japanese invaded Korea in 1592 they brought back some metal types and there was a short though highly prolific burst of movable-type printing in Japan between the years 1592–1640. As a result of this the position of the manuscript was not quite the same as in medieval Europe or in the countries of the Near East. Manuscripts were still held in great esteem; they could be admired for the beauty of their script, the charm of their illustrations, but they could also be copied with relative ease. At least as far as the text was concerned they were no longer unique. Calli-graphy has always been one of the most highly prized arts in China and Japan but with the advance of printing, especially a certain class of luxury printing which often reproduced the hand of famous calligraphers, the book as we know it today began to usurp a far higher place far earlier than anywhere else in the world.

A few Chinese books had been included in the foundation collections of the British Museum. In 1834 the East India Company's monopoly in China ceased. In the following decades the Museum could therefore acquire most important collections which reached England without losing a share to the Company's Library. An important acquisition was made in 1847 when the Government purchased 11,509 volumes from the collection of John Robert Morrison who, like his father, had spent many years in China. His library included works on the drama (a new element in the Museum), on law, history, geography and Buddhist religion. Towards the end of the nineteenth century

312

several other important purchases were made. Today, with over 50,000 printed books, the Department's collection is large and representative. It ranges from ninth century block-prints to the *Thoughts of Chairman Mao*. There is a large nucleus of works on Christian religion published before 1770 which, incidentally, provides interesting material for the study of local dialects.

No Japanese books seem to have reached Europe between the discovery of the islands in AD 1542 and the expulsion of foreigners a century later. In 1693 the German traveller Engelbert Kaempfer returned with a number of Japanese books which Sir Hans Sloane later purchased from Kaempfer's widow. Though the collection was small it had the unique distinction of being the only one in England; perhaps even in Europe. Only a small number of books were acquired during the eighteenth century, but the purchase of the two large collections of Alexander von Siebold and Sir Ernest Satow in 1868 and 1884 respectively put the Museum's Oriental library on a new footing. Satow's collection included two of the Empress Shōtoku's Buddhist charms, early examples of movable-type printing of the period 1590–1640 and a Chinese version of the *Lotus Sutra* printed in Japan in the thirteenth century. The *Lotus Sutra* had enjoyed great popularity in Japan; 81 editions are believed to have been printed between AD 1080 and 1614. Other valuable items of the Japanese collection are novels, mostly illustrated, of the Edo period (1600–1867), books published in the Meiji period (1867–1912) and picture books of the seventeenth, eighteenth and early nineteenth centuries illustrated with woodblock prints.

312

Since the end of the last war important manuscripts from Asia have become almost unobtainable. At times, treasures like the *Akbarnāmeh* can still be purchased in the auction room or whenever a private collection is suddenly put on the market. But most Asian countries have placed firm restrictions on the export of their manuscripts, treating them, rightly, as an integral part of their national heritage. There can be no more expeditions like those led by Sir Aurel Stein, no great diplomat-collectors like Claudius Rich, certainly no scholars accompanying military expeditions. But while manuscripts are getting rarer and rarer the printed material from Asia and Africa is rapidly increasing year by year.

298

Printing in Asia was originally closely associated with the propagation of religion. Already in the seventh century AD Buddhist monks in China had recognized the potential power of quickly produced religious literature. Printing and Buddhism spread all over the Far East. A thousand years later the whole process repeated itself. Christian missionaries coming from Europe set up printing presses in India and in the countries of the Near East in order to supply their new converts with quickly made translations of the Scriptures. The Department has a valuable collection of such early imprints: books printed in Burma between 1770–80, the productions of the Baptist Mission Press in Serampur which includes a Bengali version of the Scriptures prepared by Dr William Carey (1761–1834) and a large number of early Tamil

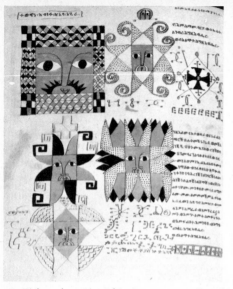

313 Eighteenth-century Ethiopian ms. on magic and indigenous medicine with various forms of the cross thought to avert the evil eye

314 Page from the *Manāfi ʿal-hayawān* of Ibn Bakhtīshū, a work on the medical properties of various animals. Mesopotamian school, *c.* AD 1250

315 Persian made in AD 148 *Shāhnāmeh* by ausī, an epic relating the histo the kings of Persi

316 Ornamental page of a *Kora* seven volumes, w and illustrated for I ad-Dīn Baibars, wards Sultan Ba II, in Egypt in 1304

imprints published after 1714 by the Danish Lutheran mission in Tranquebar. In the twentieth century printing in Asia became increasingly associated with national sentiments. New editions of old classics appeared, experiments were made by young writers, books and pamphlets published for the sake of political propaganda. Since the middle of the century, when the majority of these countries attained political independence, printing in Oriental languages has rapidly increased. A recent estimate has shown that the annual book production in Asia and Africa forms about one sixth of the world's total. The Department's yearly intake of printed material (books and periodicals) fluctuates between 25,000 and 30,000 items. The majority is directly bought from Asian or African countries but one third is acquired by exchange. The Department covers all subjects save those connected with pure science and technology. Altogether 200 different languages are represented in the collection (this includes printed books as well as manuscripts) written in a large variety of different scripts. Apart from the major collections in Arabic, Hebrew, Persian, Turkish, Chinese, Japanese and Indian languages there are smaller, though not necessarily less important, collections in Korean, Tibetan, Mongol, Manchu, the Iranian groups, Syriac, Amharic, Coptic, Aramaic, Armenian, Georgian, Judaeo-Persian and in the many languages of Central and south-east Asia and the Chinese borderlands.

One of the reasons for the foundation of the Department had been a desire on the part of the Trustees to ensure that the growing quantity of valuable Oriental material was described and classified by qualified scholars. In the early days of the Museum's history new acquisitions were simply included in the current catalogues of the two parent Departments or not catalogued at all. The first catalogue entirely devoted to Oriental material was begun by F. August Rosen in 1838 and completed by the Rev. Josiah Forshall and others in 1847. It bore the impressive title *Catalogus codicum manuscriptorum orientalium qui in Museo Britannico asservantur*, and was written in Latin. It was the only attempt at a general catalogue. Subsequent catalogues have been written in English and devoted to one language only. Today nearly all collections have their own catalogues, either in printed form or in the form of catalogue cards and manuscript lists.

There remains but one question. What is the most important item in the whole collection? It would be difficult to say. Anybody who has once been enchanted by the sheer loveliness of Persian miniatures, the richness of gold-embellished Hebrew book illumination or the metaphysical austerity of Arab calligraphy might think himself near an answer. But under certain circum-stances a tiny pamphlet printed on a few sheets of shabby paper can be of equal value to the scholar. The real importance of the collection does not lie in one single item, perhaps not even in one special branch. It lies above all in the immense variety of the material which is like a window permanently open towards the East.

A. GAUR

CHAPTER TEN

Prehistoric and Romano-British Antiquities

Towards the middle of the nineteenth century a great interest in British national antiquities developed among amateur archaeologists. Nevertheless, although the British Archaeological Association and the Royal Archaeological Institute had a great concern for British antiquity, the educated public in general regarded the ancient Britons as barbarous and unworthy of serious study. This disdainful attitude was shared by the Trustees of the British Museum and although the British Archaeological Association had prepared a resolution which expressed indignation at the neglect of British antiquities in the British Museum, a commission enquiring into the affairs of the Museum was told by the Trustees in 1849 that no consideration had been given to the extension of the collection of British antiquities or their establishment in a separate Department.

A manifestation of the public concern for due representation of national antiquities in the national museum was the offer by Lord Prudhoe in 1844 of the hoard of Iron Age bronzes from Stanwick to the British Museum 'provided that a room were appointed in the Museum for the reception of national antiquities'. The bronzes were accepted but not until the end of 1850 was a room completed for the display of smaller British antiquities to supplement the RomanoBritish monuments which in 1848 had been assembled in what is now the Publications Gallery. This event may be regarded as the first gleam of the dawn of recognition of national antiquities in the national museum, but British antiquities were eclipsed by the arrival of the Assyrian sculptures in 1849 and during the 1850s by the completing of important new Greek and Roman Galleries and the Reading Room.

The beginning of a new era may be discerned in the appointment of Augustus Wollaston Franks in 1851 as Assistant Keeper in the Department of Antiquities. Shortly afterwards, in 1856, the great Roach Smith collection, mostly of RomanoBritish antiquities from London, was purchased. This signalled a new willingness on the part of the Trustees to expend their resources on antiquities from British soil, but the real launching of this part of the collections came in 1866 when the Department of British and Medieval Antiquities and Ethnography was formed with Franks as the Keeper. By 1887 there was relatively generous provision for the public to study their native antiquities in a prehistoric saloon and in separate galleries for RomanoBritish, AngloSaxon and Medieval antiquities. By this time foreign antiquities were being included in the Prehistoric collection.

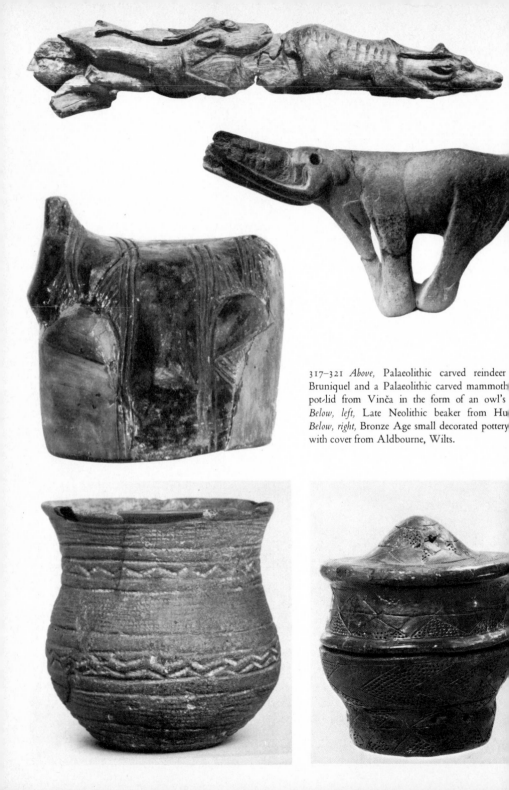

317-321 *Above,* Palaeolithic carved reindeer
Bruniquel and a Palaeolithic carved mammoth
pot-lid from Vinča in the form of an owl's
Below, left, Late Neolithic beaker from Hu
Below, right, Bronze Age small decorated pottery
with cover from Aldbourne, Wilts.

322–324 *Left,* one of the three Early Bronze Age carved chalk drums from Folkton, Yorks. *Centre,* detail of the terminals of one of the group of Iron Age gold torcs from Ipswich, Suffolk (*see also Pl. 328*). *Below,* Bronze Age decorated gold cape from Mold, Flint-shire

During the Second World War the Prehistoric Saloon and Roman-Britain rooms were destroyed by bombing. Fortunately the collections had been evacuated to safe storage and suffered no losses apart from a few trifling items exhibited in a small wartime exhibition.

Within a few months of the end of the war a small series of prehistoric and Romano-British antiquities was on display in a section of the inter-departmental exhibition in the Edward VII Gallery. A temporary exhibition was then prepared under a corrugated iron roof in the Roman Britain room, and opened in August 1951. This was supplemented by a Stone Age exhibition in the south wing of the Central Saloon which was completed in 1958. It was not until 1963 that the permanent rebuilding of the Department's galleries began. Outstanding antiquities such as the Desborough mirror, Iron Age helmets and shields and the Mildenhall Treasure were mounted in a Masterpiece Exhibition in the old Early Christian room and remained on display without interruption except for an interval of a few days.

While the rebuilding of the main galleries was in progress, a series repre-senting prehistoric and Romano-British antiquities was exhibited in specially constructed cases in the Iron Age Gallery.

On 1 April 1968, the exhibitions in the rebuilt Prehistoric galleries and Roman Britain room were opened to the public.

The rebuilding of the new galleries and installation of the new exhibitions was accompanied by much reconstruction behind the scenes, but already the old storage basement, where after 1946 the Quaternary collections were stored in conditions exceedingly unsatisfactory from every point of view, had been transformed. New specially designed boxes and racking were installed, the pervasive London grime was banished by air-conditioning, and proper lighting was provided. The room became an example of what might be done with basically unsatisfactory accommodation, and in the end became entirely satisfactory for the storage and study of the Palaeolithic and Mesolithic collec-tions.

Whilst three of the old basements were necessarily still used for storage with only minor modifications, full advantage was taken of the rebuilding programme to provide accommodation for the most significant part of the prehistoric and Romano-British reserve collections adjacent to the new exhibition galleries. It was possible to include in the rebuilding programme not only two additional floors in the north wing of the Central Saloon, but also an entirely new wing running north from this, above a section of Printed Books accommodation. On the top floor of the north wing was constructed a new students' room, while on the lower floor is a conservation workshop carefully designed and equipped to meet all the conservation needs of the Department. In 1968 the Department set foot outside the main Bloomsbury building by establishing in the outhouse accommodation at Shepherdess Walk a workshop for the con-servation and study of the newly acquired painted plaster from the Roman villa at Lullingstone in Kent.

In April, 1969, the Department of British and Medieval Antiquities was divided into two new departments, the Prehistory and Roman Britain section, hitherto a sub-department, becoming the Department of Prehistoric and Romano-British Antiquities. The collections of the Department include material from Quaternary cultures (Palaeolithic and Mesolithic) from all over the Old World; later prehistoric material from Europe is included besides antiquities from the Roman province of Britain.

The collection of flint and stone implements representing Palaeolithic and Mesolithic cultures is a very large one. Palaeolithic art is well known from the cave paintings, but also includes portable objects, some of which are included in the Department's collection. Two of the finest of these are carvings, one of two reindeer and the other of a mammoth, animals important in the economy   317, 318 of a hunting society. The reindeer are carved in mammoth ivory and the mammoth in reindeer antler. These objects are products of the late Magdalenian culture of the Upper Palaeolithic, and date from about 10,000 BC. They were acquired in 1887 and paid for from the Christy Fund, founded by the famous nineteenth-century archaeologist and benefactor of the Museum.

Much of the Department's collection consists of the domestic products, mostly pottery, of agricultural and pastoral societies dating between the introduction of agriculture into Europe during the fifth millennium BC and the middle of the first millennium BC. Such pottery is hand-made and un-sophisticated, but displays distinctive decorative traditions. Though the artistic aspect of most of such material is purely decorative, the pot-cover from the Neolithic settlement at Vinča (Yugoslavia), dating from the fourth millennium BC, carries an owl-like face which is characteristic of a developed tradition of   319 representational art, current in south-east Europe at that time. Late Neolithic beakers are well represented by examples from widely separated European sites. The form, good-quality reddish ware and comb-impressed ornament of   320 these represent a ceramic widespread in Europe about 2000 BC. Beakers are normally found in the graves of the people named after them, who were responsible for the earliest working of copper and gold in much of Europe.

The cup with cover, decorated with incised geometric ornament, was found   321 in a barrow at Aldbourne, Wilts, with a cremation burial. It is an example of the group of pottery, Aldbourne cups, named after this site, which is characteristic of the second phase of the Early Bronze Age 'Wessex' culture. 'Collared' urns, such as that from a barrow on Stockbridge Down, Hampshire, were used to contain or cover cremated bones during the later part of the Early Bronze Age and the Middle Bronze Age. They bear simple geometric ornament executed by impressing with a cord. The Stockbridge Down example belongs to the later part of the 'Wessex' culture, c. 1550–1400 BC.

Returning to the Continent, pottery of the Lusatian culture dates from c. 1400–700 BC, the type with large bosses ante-dating that where the ornament consists of concentric grooves. It is found in Central and Eastern Europe, and the pots contained or accompanied cremated bones deposited in large cemeteries.

325 The Desborough mirror, with its curvilinear decoration and intricate handle, represents the highest point in the development of Celtic mirror art of the Early Iron Age

During the Bronze Age in Europe a high standard of metal⁄working developed. This is represented principally by tools, weapons and other articles of bronze, but also ornaments of gold. An outstanding example of the latter class is the sheet gold cape from Mold, Flintshire. This was found under a 324 cairn with a skeleton, amber beads, pieces of sheet bronze and fragments of a cloth fringe. It has been dated to the Middle Bronze Age, *c*. 1400–1000 BC. The object was broken up after it was found and the pieces now in the Museum were acquired at intervals between 1856 and 1927.

Few prehistoric antiquities are unique, but the Mold gold cape is so, and also the carved chalk drums from Folkton, Yorkshire. These carved chalk 322 cylinders were found with the skeleton of a child, under a barrow of which the primary inhumation was associated with a cordoned beaker dating from between 1800 and 1600 BC. The burial with the drums is probably contemporary with the primary burial. It is not possible to find the origins of the decorative motifs on the drums in the same area in which they were found. The whole character of the drums is unique, and it is perhaps not unexpected that parallels for the ornament must be sought farther afield. Thus, the pair⁄of⁄eyes design found on the drums occurs also on pottery found in chambered tombs of the Spanish peninsula and also on Copper Age cult⁄objects in the same area. The 'pick⁄axe face' is a common motif in the context of chambered tombs in Western Europe and the Mediterranean area. The form of the drums resembles that of certain lidded pots from the Spanish peninsula, but it is also possible that they are copies of wooden vessels.

The Folkton Drums come from the collection of Canon Greenwell, the noted nineteenth⁄century antiquary. His collection was acquired by the British Museum, mostly in 1879 and 1909, and includes a very important series of Bronze Age antiquities from his excavations.

The Department is exceptionally rich in examples of Early Celtic art and craftsmanship which represent the great artistic tradition of the La Tène culture that flourished in Central and North⁄western Europe, including Britain, between the fifth and first centuries BC. These articles are finely decorated weapons, shields, helmets and other objects of display pertaining to the warrior aristocracy of a 'heroic' society. 325

The bronze mirror with decorated back from Desborough, Northants., is an outstanding example of a British tradition of curvilinear decorative art. This is used on the backs of a succession of bronze mirrors dating from the last quarter of the first century BC and the first quarter of the first century AD. The ornament is executed by chasing, the flowing patterns being skilfully made up of negative (plain) areas and positive areas filled with 'matting'. Although on many mirrors the pattern has a trefoil layout, in later examples such as that from Desborough, the design acquires a 'fold⁄over' symmetry which has been attributed to Roman influence.

The Battersea shield is perhaps the best known piece of early Celtic craftsman⁄ ship from Britain. It was recovered from the Thames in 1857 and acquired by 326

326 Bronze facing for a shield from the river Thames at Battersea, London. It is one of the finest pieces of Celtic metalwork and certainly one of the best known. Its decoration of embossing and red glass studs is rather mechanical in its precision and may indicate Roman influence

the British Museum in the same year. What is preserved is the decorated bronze facing for a backing of wood or leather.

The embossed ornament on the discs or roundels of the Battersea shield includes scrolls and palmette derivatives familiar from other pieces of Celtic craftsmanship, and technically is superbly accomplished. Nevertheless, its almost mechanical precision and its linear nature may be considered alien to the main British tradition of the first century BC and the first century AD. Even Roman influence may be discerned, and one expects the Battersea shield to come late in the sequence of early Celtic art in Britain. Besides the embossed

327 Celtic horned helmet from the river Thames at Waterloo Bridge, London. Decorated in the 'Snettisham' style (*see also Plate 329*), it is the only known example of such a helmet although the type is familiar from sculptural representations and classical authors

ornament the decoration of the Battersea shield includes red glass studs. These studs are made in the same way as those from the Hertford Heath and Lexden burials, both of which must date from the middle of the first century AD. The evidence of these very distinctive features therefore supports that of the style of the embossed ornament in dating the shield to the first half of the first century AD. The Battersea shield provides interesting examples of the way in which the Celtic artist combined a formal pattern with an apparent representation of human or animal features. The motifs between the central and terminal roundels, though superficially merely formal, may well have been intended to represent the antlered heads of stags, while the pairs of studs in the central roundel on the longitudinal axis, surely represent the eyes in owl-like faces.

Of the same three-disc layout as the Battersea shield, though of more elongated form, is the bronze facing for a shield found in the river Witham. The 'shadow' may be traced on the front of the shield of a conventionalized outline figure of a boar once attached by rivets, but now lost. The decoration of the central roundel of the Battersea shield echoes that of the central boss of the Witham shield, which is perhaps ancestral to it. Ornamentation by red-coloured studs, though of very different types, is also common to both shields, the central boss of the Witham shield bearing three studs of a pink coral-like substance.

The terminal bosses of the Witham shield are decorated with a fine, incised tendril design. This type of design is one of the principal elements in the earliest British school of La Tène art, and it has been argued that this school was active between c. 250–150 BC.

329   The Snettisham torc is the finest example of a series of multi-strand ring terminal torcs best represented in Norfolk. The torc is made of an alloy of gold and silver, the hoop being made up of a number of separate twists, the ends of which are inserted into large hollow ring terminals splendidly decorated in an early Celtic tradition. The particular kind of ornament found on this great torc from Snettisham may be named after it as the 'Snettisham' style. Elements in this style of embossed ornament are a pattern of curved ridges enclosing areas of incised 'matting' (hatching) and also small spherical bosses sometimes impressed with three fine punch marks.

323, 328   The same style of ornament is found on the magnificent gold torcs from Ipswich although, since these were never completed, the effect is relatively crude when compared with the beautifully finished work on the great Snettisham torc. One of the hollow terminals of this large torc actually contained a coin of the tribe of the Atrebates of a type known to archaeologists as Gallo-Belgic Dc. This coin may have been minted either in Gaul or in Britain. A worn specimen of the type was found on Jersey in the Le Catillon hoard which was deposited between 56 and 51 BC, so that the type of coin and the great Snettisham torc itself may be dated a little later.

The gold torc from Snettisham was the finest piece in a series of deposits found in the area in 1948 and 1950. It was acquired by the British Museum as

Treasure Trove in 1951, the price of the award to the finder being paid by the National Art Collections Fund.

The famous horned helmet from the Thames at Waterloo Bridge was deposited in the British Museum on loan by the Thames Conservancy in 1868. The ornament of the helmet consists of five (originally six) bronze studs, cross-scored to take red enamel, and a repoussé design on the front and back. This design is in the Snettisham style. A comparison of the ornament on the large torc from Snettisham and that on the Thames helmet demonstrates the resourcefulness of the early Celtic artists in adapting ornament employing the same elements to the form of the objects to be decorated. The compact design of the Snettisham torc provides a striking contrast to that on the helmet which is extended in the way required by the much larger surface to be decorated. The date in the first century BC indicated for the Thames helmet by its Snetti-sham style ornament is endorsed by its cross-scored and enamelled studs; such studs are very characteristic of finds from the La Tène III period on the Continent.

Actual horned helmets worn by early Celtic warriors do not survive else-where. The type was, however, undoubtedly extensively used, as is indicated by Diodorus Siculus and by a number of representations on Roman sculptures. A figure on the cauldron from Gundestrup (Denmark) demonstrates, from a native point of view, the use of horned helmets among the Celts around 100 BC. It is possible that the original helmets have not been preserved because they were made of leather rather than metal. The Thames helmet can hardly be accepted as a functional piece of battle equipment. It is of frail construction and does not fit the head satisfactorily. It can only be interpreted as a ritual article, and this character is supported by its having been found in the river, where it came most likely as a votive deposit.

The Ipswich torcs are five outstanding examples of early Celtic craftsman-ship of exceptional technical interest and great sociological and economic significance. They are one of the most important archaeological finds ever made in this country. They were discovered on 26 October, 1968, during mechanical earth-moving connected with building operations on the eastern outskirts of Ipswich. The torcs were declared Treasure Trove and the British Museum exercised its option and acquired them. An *ex gratia* payment of £45,000, the full market value of the torcs (and the highest price ever paid by the British Museum for Treasure Trove), was made to the finder, Mr Malcolm Tricker. Generous contributions were made by the National Art Collections Fund, the Goldsmiths' Company and the Pilgrim Trust. The torcs are of gold alloyed with a small proportion of silver. One has plain ring terminals while those of the other four are decorated with embossed ornament, in what has been called the 'Snettisham' style. Their unfinished condition reveals important evidence of the methods used by the craftsmen of the first century BC, and they are therefore of outstanding interest for the history of technology. A sixth torc, undoubtedly from the same hoard, was found nearby in 1970.

327

cf. 329

323, 328

328, 329 The Ipswich torcs *(above)*, and the Snettisham torc *(below)* were all acquired as Treasure Trove. The torcs (and a detail in Plate 323) all show unfinished decoration in the 'Snettisham' style, named after the great torc, *below*

110 Bronze statue of
the emperor Nero dec-
orated with inlays of
copper, silver and niel-
lo. The pose is typical
of official Roman im-
perial statuary

PRESENTED BY EARL OF ASHBUR

336, 337   The wooden bucket with decorated bronze plating and handle mounts in the form of human heads from Aylesford is one of the most interesting examples of Early Celtic art from Britain. The handle mounts provide one of the comparatively rare examples of representational Early Celtic art from this country, but even these are highly stylized as are the animal figures in the repoussé frieze on the uppermost bronze band. The bucket contained cremated bones and bronze brooches. It comes from the cemetery at Aylesford, Kent, which, with its companion at Swarling, gives the name to an Iron Age culture of South east England, of which the main period may be dated 50–10 BC.

331   The finest item in the Department's collection of early Celtic art is the pair of bronze wine flagons from Basse Yutz in the Moselle Department of France. They were found in 1928 with two Etruscan bronze jars. The four vessels must have formed part of the rich table furniture of a Celtic chieftain, and the flagons date from the fourth century BC. The decoration is lavishly inlaid with coral imported from the Mediterranean and the beasts on either side of the mouth and on the upper part of the handle are decorated with red champlevé enamel. The ornament on these flagons is a splendid example of the Early La Tène style and the different elements well demonstrate the diverse origins of La Tène art. A motif derived from the Greek palmette occurs on the throat and on the handle, the beasts are Oriental in feeling, and the little duck on the spout may be of Hallstatt ancestry.

    Other important examples of Early Celtic art from the Continent of Europe are included in the Morel collection, in which are numerous objects from the rich graves of the La Tène culture found in the Marne region of North east France. The Morel collection was purchased by the British Museum in 1901. The bronze torc from Courtisols carries below each 'buffer' terminal a human

335   face of typical Celtic character, which may be compared with those on the Aylesford bucket. The Celtic love of an intricate combination of representationalism and abstract design is shown by the placing of three faces, one above the other, the lowest being inverted.

    In the La Tene culture of the Marne the artistic quality of the pottery equals

334   that of the metalwork. Two pieces demonstrate this. The urn from Le Mesnil les Hurlus owes its beauty entirely to its form and comes from a woman's grave of the La Tène I period, c. 475–250 BC. The second example, an urn from Prunay, is not only beautiful in shape but is richly painted with a sweeping curvilinear design; it dates from the later part of the La Tène I period, or the earlier part of the La Tène II period (La Tène II, c. 250–100 BC).

    In contrast to the examples of Celtic art detailed above, one may show the

333   bronze figurine of a priest from Despeñaperros, Spain. This is a votive figurine from a sanctuary of the Iberians, the inhabitants of southern Spain during the Early Iron Age.

    When Britain became a Roman province, the relative complexity of Roman culture was reflected in art. On the one hand, new media appeared such as

345, 346   mosaic pavements and mural paintings, both associated with elaborate

331 One of a pair of beaked bronze wine flagons with coral inlay from Basse-Yutz, Lorraine. Early La Tène

332 Unique set of glass gaming-pieces from a Belgic chieftain's burial at Welwyn Garden City, Herts.

333–335 *Left*, Iberian bronze figure of a priest from Despeña-perros, Spain. *Below left*, angular La Tène pottery urn copying a metal shape, from the Marne, France. *Below*, bronze torc from Courtisols, Marne, with Plastic Style ornament in faces and scrolls

336, 337 Stave-built bucket with bronze attachments from a Belgic cremation grave at Aylesford, Kent. *Right,* a detail of one of the human heads on the handle attachments

338, 339 *Above,* Two of the smaller silver dishes, with Bacchic scenes, from the great hoard of Roman silver table ware found at Mildenhall, Suffolk. *Right,* a Roman blue and white marbled, pillar-moulded, shallow glass bowl from Radnage, Bucks.

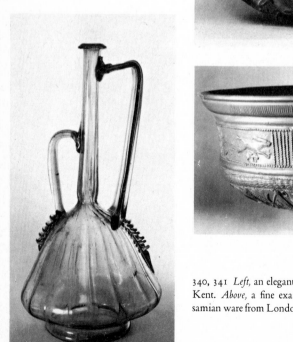

340, 341 *Left,* an elegant, pale olive green, Roman glass flagon from Bayf Kent. *Above,* a fine example of a typical form of shallow bowl in Ron samian ware from London

342, 343 Christianity in the Roman province of Britain. *Right,* a detail of the central roundel in a mosaic pavement from Hinton St Mary, Dorset. It shows an early Christian representation of the head of Christ with, behind Him, the Chi-Rho monogram. *Below,* a partly restored section of the wall-paintings found in the early Christian chapel in the villa at Lullingstone, Kent. They show a series of *orantes* in typical attitude and, elsewhere on the wall, there was a large Chi-Rho monogram

344 Castor ware beaker, with a chariot-race sc
barbotine, from Colchester, Essex

345, 346 Romano-British mosaic pavement with
of chariot- and horse-racing in a circus, from Hor
Lincs.

347, 348 Two bronze heads of Roman emperors from large-scale statues: *left*, Hadrian, from the river Thames at London; *right*, Claudius, from the river Alde, Rendham, Suffolk

349 Bronze cavalry parade helmet from Ribchester, Lancs.

buildings. Other new vehicles for art were industrial products, usually imported,
339, 341 such as glass vessels, the mass-produced shiny red pottery commonly known
340 as Samian ware, and elaborate metal vessels of bronze, or, as in the case of the
Mildenhall treasure, of silver. On the other hand, the mainly decorative Celtic
artistic tradition was, in general, replaced by the naturalistic classical tradition.
This finds its most impressive manifestation in official statues such as the large
347, 348 figures from which came the bronze heads of Claudius and Hadrian, or the
330 smaller figure of Nero from Barking Hall which is skilfully inlaid with copper,
silver and niello. The newly-introduced classical style did not, however,
completely supplant the native tradition. The latter survived in minor arts, such
as enamel work, and also on pottery produced by British industries, such as the
344 'hunt cup' with a chariot race scene from Colchester. It is, however, most
strikingly embodied in provincial sculpture of which the most notable example
in the collection is the head from Towcester which combines Celtic and
classical elements to great effect.

One of the most impressive items in the Romano-British collection is the
Mildenhall treasure. This consists of 34 pieces of silverware – dishes, bowls,
goblets, ladles and spoons – made during the fourth century AD, the best
pieces of which at least were imported from the Mediterranean or Gaul.
It was acquired by the British Museum as Treasure Trove in 1946 and was
reported to have been accidentally ploughed up during the war of 1939–45.
The treasure is exceptionally well preserved, and had no doubt been buried by
its owners in order to preserve it from the Saxon raiders who harassed the
eastern parts of Britain during the fourth century. The finest piece is the great
dish, which is 1 ft 11¾ ins in diameter and weighs 18¼ lbs. The outer frieze
of relief figure ornament shows in a lively fashion the triumph of Bacchus,
god of wine, over Hercules. Silenus and Pan are also shown, besides maenads
and satyrs. There is an inner frieze of nereids riding on the backs of sea
monsters, and in the centre is a striking relief of Neptune or Oceanus. Two
338 platters are also decorated with Bacchanalian figures in relief. The figures on
all three pieces are naturalistic and classical in style, and perhaps these pieces
were made quite early in the fourth century. Less spectacular, but equally
interesting, are the spoons. Two of these bear inscriptions, *Papittedo Vivas* and
Pascentia Vivas, wishing long life to Papittedo and Pascentia respectively. It is
believed that such spoons were given as christening presents. In the bowl of
three other spoons appears the Christian Chi-Rho monogram between the
Greek letters Alpha and Omega, also used as a Christian symbol. It is not as
rare as might be thought to find, in Late Antique art, evidences of Christianity
juxtaposed with such thoroughly pagan representations as those on the great
dish and two platters.

The relics of Christianity in the Mildenhall Treasure lead us to two most
important items from Roman Britain, the early Christian mosaic pavement
from Hinton St Mary, Dorset, and the mural paintings from the Christian
chapel at the Lullingstone Roman villa.

The Hinton St Mary pavement was accidentally discovered in 1963 when Mr W. J. White, a blacksmith, was digging foundations for an extension to his smithy. The pavement measures about 30 by 20 ft and covered the floors of two inter-connecting rooms. In the centre of the smaller section is a roundel containing a much damaged representation of Bellerophon killing the Chimaera. On either side is a hunting scene. On each side of the larger section is a lunette, three of which contain hunting scenes and the fourth a tree. In each corner is the head and shoulders of a human figure. It is, however, the central feature of the larger section which gives great importance to this pavement. This is a roundel containing the head of a man with the Chi-Rho monogram behind it. This can only be a representation of Christ. The pavement was laid in the early fourth century and probably carries the earliest representation of Christ made in Britain. The four heads in the corners of the larger section may be the four Evangelists.

342

The early Christian paintings from Lullingstone came from a Christian chapel in the Roman villa there. Thousands of fragments of the wall plaster carrying the paintings were discovered in 1949. Although it has still only been possible to restore a relatively small portion of the plaster, the paintings may be reconstructed almost completely. The principal feature in the chapel was a frieze of six human figures standing in an attitude of prayer between columns. The figures are all almost the same height as the columns, which are about 32 ins high. The illustration shows the most complete of the figures which is that of a young man robed elaborately in a tunic with long tight fitting sleeves and in a Dalmatic-like over-garment, with edgings of pearls. Facing the door of the chapel was painted a large Chi-Rho monogram surrounded by a wreath, and the same device was painted in an ante-chamber. There can be little doubt that the Christian chapel at Lullingstone was a house-church used for liturgical worship. Only one or two other examples of such house-churches are known, so that the Lullingstone chapel is of outstanding significance not only in Britain but in the Roman empire as a whole.

343

The paintings date from about AD 350, and with the evidence of the Milden-hall treasure and the Hinton St Mary mosaic, have revolutionized our concept of Christianity in Roman Britain, which now clearly appears to have been not only distinctive in character but far more influential in the life of the Province than had previously been apparent.

J. BRAILSFORD

350 *Night Landscape with Figures round a Fire*, Adam Elsheimer (1578–1610)

351 *Fairlop Fair*, Thomas Rowlandson (1756–1827)

Although Sir Hans Sloane's bequest of 1753 included drawings of great importance, it was not until 1808 that the care of the British Museum's collection of Prints and Drawings was allocated to a department separate from the Library. The last keeper to have joint charge of both books and prints was the Rev. William Beloe (1756–1817), during whose term of office a serious breach of security forced the Trustees to reconsider the accommodation of such easily removable material as sheets of drawings and engravings. The caricaturist Robert Dighton (?1752–1814) was discovered in 1806 to have been systematically filching prints from the guard-books in which they were pasted, replacing them with copies. Most of the stolen material was recovered, but the Trustees took steps to ensure that such a thing did not occur again: they instituted a new, separate department in 1808 and William Alexander (1767–1816), the topographical draughtsman who had accompanied Lord Macartney on his famous embassy to China in 1792, was appointed to the curatorship with the title of 'Assistant Keeper of the Antiquities Department'.

The roguish air which Alexander gives himself in the self-portrait now 374 in the Department, with its suggestion of a piratical eye-patch, is belied by the responsible manner of his application to the task of organizing the collec- tions. These had already grown to impressive proportions. The Sloane bequest was, in the first year of the Museum's life, extended by the acquisition of the John Bagford collection, and to this core of material the bequest of William Fawkener in 1769 added thirty-nine volumes of prints and drawings; the Earl of Exeter gave a collection of drawings in 1779 and 1789; and in 1799 the Rev. C. M. Cracherode bequeathed many important prints and drawings. These examples show how, from its earliest days, the Museum was recognized as a national repository of graphic art and attracted fine gifts in the form of presented or bequeathed collections. Alexander arranged the prints, a memor- andum of 1810 records, 'as far as circumstances would permit, according to the respective schools of Painting, and pasted them into Portefolios provided for the purpose', of which 'Eighty three Volumes are finished, and delivered into the hands of Mr Alexander, after being stamped and marked as far as they are known, with the Initials of their respective Donors . . . there are nine more Volumes arranged, to be pasted in – Besides Six Volumes of Original Draw- ings, which are placed in volumes to be pasted in.'

The collections had become so extensive, in fact, that Alexander seems never to have got as far as the original Sloane drawings: these were transferred from the Library to the Print Room under the keepership of John Thomas Smith (1766–1833), and the task was not completed until 1832. Smith was himself a considerable draughtsman, specializing in records of the old buildings of London; he was the author of *Nollekens and his Times*, a major source of information about artistic life in London in the late eighteenth century. Two of his drawings in the Print Room give some idea of life there in his day: one shows J. M. W. Turner leafing over prints in an album; the other is a portrait of 'faithful Christopher Pack', one of the first of the Print Room assistants. At this time the Department was housed in 'a long narrow room, in the north-east side of Montague House, above that containing the Towneley Marbles, approached by a separate stone staircase, leading to a small vestibule, in the centre of which was the Portland Vase. Passing through a large apartment . . . the Print Room was beyond, shut in with a heavy iron door.' Into this sanctuary works of art and objects of historical interest flowed abundantly. In particular, Richard Payne Knight, one of the foremost connoisseurs of his day, bequeathed in 1824 a superb general collection of prints and drawings including one of the finest representations of Claude Lorrain in existence.

Smith died in 1833; the man who replaced him was well suited to the next great task of the keepers: the cataloguing of the Department's holdings. He was William Young Ottley (1771–1836), a fine artist in his own right who is now well represented in the Museum, and a connoisseur of standing whose own collection became the basis of the famous one acquired by Sir Thomas Law-rence, subsequently dispersed. Ottley's efforts as a publisher of facsimiles of German and Italian Renaissance prints were landmarks in the spread of knowledge on the subject, and he made extensive catalogues of the Department's material. Under its next Keeper, Henry Josi (1802–1845), the Department was moved into 'the North West angle' of the new building designed by Sir Robert Smirke. The old conditions of mightiest impregnability seem to have been maintained here; indeed they were no doubt improved upon since the new Museum, unlike the old Montagu House, was designed for its function. With the prints and drawings in their portfolios 'admission to the Print Room would be interesting', it was agreed, 'only on condition of opening the portfolios and examining the prints – a course which would speedily lead to their injury'. The impasse was partially overcome in 1858 by the mounting of an exhibition in the King's Library. Two further exhibitions, in 1885 and 1890, were held in 'the second Northern Gallery, adjoining the Egyptian Gallery on the Upper Floor'. But exhibition had not at this date taken its place among the first pre-occupations of the Department. For Josi's successors, William Hookham Carpenter (1792–1866), and George William Reid (1819–87), acquisition and conservation had, as for Alexander and Ottley and as at the present day, first priority. Reid had joined the Museum staff as an attendant in 1842 and was the first officer in the Department to have made his career in the Museum.

A significant development took place in 1871; the Trustees' Resolutions of that year include this entry: 'Mr Reid having called the attention of the Trustees

52 *Seated Arab*, Eugène
Delacroix (1798–1863)

53 *Landscape*, Sir Antony
van Dyck (1599–1641)

354 *Abundance*, Sandro Botticelli (1444/5–1510)

355 *Allegory of Vice and Virtue*, Andrea Mantegna (1436–1506)

6–359 *Above, left, Head of a Woman*, Andrea
errocchio (1438–88); *Head of a Young Man*, Hans
olbein the Younger (1497/8–1552). *Right, Bust of
Warrior*, Leonardo da Vinci (1452–1519); *Portrait
a Young Man*, Albrecht Dürer (1471–1528)

360–362 *Left*, *Study for a Pieta*, and *Male*
Michelangelo Buonarroti (1475–1564).
Study for the Phrygian Sibyl, Raphael (1483

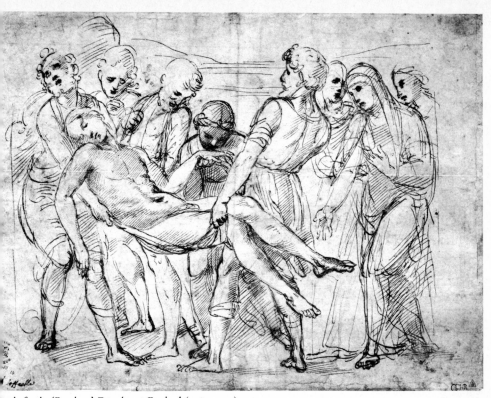

udy for the 'Borghese' *Entombment*, Raphael (1483–1520)

364 *Capriccio with Tombs*, Giambattista Piranesi (1720–78)

to the injury which had been done to prints and drawings whilst in the book'
binder's shop for the purpose of being mounted, it was resolved that the
mounting of prints and drawings be done in the Department by men working
under the supervision of the Keeper: and that the Principal Librarian be
authorized to employ these men to be paid by piece'work for the number of
prints and drawings mounted and stamped, until the arrears, referred to in
Mr Reid's report, shall have been reduced.'

The size and rate of growth of the collections have made for a more or less
constant problem of 'arrears'; but the Department's independent Conservation
room has also grown; especially during the last ten years it has become equipped
with staff and machinery giving it a position of the first rank among paper
restoration centres, an absolutely necessary corollary of a large and important
collection of prints and drawings. After Reid's acquisition of this valuable
facility, Sir Sidney Colvin (1845–1927) was able to make extensive improve'
ments in the storing and organization of material. It was now possible to make
general the practice, which had already been in restricted use, of mounting the
drawings individually on firm card or board rather than pasting them into
albums, or attaching them to sheets of heavy paper.

Colvin became Keeper in 1884, the year following Reid's retirement, and
in 1888 the Department moved to new premises in the 'White Wing'. Before
the end of his keepership in 1912 yet another move was in preparation. In 1914
the new block to the north of Smirke's building, the Edward VII Galleries,
was opened and the Print Room then came to its present quarters with furniture,
panelling and galleries transplanted from the White Wing. All these fittings
are still in use. During the 1914–18 War the public were not admitted, but
normal service was resumed thereafter.

Colvin's successor, Campbell Dodgson (1867–1948), took up office at a
moment when not only the location of the Department was to be changed,
but also its very constitution. There had recently been acquired two major
groups of oriental objects, the Wegener collection in 1910, and the Morrison
collection in 1913; these additions to the Departmental holdings precipitated
a decision to isolate Eastern from Western art, and a new sub'department of
Oriental Antiquities was put in the charge of Laurence Binyon (1869–1943),
assistant keeper under Colvin, who had already produced a four'volume
catalogue of the Department's English drawings. In 1932 Binyon became
Keeper of the Print Room for a year, on the retirement of Campbell Dodgson.

Dodgson's acquisitions, during a keepership of twenty years, are a monument
of catholicity and connoisseurship; and by following his particular preference
for early German prints he built up this branch of the collection to a richness
and comprehensiveness unrivalled anywhere. His catalogue of Early German
and Flemish woodcuts in the Print Room is a parallel achievement. His final
act of generosity to the Department was the bequest of his own collection,
which came to the Museum in 1949, adding substantially to the range and
quality of nearly all sections. Arthur Mayger Hind (1880–1957) followed

Dodgson as a cataloguer, especially of Dutch and Flemish prints and drawings (including Rembrandt's etchings) and his successors, Arthur Ewart Popham who became Keeper in 1945, and Edward Croft-Murray, Keeper since 1954, have begun similar work on the Italian and English schools respectively. Since Binyon at the beginning of the century, assistant keepers have taken an increasingly prominent part in the production of such catalogues in association with the keepers; the curatorial staff now numbers five, and responsibility for different schools is divided among them.

The history of the Print Room can thus be told in terms of its staff and the methods employed by its Keepers in the carrying out of their responsibility towards the valuable material they care for. But it must also be seen as an illustration of the development of a single idea: the English genius for connoisseurship to which Sir Hans Sloane's bequest was the first national memorial, and which has been visible in the British Museum's collection at all stages of its evolution. The result has been an extraordinarily full representation of the arts with which it is concerned, with major collections of nearly all the great draughtsmen and printmakers of Europe since the end of the Middle Ages. Its concern is to secure these objects against damage and decay; to make public inspection of them as convenient as possible by conservation, storage and exhibition; and to further scholarship in relevant fields both by the work of its own staff and by co-operation with students. All three functions are linked and inseparable. What is important is that they apply to the whole collection; no portion of the many hundreds of thousands of items is less important than another, and the Print Room is not only a repository of many of the greatest works of European draughtsmanship: it holds vast resources of historical and topographical material. The Burney collection of theatrical portraits was acquired in 1818, and in the same year Miss Sarah Sophia Banks gave her family collection of visiting tickets, shop bills, political cartoons and other ephemera. The Henry W. Martin collection of French costume and historical prints came to the Department in 1861; Frederick Crace's huge accumulation of views of London in 1880; Lady Charlotte Schreiber's fans and fan leaves in 1891, followed by her bequest of playing cards at her death in 1895. In 1897 A. N. Frank bequeathed a large collection of book-plates, which was extended by 8,000 more with G. H. Viner's gift in 1950. In such material the Print Room is extremely rich; but it is its collection of great masterpieces which most clearly illustrates the long tradition of connoisseurship in England from the time of Sir Hans Sloane.

Sloane's own collection included a large number of zoological and botanical studies, some of which remain in the Department although many have been transferred elsewhere. The most distinguished, and indeed perhaps the rarest and finest of such studies, are those executed by John White (fl. c. 1583–93) in the American colonies in the latter part of the sixteenth century. These came to the Department in 1906, but Sloane owned an important series of early copies. Their lively concern for the scientific realities of a totally strange way of life,

365–367 *Christ on the Cross with the Virgin, St John and the Magdalen*, Sir Antony Van Dyck (1599–1641); Stud
Eve, Correggio (*c.* 1494–1534). *Below, A Bishop in his Study*, Vittore Carpaccio (1455–1525)

368 *Fall of the Damned*, Sir Peter Paul Rubens (1577–1640)

buildings, animals, landscape, men and women is recorded in watercolour with a characteristically English disregard for every effect save clarity and information. Sloane also assembled a fine group of jewellery drawings by Hans
357   Holbein the Younger (1497/8–1552), examples of a spirit of accurate representation similar to that of White though in a wholly different application; these are, in fact, some of the most exhilarating of Holbein's marvellously brilliant drawings. They contrast strongly with the drawings of his contemporary Albrecht Dürer (1471–1528) which also belonged to Sloane. Dürer's work pulses with the vivid life which the artist saw in everything about him: the passing expression which animates the twinkling eyes of the young man in one of Sloane's finest specimens is rendered with vigorous conviction. On the other hand, the *Pine Trees by a Lake*, one of a series of remarkable watercolours done in Nuremberg at the beginning of Dürer's career, embodies a tranquil melancholy, epitomizing the Teutonic landscape simultaneously in intense details of grass and foliage and in broad atmospheric effect. A collection of Dürer's equally important prints – lineengravings and woodcuts – was later bequeathed by the sculptor Joseph Nollekens (1737–1823), through Francis Dance, in 1834; and Sloane himself provided the foundation of another major print collection: that of etchings by Rembrandt (1606–69), of which the Museum possesses an almost unrivalled representation. This is matched by a collection of Rembrandt drawings including such masterly
370   examples as the treatment of the *Good Samaritan* subject, acquired in 1860. It is one of Rembrandt's many explorations of the theme, which seems to have appealed to him particularly on account of its very human concern with friendship, suffering, physical weakness and moral strength, which he was so fond of depicting.

Of the later eighteenthcentury collectors, apart from Joseph Nollekens who has been referred to, C. M. Cracherode and Richard Payne Knight are prominent. Both bequeathed fine general collections of prints and drawings
355   by old masters. Payne Knight contributed the *Allegory of Vice and Virtue*, by Andrea Mantegna (1436–1506), one of a group of Mantegnas now in the Print Room which make a unique representation of this great and rare artist. The *Allegory* is executed in monochrome on a prepared black background giving the figures a faintly Classical quality which aptly expresses the strange mixture of classical mythology and medieval Christianity in the *Allegory* itself. It is a work very typical of the early Renaissance, and of the intellectual mind of Mantegna in particular. Of a quite different kind is Payne Knight's
350   beautiful little *Night Landscape with Figures round a Fire* by Adam Elsheimer (1578–1610), a German working in Italy whose delicately composed and exquisitely painted landscapes (often night scenes like this one) foreshadow the work of Claude Lorrain (1600–82). Payne Knight's Claude collection can hardly be equalled. It is a complete record of this artist's very large output of drawings, all of them interesting, many wonderfully beautiful, as is the
369   *Landscape with a River*, drawn in bold strokes of a brush heavily loaded with

sepia ink, obviously executed rapidly, and yet very precisely evocative of the tree-studded Campagna, with a river reflecting sunlight in its centre.

Another great eighteenth-century Claude collection was that of the second Duke of Devonshire, from which the Museum acquired in 1957 Claude's famous *Liber Veritatis*. This is the artist's own record of nearly all the compositions which he executed for patrons throughout his life, and besides being a most valuable document of his career contains 145 drawings, done either in sepia ink or in black and white chalk on blue or grey paper. These reproduce more or less accurately the details of finished pictures, and compare interestingly with the more spontaneous studies directly from nature which make up most of the Payne Knight group. They illustrate the process by which Claude's knowledge of the countryside, learnt by careful study of individual plants, views, animals and buildings, was used and transformed in the studio to create ideal landscapes which, again and again, achieve a perfection of structure, gentle lighting and atmosphere, and delicate colour harmonies which never cease to convince. The 'working drawings' straight from nature explain this miracle in some degree.

The Devonshire collection included some landscapes of Claude's Flemish contemporary, Antony Van Dyck (1599–1641), who made many lovely watercolours generally supposed to show the English countryside in the 1630s. Another of the same type is the *Landscape* acquired in 1936. Although very different from Claude's work, its lyrical mood and subdued colour make it a worthy counterpart from northern Europe. The sketch for a picture of *Christ on the Cross with the Virgin, St John and the Magdalen*, acquired in 1910, contains more of the characteristic Van Dyck fire; it is a study for a painting now at Lille, which was finished in about 1632, with many variations from the design in this drawing. Although it bears the marks of Van Dyck's very personal manner, it inevitably recalls the strenuous figure compositions of his master Peter Paul Rubens (1577–1640). A large and typical example of this most physically exciting of all artists is another Payne Knight drawing: the sheet of studies for the great *Fall of the Damned* at Munich. The sheet contains twenty figures in two principal groups and must have been drawn between 1614 and 1618 when the canvas was in progress.

At the time when the Payne Knight bequest came to the Museum, Sir Thomas Lawrence (1769–1830) was building up his magnificent collection; and although, as has been mentioned, this was broken up, the Print Room did acquire some individual items from it. One of these, an important study for the 'Borghese' *Entombment* of Raphael (1483–1520), came with the Chambers Hall bequest of 1855 (which also included a group of watercolours by Thomas Girtin, 1775–1802). Raphael's *Entombment* drawing is a composition study in pen and ink for the famous picture in Rome, which probably dates from 1507. It illustrates well the way in which Raphael sought to express metaphysical and religious ideas in terms of the visual relationship of human figures. A later Raphael drawing is the more finished *Study for the Phrygian Sibyl* in a fresco

353

365

368

363

362

369 *Landscape with a River*, Claude Lorrain (1600–82)

370 *The Good Samaritan*, Rembrandt Van Rijn (1606–69)

371, 372 A sheet of studies of heads, and *Woman seated on the Ground*, Antoine Watteau (1684–1721)

373 *Family Group*, William Hogarth (1697–1764)

374 *Self-portrait*, William Alexander (1767–1816)

375 *Duke and Duchess of Cumberland*, Thomas Gainsborough (1727–88)

Study for a female Nude for an Odalisque,
Auguste Ingres (1780–1867)

Adoration of the Magi, John Flaxman
(5–1826)

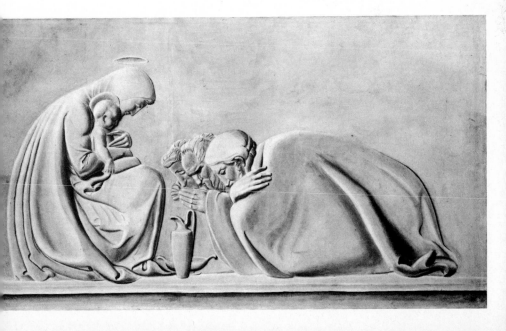

at Santa Maria della Pace in Rome, acquired as recently as 1953. This drawing was owned by another great English collector, the eighteenth-century painter Jonathan Richardson (1665–1745). Some of the finest old master drawings in the Print Room were at one time in his collection. Richardson wrote a note about the drawing on its old mount, in which he says that the figure in the fresco 'has the same perticularity [sic], a sort of Stiffnes about the Head and Neck as in this Drawing'. It is, nevertheless, a wonderfully graceful design, typical of Raphael in its combination of feminine delicacy with masculine strength. The turns of the body and the balancing of the masses of limbs and drapery are resolved into a dignified repose which in Michelangelo's hands would probably have suggested restlessness and action: Raphael's figures are not struggling to break free; they are part of a universal, divine tranquillity.

Both Raphael and Michelangelo (1475–1564) are extremely well represented in the Print Room. In 1887 Henry Vaughan presented a group of very fine Michelangelo studies, of which an example is the *Male Nude*, part of Michelangelo's preparatory work for the group of bathers in a projected wall-decoration for the Great Council Hall in Florence, *The Battle of Cascina*. This was to have been paired with a fresco by Leonardo showing the *Battle of Anghiari*, but neither work was finished. The study probably dates from about 1504. It sums up Michelangelo's power to invest the human body with majesty and strength even while he is effortlessly performing miracles of draughtsmanship in the rendering of complex poses. The *Study for a Pietà*, acquired in 1896, is a contrasting work of about 1535, in the artist's later style. It has something of the bleak grandeur of the two late sculptures of the same subject, although the soft modelling of the forms in black chalk, common in Michelangelo's drawings of this period, does not suggest their rather gaunt carving. It is perhaps an idea for a painting rather than for a work of sculpture.

Many other drawings by Michelangelo had been acquired in the year previous to the purchase of the *Pietà* study, for in 1895 the John Malcolm collection, certainly one of the greatest collections of old master drawings ever to be assembled, was purchased at what even in those days was a bargain price of £25,000. In addition to Michelangelo, most of the supreme Italian masters were magnificently represented; Leonardo (1452–1519), for example, with his youthful fantasy on a theme provided by a work of his master, Verocchio: the *Bust of a Warrior* was probably done when Leonardo was still in Verocchio's workshop, and seems to be derived from that artist's bust of *Darius* (now known by a copy in Berlin). But the drawing is a purely and vividly imaginative work, typical of Leonardo himself and foreshadowing many of the interests which were to occupy him throughout his life: military costume and equipment, human physiognomy and so on. Another outstanding drawing from the Malcolm collection is the *Abundance* of Botticelli (1444/5–1510), possibly the finest surviving example of this artist's lyrical, sinuous draughtsmanship. The design is connected in spirit with the Uffizi *Primavera*, and it may be that this floating figure in fluttering, diaphanous drapery, accompanied by children

361

360

358

354

with cornucopiae is in fact a personification of Autumn, intended perhaps for a companion picture.

Since the beginning of the century, a number of gifts have greatly widened the scope of the English collections in the Department. In 1902 the Museum purchased a large number of Norwich School drawings from the well-known collection of James Reeve. This meant primarily a very distinguished group by John Sell Cotman (1782–1842), including the *Dismasted Brig* and *Greta Bridge*, in which the artist's very personal idiom is fully developed. The Department had already acquired, in 1859, a rare and magnificent early Cot-man, the *St Mary Redcliffe, Bristol: Daybreak* of 1801. The stunted spire of the great fourteenth-century church dominates a lowering industrial townscape wreathed in smoky twilight: a thoroughly Romantic exercise in which Cotman approaches closer to Turner (1775–1851) than at any other moment in his career. 381

Turner was represented by some fine drawings in the bequest of George Salting of 1910. This bequest also includes a splendid example of an *Imaginary Landscape* by Gainsborough (1727–88), which shows to what heights of drama and atmospheric poetry this artist could bring a simple formal idea. The details, trees, rocks, distant buildings, stormy sky, can be found in many Gainsborough drawings, and in each they are given fresh reality by inspired organization – each is a new formal solution to the problem of landscape composition and at the same time a convincing evocation of nature, often, as in this drawing, conceived in a sombre twilight which gives scope for Gainsborough's love of 375 fitful lighting effects. The speed and deftness of Gainsborough's suggestion of light, air and space with apparently casual strokes of black and white chalks on grey-blue paper are, however, characteristic of a painter in oils and compare interestingly with the work of Gainsborough's contemporary, Richard Wilson (1712–82), another landscape artist whose drawings, Farington said, 'have all the quality of his pictures except the colour'. Many fine chalk studies and finished drawings came to the Print Room with John Deffett Francis's important gift of 1881. These eighteenth-century masters preceded the full development of the watercolour in the hands of the Norwich School and others of the early nineteenth century like Richard Parkes Bonington (1802–28), of whose achievement in watercolour there is a superb record in George Salting's bequest. In the *River Scene*, the daylight dazzles with its brilliance 378 and the very simple composition emphasizes that the concern of such master-pieces as this is with communicating the atmosphere and climate of a landscape, not, as it had been earlier in the Romantic movement, with the sublime awesomeness of mountains, storms and waterfalls.

In 1888 another artist of this period, John Constable (1776–1837), was added in quantity to the collections. These drawings were presented by the artist's daughter, Miss Isabel Constable. Some are rapid sketches from nature; others the more careful pencil or watercolour studies which Constable loved to make in the open air. There are also examples of his preparations for the famous

378 *River Scene*, Richard Parkes Bonington (1802–28)

379 *Coventry*, J. M. W. Turner (1775–1851)

380 Study for the *Leaping Horse*, John Constable (1776–1837)

381 *St Mary Redcliffe, Bristol: Daybreak*, John Sell Cotman (1782–1842)

382 *La Crau from Montmajour*, Vincent Van Gogh (1853–90)

383 *Sunday Afternoon on the Grande Jatte*, Georges Seurat (1859–91)

painting of the *Leaping Horse*, finished in 1825. These studies, in which only a   380
brush and black ink are used, convey all the variety of movement and light
which Constable's diligent and delighted eye saw in the countryside of Suffolk.
The surface of the drawing is scratched all over, just as the finished picture was
to be scumbled with white paint, to express the sparkling wetness of foliage,
grass and the very air itself.

If Bonington and Constable painted the scenes in which they lived, Turner's
unquenchable fascination with all natural phenomena led him to perpetuate
much more than these artists did the ideas of eighteenth-century landscape. He
bequeathed the entire contents of his studio to the nation at his death in 1851,
and in 1930 the sketchbooks and unmounted drawings were transferred from
the Tate Gallery to the British Museum. This mass of material, amounting to
some 19,000 items, shows the full range of Turner's interests and achievements,
from the iridescent *More Park* of about 1824, in which he approaches the
English countryside painstakingly and rather in the spirit of Constable, to the
brilliantly free *Passau* of about 1840, an exultation in the mountainous, airy
expanses of the Continent. There are many sketchbooks which record moment
by moment the occupation of his busy mind; rapid jottings from the windows
of coaches in France, Italy and Switzerland; studies and composition sketches
for pictures destined for the walls of the Academy, and nude studies done
actually in the Academy Schools; designs for book illustrations; all the watercolours connected with Turner's fruitful stay with Lord Egremont at Petworth
in 1830. More valuable examples of Turner's work, a fine series of finished
watercolours, came with the bequest of R. W. Lloyd in 1958. These consist
largely of work of the 1820s and 1830s, with many of the colourful and dramatic
views of towns which are among Turner's most important watercolours.
Among them is the view of *Coventry*: a vista in which the two majestic spires   379
of the city rise into a swirl of stormy light which beats diagonally down, across
the scene, unifying the panorama in a single visual movement.

A further great contribution to the holdings of English drawings was Henry
Vaughan's bequest in 1902 of work by John Flaxman (1755–1826) and
Thomas Stothard (1755–1834). Flaxman led the Neo-Classical movement
both in this country and on the Continent and, unlike many artists who
deliberately adopted a 'Greek' style, he found for himself an entirely natural
language. The bequest of Dr Eric Millar in 1967, which greatly enriched the
nineteenth-century English collections of the Print Room, included Flaxman's
Adoration of the Magi, a design for a lunette in bas-relief now in the Soane   377
Museum, for which the Department already had a preliminary sketch. The
simplicity of this design achieves a dignity which rises above the often rather
petty imitation of early nineteenth-century sculpture, and indeed seems closer
in mood to the present century than much of the work which immediately
followed it.

In addition to the English drawings, Henry Vaughan's bequest made notable
contributions to other schools. A superb sheet of studies of heads by Watteau   371

(1684–1721) deserves attention; it is a characteristic group of sketches from the life and includes a portrait of the actor Paul Poisson which recurs in the painting *L'Amour au Théâtre Français* in Berlin. The subtle balance between the theatrical and the simply real which can so often be felt in Watteau's pictures is clearly suggested here. It sometimes reaches an attenuated poignancy capable of being very moving, and perhaps part of the sadness common in the work of artists destined for an early death, as was Watteau. Another Watteau drawing in the Print Room, the *Woman seated on the Ground*, displays the artist's wonderful skill in depicting fabrics, suggesting their texture and their relation to the body they clothe, as well as the charm of their folds and the elegance of the wearer's pose. As with the faces on the other sheet, Watteau is able to infuse a sad but real life into this simple subject.

372

Another fine French drawing of the eighteenth century in the characteristic red chalk of the time is the *Church at Tivoli* by Hubert Robert (1733–1808), acquired in 1963. The artist's technical resource here is a cause for wonder. The chalk is made to suggest sunlit stone walls, old woodwork and the shimmering movements of poplar trees and, although the subject is un-pretentious, Robert makes it splendidly grand simply by the beauty and seriousness of his treatment. The small, lively study of a *Roof of a Building* by G. B. Tiepolo (1696–1770) is a contrast provided by one of Robert's most illustrious Italian contemporaries. It was presented by the artist Charles Ricketts (1866–1931), a great benefactor of the Museum and one of the fore-most connoisseurs of his time. Tiepolo's sketch is a mere detail – a tiled roof and urn-decorated pediment glimpsed, as it were, over a wall; but it is a masterly fragment, full of Italian light conveyed in Tiepolo's typical vigorous brown ink and wash.

Of works by nineteenth-century French and Dutch masters a superlative group of sixteen choice examples was bequeathed to the Museum in 1968 by César Mange de Hauke. The drawings range from the Romantics to the Post-Impressionists, including a Delacroix (1798–1863) *Seated Arab*, and the *Portrait of Charles Hayard and his Daughter* by Ingres (1780–1867), two drawings which illustrate the strange contrast between Delacroix's richly Romantic outlook and Ingres's cool, precise draughtsmanship. From the latter part of the century are an important study for *Sunday Afternoon on the Grande Jatte*, the large painting by Seurat (1859–91) now in Chicago, and *La Crau from Montmajour*, a landscape in pen and ink by Van Gogh (1853–90), done in 1888, one of several large drawings by him in this medium.

352

376
383

382

The post-impressionist drawings herald the twentieth century, a new epoch in draughtsmanship as every previous century has been, and one in which technical excellence and inspired perception are, as much as ever, the character-istics of great art. If such qualities are as highly prized in the future as they have been in the past, the Print Room can hope to maintain the tradition of connoisseurship which has created it.

A. WILTON

CHAPTER TWELVE

Printed Books

Since the opening of the Museum in 1759, the Department of Printed Books has had two duties to perform – to act as a museum of the printed book in all its forms and to be the national reference library. In the early days the former role was emphasized, in that the Keeper saw his main duty as keeping the collections intact, and only a few distinguished readers gained access to the books. A more enlightened policy, however, was soon adopted culminating in 1836 in Antonio Panizzi's noble declaration: 'I want a poor student to have the same means of indulging his learned curiosity, of following his rational pursuits, of consulting the same authorities, of fathoming the most intricate enquiry, as the richest man in the kingdom.' From that moment the Department had taken over its role as the national library. Aided by the operation of the successive Copyright Acts it has the greatest collection of English books in the world. Thanks also to its various accessions by purchase and gift over two centuries no other library has such a fine all-round representation of the early printed literature of other European countries.

The main foundation collection of printed books, the library of Sir Hans Sloane (1660–1753), was a general working library, illustrating its owner's very wide interests which were by no means confined to medicine and science. Before the Museum opened its doors, King George II added, in 1757, the Old Royal Library, which certainly did not lack quality, although the manuscripts were more important than the printed books. The printed books fall into two sections, the books from all the royal palaces which had been gathered at St James's by 1649 and the additions made to the St James's Library after the Restoration. The later group, apart from the library of John Morris added in 1661, consisted largely of the English books deposited under the Licensing Acts of 1662 and subsequent years and the later Copyright Acts; there are no presentation copies to sovereigns later than Charles I among them. Many are to be found in the earlier section of the library, which also includes that formed for James I's eldest son, Henry, Prince of Wales. This in turn incorporated many books from Archbishop Cranmer's library and those of Henry, Earl of Arundel, and his son-in-law, John, Lord Lumley.

The Old Royal Library was not the only royal collection of books to reach the British Museum. In 1762 George III presented the invaluable collection of tracts formed between 1640 and 1660 by George Thomason, a London bookseller who, with remarkable prevision of what would be of use to future

8

historians, set himself to collect any possible printed item except folio books from the great flood of ephemeral literature let loose by the breaking down of literary censorship in the Civil War period. The gift was an act of considerable self-denial on the part of the King, who was the first British sovereign to be an enthusiastic collector. He built up the splendid collection of about 70,000 volumes which is now housed in the long gallery known as the King's Library. It included books from the private libraries of his predecessors from Charles II onwards, a fine Italian library bought in 1763 from Joseph Smith, British Consul at Venice, and the result of over fifty years' intelligent collecting. With the exception of thirty of the finest books it was transferred to the Museum by George IV in 1828.

With its arrival the Department's collections were for the first time worthy of the National Collection of what was then the wealthiest country in the world, although a number of other very important accessions had meanwhile been secured. The majority of the Museum's unsurpassed collection of Shakespeare's plays in quarto had been bequeathed – most appropriately – by the great Shakespearean actor, David Garrick, in 1779. A more general library of great distinction was bequeathed twenty years later, that of C. M. Cracherode, a clergyman of retiring disposition but admirable taste, who shared the prevailing interest in the early editions of the classics, and paid special attention to the beauty and the bindings of the copies he acquired. Some twenty years later the library of the great naturalist Sir Joseph Banks was also bequeathed, bringing to the Department a great wealth of zoological and botanical colour plate books, as well as a splendid collection of early as well as contemporary scientific books.

A third big bequest was the finest of all, the library of Thomas Grenville, who died in 1846. It is wonderfully strong in early Bibles, in classical, English, Italian and Spanish literature, history, voyages and travels, and nearly all the 20,000 volumes are splendid copies.

The Museum benefited by a new form of bequest in 1910, when Alfred H. Huth left to the Trustees the choice of fifty volumes from the vast library which his father Henry Huth had formed. Thirty-seven of those selected were printed books and the opportunity was taken to add some very important fifteenth- and sixteenth-century books including three Shakespeare first quartos and a famous collection of Elizabethan ballads.

Most of the special collections so far described tended to concentrate on early books, and by 1937 the eighteenth- and nineteenth-century holdings of English books were relatively of poorer quality. The opportunity was therefore taken in 1937 to acquire the library of T. J. Wise which was particularly strong in these periods. Despite its owner's nefarious practices in his earlier days, when he created bogus first editions of nineteenth-century authors, and stole, or arranged to have stolen, leaves from Museum books, it remains an outstanding collection, particularly of the Romantic poets, of Rossetti and Swinburne, and of poetry and drama from the seventeenth to the twentieth centuries.

The books to be illustrated here have been chosen primarily as museum specimens, and the stress is naturally on fine printing, illustration and book-binding, on decorative music and maps. But it is as texts that books primarily exist, and the first three examples have been selected with that in mind.

The first printing of Chaucer's *Canterbury Tales* by William Caxton forms   384 a solid foundation – England's first great poet published by her first printer. Born in the Weald of Kent about 1420, Caxton had spent some thirty years in the Low Countries, before learning to print in Cologne. After printing for a year or two in Bruges, by 1476 he had returned to England and established himself in the Sanctuary of Westminster Abbey, where he printed nearly a hundred books before his death in 1491. He was deeply interested in English and French Literature and much of his time must have been spent translating and editing the books which he printed. They included the poetry of Gower and Lydgate as well as that of Chaucer; Malory's *Morte d'Arthur* and other favourite romances; history books such as the *Chronicles of England* and Higden's *Polychronicon*; and his own English translations of Aesop and of Vergil's *Aeneid*.

No book has had a greater influence on the English character than the Bible. Beginning with the only known copy of Tyndale's translation of part of the New Testament which was printed at Cologne in 1525, the whole history can be followed in the Museum's collections from Coverdale's first complete English Bible of 1535, through the Great Bible of 1539, the Geneva translation (1560) which was that used in English homes for the next fifty years, the Bishops' Bible of 1568, which was the one used on the lectern in churches, and the Douay-Rheims Catholic versions of the New and Old Testaments (1582, 1609). The culmination was the production – astonishingly by a com-plicated series of committees – of the so-called Authorized or King James   385 Version printed in 1611 which rapidly became the accepted version and whose noble words were to exert an unrivalled influenced on the language as well as the minds of its readers.

The third choice is equally inevitable – the first collected edition of the plays of Shakespeare. John Heminge and Henry Condell, two actors from Shakespeare's old company undertook the editing of a complete edition which appeared in folio size in 1623 and is usually called the 'First Folio'. It contains thirty-five plays, and it remains the primary authority for the text of the world's greatest playwright. The Museum possesses five copies, of which the most interesting is the one which was used in turn by three great Shakespearean critics – Theobald, Dr Johnson and Steevens – and the example illustrated,   386 purchased in 1922, which is one of three known copies in which the portrait of Shakespeare on the title-page by Martin Droeshout is in its earliest state.

Turning now to the book as an art-object, we find that the first substantial printed book, the Latin Bible with forty-two lines to the column, completed at   388 Mainz by September 1456, is among the most beautiful books ever to be printed. It was planned by Gutenberg, who probably devised the apparatus for casting

384–386 *Above*, Chaucer's *Canterbury Tales*, printed by Caxton *c.* 1478. *Right*, first edition of the Authorized Version of the *Bible*, London, 1611. *Below*, First Folio Shakespeare, London, before 1623

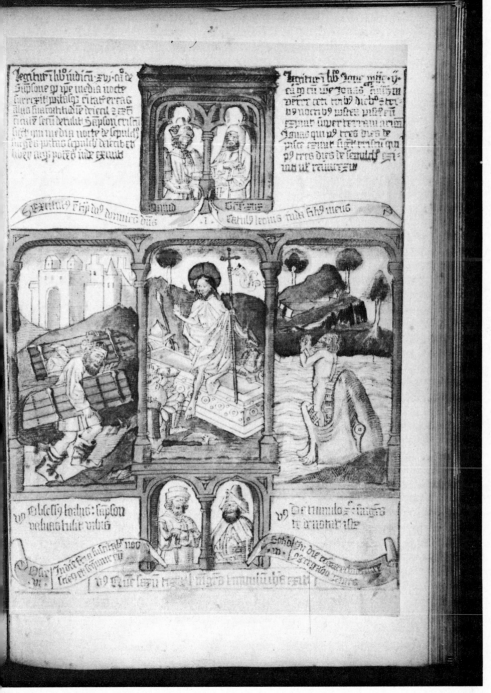

blia Pauperum, a Blockbook of *c.* 1463

Incipit liber Bresith quem nos Genesim dicimus. In principio creauit deus celum [et] terram. Terra autem erat inanis et vacua: et tenebre erant super faciem abissi: et spiritus dei ferebatur super aquas. Dixitque deus. Fiat lux. Et facta est lux. Et vidit deus lucem [quod] esset bona: et diuisit lucem a tenebris appellauitque lucem diem et tenebras noctem. Factumque est vespere et mane dies unus. Dixit quoque deus. Fiat firmamentum in medio aquarum: et diuidat aquas ab aquis. Et fecit deus firmamentum: diuisitque aquas que erant sub firmamento ab hiis que erant super firmamentum: et factum est ita. Uocauitque deus firmamentum celum: et factum est vespere et mane dies secundus. Dixit vero deus. Congregentur aque que sub celo sunt in locum unum et appareat arida. Et factum est ita. Et vocauit deus aridam terram: congregationesque aquarum appellauit maria. Et vidit deus [quod] esset bonum. et ait. Germinet terra herbam virentem et facientem semen: et lignum pomiferum faciens fructum iuxta genus suum: cuius semen in semetipso sit super terram. Et factum est ita. Et protulit terra herbam virentem et facientem semen iuxta genus suum: lignumque faciens fructum et habens unumquodque sementem secundum speciem suam. Et vidit deus [quod] esset bonum: et factum est vespere et mane dies tercius. Dixitque autem deus. Fiant luminaria in firmamento celi: et diuidant diem ac noctem: et sint in signa et tempora et dies et annos: ut luceant in firmamento celi et illuminent terram. Et factum est ita. Fecitque deus duo luminaria magna: luminare maius ut presset diei et luminare minus ut presset nocti: et stellas. et posuit eas in firmamento celi ut lucerent super terram: et

presset diei ac nocti: et diuideret lucem ac tenebras. Et vidit deus [quod] esset bonum: et factum est vespere et mane dies quartus. Dixit etiam deus. Producant aque reptile anime viuentis et volatile super terram: sub firmamento celi. Creauitque deus cete grandia et omnem animam viuentem atque motabilem quam produxerant aque in species suas: et omne volatile secundum genus suum. Et vidit deus [quod] esset bonum: benedixitque eis dicens. Crescite et multiplicamini et replete aquas maris: auesque multiplicentur super terram. Et factum est vespere et mane dies quintus. Dixit quoque deus. Producat terra animam viuentem in genere suo: iumenta et reptilia et bestias terre secundum species suas. Factum est ita. Et fecit deus bestias terre iuxta species suas: et iumenta et omne reptile terre in genere suo. Et vidit deus [quod] esset bonum: et ait. Faciamus hominem ad ymaginem et similitudinem nostram: et presit piscibus maris et volatilibus celi et bestiis uniuerseque terre: omnique reptili quod mouetur in terra. Et creauit deus hominem ad ymaginem et similitudinem suam: ad ymaginem dei creauit illum: masculum et feminam creauit eos. Benedixitque illis deus et ait. Crescite et multiplicamini et replete terram et subicite eam: et dominamini piscibus maris et volatilibus celi et uniuersis animantibus que mouentur super terram. Dixitque deus. Ecce dedi vobis omnem herbam afferentem semen super terram et uniuersa ligna que habent in semetipsis sementem generis sui: ut sint vobis in escam et cunctis animantibus terre omnique volucri celi et uniuersis que mouentur in terra et in quibus est anima viuens: ut habeant ad vescendum. Et factum est ita. Viditque deus cuncta que fecerat: et erant valde bona.

type to a uniform height which was the vital clue to the development of the printing art. During the course of printing Gutenberg was sued by his financial partner Johann Fust, lost the case, and had to surrender his share of the business to him. The printing was probably completed by Peter Schoeffer in partnership with Fust. The Museum owns two copies, one on paper from King George III's library, and one on vellum, from that of Thomas Grenville.

At about the time that successful experiments were being made in the use of movable type, another form of printing certain kinds of books was being practised in Germany and the Netherlands. The so-called Blockbooks were printed from engraved wooden blocks, with the text being produced by laboriously cutting each letter in wood. This process was only commercially practicable for short books for which a big sale was anticipated, and was largely used for illustrated books designed for the religious edification of the poorer and illiterate classes. A typical example of this was the *Biblia Pauperum* or Bible 387 of the Poor, which shows scenes from the life of Christ flanked by related scenes from the Old Testament.

Italy was the first country after Germany in which printing with movable types was practised, two Germans working at the monastery of Subiaco in 1465 before going on to Rome. It was in that city and in Venice that most Italian fifteenth-century books were produced, and by the 1480s the trade was largely in the hands of Italians. Perhaps the most famous of the early printers at Venice, however, was a Frenchman, Nicolas Jenson, who worked there from 1470 to 1480. He produced some particularly fine editions of the classics, using a fount of roman type which has been a source of inspiration to many modern type designers. This copy of the 1475 Cicero from Cracherode's 394 library is finely printed on vellum.

Another foreigner to print in Venice was Erhard Ratdolt, who was born in Augsburg, but worked for ten years in Venice before returning to his native city in 1486. His books are notable for their fine decorative borders and initials and he was also the first to solve the problem of producing the necessary geometrical diagrams for the first edition of Euclid. This is the 389 dedication copy which he presented to the doge of Venice, Giovanni Mocenigo; it is on vellum with the dedicatory letter printed in gold ink and with the illuminated arms of the doge. It belonged to King George III.

The most famous of all Venice printers was Aldus Manutius. He was the first of the great scholar printers, who did so much to spread the classical ideals of the Renaissance throughout Western Europe, being interested at first in the publishing of Greek authors and then from 1501 onwards specializing in pocket editions, the 'Aldine' classics, carefully edited and printed in an italic or cursive type. This lacked the beauty of his roman, seen at its best in the finest illustrated book of the fifteenth century, the *Hypnerotomachia Poliphili* by 396 Franciscus Columna. The finest copy of this book in the Museum is in an outstanding French binding, *c.* 1550, by Claude de Picques for Thomas Mahieu.

The general standard of printing in England during the fifteenth century was low and Caxton's contemporaries and successors did not normally improve on his distinctly uninspired work. His press was taken over at his death in 1491 by his foreman, Wynkyn de Worde, thought to have been a native of Wörth in Alsace. De Worde was active until his death in 1535, but he never

395 improved on the English translation of *De proprietatibus rerum*, an encyclopaedic work by Bartholomaeus Anglicus, which he printed about 1495. The wood-cut illustrations are seen to particular advantage in this exceptionally clean copy from the Grenville Library with its splendid margins. The paper, which has lasted so well, was made by John Tate of Hertford, the first English paper-maker.

In Germany gothic types were preferred and a particularly tortuous version known as 'Fraktur' (broken) became the typical German letter for four centuries. Based on the hand used by the clerks in the Imperial chancery it was originally cut about 1510 for Johann Schönsperger, the court printer to the Emperor Maximilian I. It is seen at its best with special flourishes in the upper

397 and lower margins in the *Theuerdank* of 1517. This is an elaborate allegorical romance in which the wooing of Mary of Burgundy by the emperor is described. Planned by Maximilian himself and edited by Melchior Pfinzing, it was illustrated with numerous woodcuts from designs by Hans Leonhard Schäuffe-lein. This copy, on vellum, is again from Grenville's library.

By the second half of the sixteenth century Christopher Plantin had made Antwerp the centre of European printing. At one time he had twenty-two presses at work, and his types, illustrations and press work were worthy of his distinguished list of authors. His most impressive work was his Polyglot Bible in eight volumes, produced between 1569 and 1572 under the patronage of, but without the promised financial aid from Philip II of Spain. The languages in which the text is printed in parallel columns include Hebrew, Aramaic,

398 Greek, Latin and Syriac. This copy, one of thirteen on vellum, was presented in the name of Philip II to the Duke of Alva, the tyrannical Spanish governor of the Netherlands, by the editor Arias Montano on 4 November, 1572. It was purchased in 1840 by the Museum, which also possesses a set on paper given by Plantin to the Archduke Mathias.

The first forty years of the seventeenth century were marked all over Europe by a disastrous lowering of standards in everyday printing, but a partial revival was achieved in France in 1640 with the foundation by Louis XIII of the Imprimerie Royale. The king was acting on the advice of Cardinal Richelieu, whose personal bookseller, Sébastien Cramoisy, was put in charge of the seven presses which were set up in the Louvre. One of the first books to be

400 put in hand was a fine Latin Bible and this was completed in eight volumes by 1642. The new roman type closely resembles Jean Jannon's *gros canon* of which the Imprimerie Nationale still possesses the original punches. This copy came from the great collection of Bibles formed by George III's sixth son, the Duke of Sussex.

Preclarissimū opus elementoꝝ Euclidis megareñs vna cū cō/
mentis Campani pspicacissimi in arte geometriā incipit feliciť.

Punctus est cuius ꝑs non est. ꝅ Linea est
longitudo sine latitudie cuius quidem ex/
tremitates sunt duo puncta. ꝅ Linea recta
e ab vno pūcto ad aliū breuissima exten
sio in extremitates suas vtrūqȝ eoꝝ reci/
piens. ꝅ Superficies e ꝗ longitudinē ꞇ latitu
dinē tm̄ habet: cui°termini quidē sūt linee
ꝅ Superficies plana e ab vna linea ad ali
am extensio in extremitates suas recipiēs
ꝅ Angulus planus e duarum lineaꝝ alte/
rius cōtactus: quaꝝ expansio est super su/
pficiē applicatioqȝ nō directa. ꝅ Quādo aūt angulū cōtinent due
linee recte: rectiline° angulus noiatur. ꝅ Cū recta linea sup rectā
steterit duoqȝ anguli vtrobiqȝ fuerint eǧles eoꝝ vterqȝ rect° erit.
ꝅ Lineaqȝ linee superstans ei cui supstat ꝑpēdicularis vocať. ꝅ An
gulus vero qui recto maior est obtusus dicit. ꝅ Angul° vero mio/
recto acut° appellaſ. ꝅ Terminus° e qd vniuscuiusqȝ finis e. ꝅ Figu/
ra e ꝗ termino vel terminis clinet. ꝅ Circul° e figura plana vna ꝗ
dē linea cōtenta: ꝗ circūferētia noiaſ: in cui°medio pūct°e a quo oēs
linee recte ad circūferentiā exeūtes sibiinuicē sunt equales. Et hic
quidē punct° cētꝝ circuli dicit. ꝅ Diameter circuli e linea recta ꝗ
sup ei° centꝝ transiēs extremitatesqȝ suas circūferentie applicans
circulū in duo media diuidit. ꝅ Semicirculus e figura plana dia/
metro circuli ꞇ medietate circūferentie cōtenta. ꝅ Portio circuli
est figura plana recta linea ꞇ parte circūferentie cōtenta: semicircu
lo quidem aut maior aut minor. ꝅ Rectilinee figure sūt que rectis
lineis cōtinenť quaꝝ quedā trilatere ꝗ trib° rectis lineis: quedam
quadrilatere ꝗ quatuor rectis lineis: qdā multilatere ꝗ pluribus ꝗ
quatuor rectis lineis continentur. ꝅ Figuraꝝ trilaterarum: alia est
triangulus habens tria latera equalia. Alia triangulus duo habēs
equalia latera. Alia triangulus triū inequaliū lateꝝ. Itaꝝ iteruȝ
alia est orthogoniū: vnū.s. rectū angulum habens. Alia est ambli
gonium aliquem obtusum angulum habens. Alia est origonium:
in qua tres anguli sunt acuti. ꝅ Figuraꝝ autem quadrilateraꝝ.
Alia est quadratū quod e equilateruȝ atqȝ rectangulū. Alia est te/
tragonus longus: que est figura rectangula: sed equilatera non est
Alia est helmuaym: que est equilatera: sed rectangula non est.

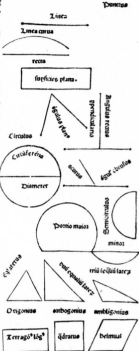

Punctus

Linea

Linea curua

recta

ſupficies plana.

Angulus plane

perpendiculare

Angulus rectus

acutus

ſigur obtuſus

Circulus

Circuferētia

Diameter

Portio maior

Semicirculus

minor

Elaterus

cuit equalia lateꝝ

triū seꝗlū lateꝝ

Origonius

orthogonius

ambligonius

Tetragó°lōg°

ꝗdratus

helmuat

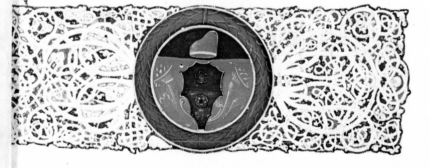

Euclid's *Elementa*, printed in Venice by Erhard Ratdolt, 1482

With the eighteenth century the illustrated book came into its own again in France and achieved a supremacy in the eyes of French collectors which it has never since lost. The best known example is La Fontaine, *Contes et nouvelles*, 'Amsterdam' 1762, actually published by J. G. Barbou in Paris and known by the name of the *Fermiers-generaux*, after the wealthy collectors of taxes who financed its production. It is one of the smaller luxury books and owes its fame to the beautifully engraved plates after Charles Eisen and the delicious head- and tail-pieces of Pierre Philippe Choffard. Grenville's copy contains many proof states and some rejected plates, together with an original design by Choffard.

399

The introduction of 'wove' paper in the 1750s with its smoother printing surface encouraged the development of 'modern-face' types, with their vertical stress and greater contrast between thick and thin strokes. This tendency is discernible in the types owned by Baskerville in England, was encouraged by Didot in France and Ibarra in Spain, and reached its apogee in the books of G. B. Bodoni in Italy. In 1768 he was put in charge of the Stamperia Reale in Parma and in 1791 was allowed also to set up his own press at which he produced fine books for the international market. He died in 1813 and five years later his widow published the *Manuale tipografico*, containing specimens of nearly three hundred of his types. This is King George III's copy.

401

English book collectors have seldom shown the enthusiasm of the French for illustrated books, but the development of aquatinting shortly before 1800 was to produce a fine series of colour-plate books, many of which were published by the German-born Rudolph Ackermann. The first of his great series of books with coloured aquatints was the *Microcosm of London*, which came out in monthly parts from 1808 to 1810. The aquatints were a composite production, since Augustus Pugin drew the buildings, Thomas Rowlandson added the lively figures and they were then engraved by a number of different artists.

During most of the nineteenth century the general standard of printing all over Europe was once more at a low ebb. The improvements in book produc- tion which have taken place more recently were greatly influenced by an Englishman, William Morris. In 1891 this socialist craftsman established at Hammersmith the Kelmscott Press. Employing professional printers, but closely supervising type, paper, ink, illustration and design himself, he produced on hand presses a series of beautiful, if archaic-looking books, culminating in the splendid *Chaucer* of 1896. It was Morris's insistence on the finest quality at every stage of production, rather than the design of his books, which paved the way to the printing revival of the present century. The Museum's vellum copy, in the binding by the Doves Bindery to a design by Morris, belonged to Sir Emery Walker, to whose technical expertise both Morris's Kelmscott Press and Cobden-Sanderson's Doves Press owed so much.

402

The study of the history of bookbinding has made important strides in recent years and thanks in particular to the numerous royal bindings, those collected by Grenville and Cracherode, and a small but choice bequest by Felix Slade in 1868, the Department has long had a fine collection. It has now been made pre⁄eminent by the Henry Davis gift of over 1000 examples from all countries, made on terms which permit the owner to retain possession of them during his lifetime but allow the Museum to exhibit some of them and to borrow them for study purposes.

Unquestionably the most popular binding exhibit in the Museum is the travelling library of Sir Julius Caesar, Master of the Rolls in the reign of James I. Forty⁄four small volumes bound in gold⁄tooled white vellum are contained in an oak case made in the shape of a folio volume covered with gold⁄tooled olive morocco. The inside of the lid of this case has a catalogue of the books painted within an architectural framework. Three other similar travelling libaries are known, all produced between 1615 and 1620. Caesar's belonged to Horace Walpole and was bought by the Museum in 1842.   407

Perhaps the most beautiful of all European leather bindings are those produced in Paris in the middle of the sixteenth century, and the most famous collector of them was the French government official, Jean Grolier. Over five hundred volumes, the great majority in their beautiful original bindings have survived from Grolier's library. His earliest books were nearly all bound in Italy where he served as Treasurer to the invading French forces in the second decade of the sixteenth century, but his later bindings are all Paris work, the one illustrated dating from about 1550. On the upper cover is his ownership inscription IO. GROLIERII ET AMICORVM – for Jean Grolier and his friends. It was bought at the J. R. Abbey sale in 1967.   390

In sixteenth⁄century England bookbinding was strongly influenced by French styles and some of the best London binders were Huguenot refugees. One of these, John de Planche, who was active in London between 1567 and 1571, was responsible for binding a copy of Nicolay's *Navigations et pérégrinations orientales*, 1568, for Queen Elizabeth I. The royal arms are painted on vellum in a sunk panel in the centre of the covers, in a style practised at Lyons, and de Planche, perhaps a native of Dijon, may have learned to bind there.   390

One of the finest printed books in the Museum was acquired from the family library of the Dukes of Devonshire at Chatsworth in 1958. It is a copy of *Les Délices de l'esprit* by Jean Desmarets de Saint⁄Sorlin, prepared for presen⁄ tation to Louis XIV's consort, Queen Marie⁄Thérèse, in 1661. The elaborate intaglio ornaments on the title⁄page and above and below the illustrations blend perfectly with similar woodcut headpieces and initials, all of which are believed to have been designed by the illustrator François Chauveau. Its binding, with its *pointillé* tooling (outlined in a series of dots instead of solid lines) and inlaid panels, is an outstanding example of Paris craftsmanship.   391

The reign of Charles II was the golden age of English bookbinding and some of the finest examples came from the shop of Samuel Mearne, the royal book⁄ binder from 1660 to 1683. The book illustrated is one of two Prayer Books 'bound suitable' to accompany two large Bibles supplied by Mearne in 1674   391

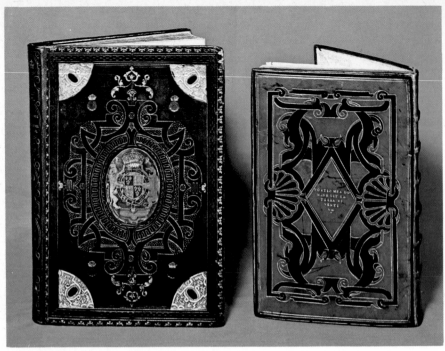

390 Bindings for Elizabeth I (left) and Jean Grolier (right)

391 Bindings for Queen Marie-Thérèse (left) and by Samuel Mearne (right)

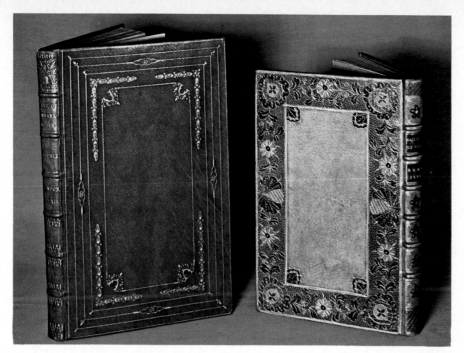

392 Bindings by Roger Payne (left) and Le Monnier (right)

for the King's own use at Whitehall Palace. The Bibles cost £20 each and the Prayer Books £15 each. They replaced a very similar Bible and Prayer Book still preserved at Steane Park, Brackley, the home of Nathaniel Lord Crew, Bishop of Durham and Clerk of the Closet, who received them as perquisites. They are in the so-called 'cottage' style, with a broken pediment painted black at head and tail, and they have the crowned cypher of Charles II, a rose and foliage painted on the fore-edge under the gold.

After a quiet period at the close of the seventeenth century Paris book-binding blossomed once more, and in the hands of three leading families, Padeloup, Derome and Le Monnier resumed its supremacy over the rest of Europe. Three new styles were developed: the *dentelle* in which the tools are disposed to form a lacework border round the covers; the *à repetition* in which they were disposed in a repeating all-over diaper pattern; and elaborate mosaic bindings in which onlays of different coloured leathers were used to build up floral, or pictorial designs. One of the most successful of this mosaic group is this Baccius, *De naturali vinorum historia*, 1597 in the Henry Davis Gift, 392 which was probably bound by one of the Le Monnier family, c. 1750.

Another very distinguished binding from the Henry Davis Gift is on a copy of Dugdale's *History of imbanking fenns and marshes*, 1661. It was bound for 392 Sir Richard Colt Hoare, the Wiltshire antiquary, about 1795, by the famous English binder Roger Payne. A native of Eton, he moved to London and before his death in 1797 had established for himself a lasting reputation, owing something to his attachment to strong drink, something to the peculiar spelling of his elaborate ill-written bills and more to his excellent craftsmanship. He was one of the few English binders whose designs were imitated in Paris.

During the nineteenth century the Department's collection of music grew largely by copyright and purchase, but in the present century two very important collections have been added. The Royal Music Library, which dates from the reign of George III, was deposited on permanent loan by King George V in 1911 and given outright by the present Queen in 1957. The whole library is kept together, and in addition to a wealth of printed material, there is an outstanding series of Handel manuscripts. The library of Paul Hirsch, acquired in 1946, greatly strengthened the holdings of foreign printed music, being particularly strong in Beethoven, Mozart, Schubert and Haydn, but with numerous other important scores and books about music of all periods.

As part of the Royal Music Library the Department of Printed Books now
404   possesses the famous manuscript of Handel's *Messiah* in the composer's autograph. This is the primary source for the text, being the actual manuscript which Handel wrote during his rapid composition of the oratorio between 22 August and 14 September 1741. It was no doubt among the 'Musick Books' which he bequeathed to his transcriber J. C. Smith the elder, whose son presented them to King George III soon after 1774.

The Museum owns the only known complete copy of what is probably the earliest known book of printed music. This is the 'Constance' Gradual – a book containing the music for the service of the Mass which was sung by the choir. It does not bear the name of its printer, the place of printing or the date, but the type used for the words is found in a Constance Breviary which is not later than 1473, and the Gradual is probably of about the same date. The plainsong music was printed from movable type in Gothic notation and decorative initials were added by hand in red and black.

In the 1580s engraved metal plates were introduced for printing music.
403   The earliest English use of this technique was in *Parthenia*, music composed for the virginals by 'three famous Masters, William Byrd, Dr John Ball and Orlando Gibbons'. The virginals were the precursor of the harpsichord, Parthenia is Greek for maidens' songs, and the engraved title page by William Hole suitably portrays a maiden seated at the instrument. The book can be dated between November 1612 and February 1613, since it was published to celebrate the betrothal of James's daughter, Princess Elizabeth, to the Elector Palatine.

The map holdings of the Department owe much to acquisitions under the Copyright Acts, to the foundation libraries and to the splendid geographical section of that of King George III. Of outstanding importance is the only known copy of the first printed map to show any portion of the New World, which was purchased in 1922. The Florentine engraver, Francesco Roselli, and the Venetian, Giovanni Matteo Contarini, were jointly responsible for

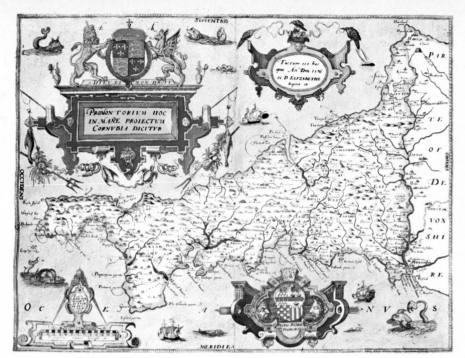

393 Map of Cornwall from the atlas of Christopher Saxton, 1576

this map of the world, which was published in 1506, and records the discoveries   405
and hopes of Columbus's fourth voyage. They seem to have shared his belief
that he had reached Cathay, and not to have grasped the existence of a continuous land barrier between the Atlantic and Pacific. Only the West Indies
and the northern coast of South America are indicated.

The first printed atlas of England and Wales was also the most beautiful,
the series of thirty-four county maps and a general map of England drawn by a
young surveyor from Yorkshire, Christopher Saxton, engraved between 1574
and 1579, and published at the behest and cost of Thomas Seckford, a Master of
Requests to Queen Elizabeth. The earlier maps were engraved by Protestant
refugees from Flanders, but some of the later ones were the work of Englishmen,
notably Augustine Ryther. The earlier issues, such as this copy prepared for
Queen Elizabeth I, were elaborately coloured by hand. Cornwall is perhaps   393
the most decorative of all the maps.

The Map Room also possesses a fine collection of manuscript portulan
charts. The Radcliff Highway, near London Docks, was the centre of this trade
during the seventeenth century and John Burston drew some of the most
ornamental and colourful of these charts, such as that of the Mediterranean and
Aegean Seas dated 1645. These charts were often laid on hinged oak panels
for protection and display, and the English ones are characterized by a profusion

323

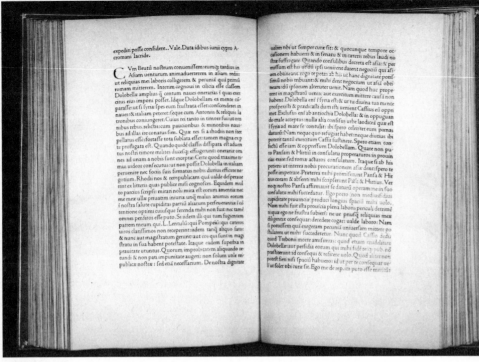

394 Cicero's *Epistolae ad familiares*, printed in Venice by Nicolas Jenson, 1475

395 Bartholomaeus Anglicus, *De proprietatibus rerum*, printed in London by Wynkyn de Worde, *c.* 1495

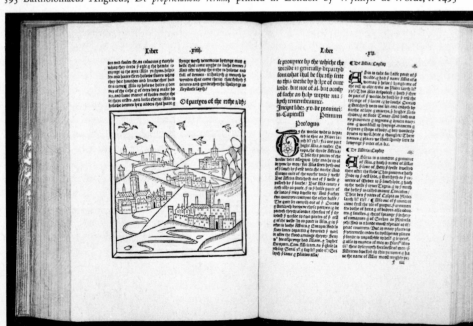

396 Franciscus Columna, *Hypnerotomachia Poliphili*, printed in Venice by Aldus Manutius, 1499

397 Melchior Pfinzing, *Der Theuerdank*, printed by Johann Schönsperger, 1517

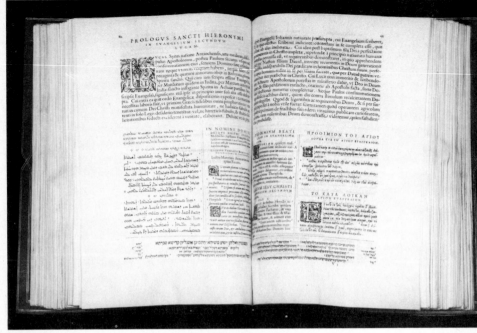

398 Polyglot *Bible*, printed in Antwerp by Christopher Plantin, 1571

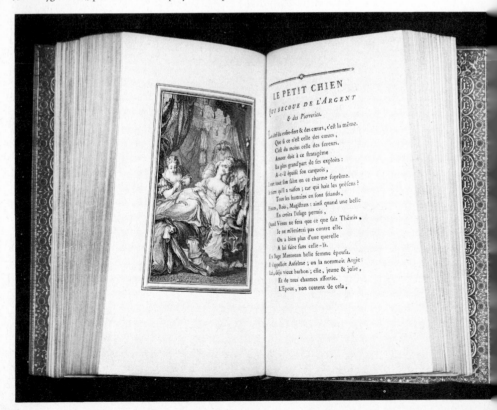

LE PETIT CHIEN

QUI SECOUE DE L'ARGENT
& des Pierreries.

PROPHETIA

SOPHONIÆ.

CAPVT PRIMVM.

ERBVM Domini, quod fa-
ctum eſt ad Sophoniam fi-
lium Chuſi, filii Godoliæ,
filii Amariæ, filii Ezeciæ,
in diebus Ioſiæ filii Amon regis Iudæ.
¹Congregans congregabo omnia a facie
terræ, dicit Dominus: ¹congregans hominem, & pecus, congregans volatilia
cæli, & piſces maris: & ruinæ impiorum
erunt : & diſperdam homines a facie

Q

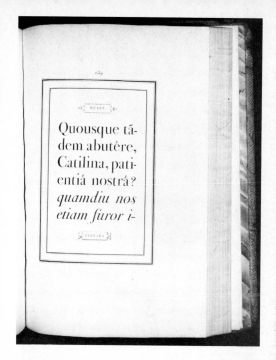

Quousque tā-
dem abutére,
Catilina, pati-
entiá nostrá?
*quamdiu nos
etiam furor i-*

La Fontaine, *Contes et nouvelles*, Paris, 1762

401 *Above, Biblia Sacra,* Paris, 1642; *right,*
ni's *Manuale tipografico,* Parma, 1818

The Kelmscott Press *Chaucer,* produced by
am Morris at Hammersmith, 1896

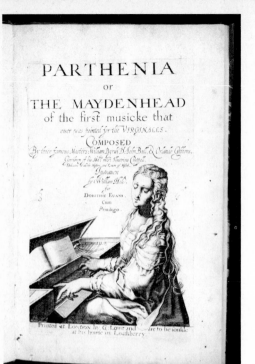

403, 404 The earliest English use of engraved metal plates for printing music was in *Parthenia*, London, 1611 (*left*) with an engraved title page by William Hole. *Below*, the autograph copy of Handel's *Messiah*, 1741. It is open at 'I know that my Redeemer liveth'

405 Contarini's map of the New World, 1506

406 Chinese Terrestrial Globe, 1623

407 The travelling library of forty-four small volumes belonging to Sir Julius Caesar, *c.* 1620

of flowers and fruits and a type of large rose compass surmounted by a flourishing *fleur-de-lis*.

The Philatelic Division of the Department contains the most comprehensive institutional collection of stamps in the world. Its nucleus is the magnificent collection of over 100,000 stamps, illustrating the first fifty years of their existence, formed by Thomas K. Tapling, M.P., and bequeathed by him in 1891, which includes almost all of the famous rarities of the period. To this has been added the duplicate collection of stamps of the world of the General Post Office from about 1890 to the present day, and through the Universal Postal Union the Museum now receives a specimen of every stamp issued throughout the world. Since 1900 the Crown Agents have supplied the Museum with specimens of all the stamps prepared for the colonies and protectorates and have recently also deposited their extensive philatelic archives. Other philatelic archives include those of the Board of Inland Revenue, whose Stamping Branch was responsible for the production of postage stamps from 1840 to 1929 and whose proof books of revenue stamps began in 1712, and of Thomas

De La Rue & Co., who have printed stamps for more than 170 postal administrations since 1853.

Important private collections given or bequeathed to the Museum include the Mosely collection of the stamps of British Africa (1847–1935), the Fitz/gerald collection of Airmails of the World, the L'Estrange Ewen collection of Railway Letter Stamps (1891–1912), the Row collection of Siam (1885–1920), the Wilson/Todd collection of the stamps of the First World War, the Model collection of German stamps, the Bojanowicz collection of Polish philately and postal history (1939–49) and the Walker collection of war/time issues of the Channel Islands.

H. M. NIXON

CHAPTER THIRTEEN

Research Laboratory

During the First World War many of the antiquities in the British Museum were stored in an unused part of the London Underground to protect them against possible damage by air raids. When these antiquities were returned to the British Museum in 1919, it was found that many of them had suffered serious deterioration, not as a result of enemy action, but because they had been exposed to adverse environmental conditions. At that time little was known about the possible detrimental effect of an uncontrolled environment on museum objects, and the Trustees of the British Museum therefore decided to request the then Department of Scientific and Industrial Research to conduct an enquiry into the condition of the antiquities that had suffered deterioration. This enquiry was entrusted to Dr Alexander Scott, a past-President of the Chemical Society, who was also well-known for his interest in the fine arts. On his recommendation a small laboratory was set up in a room near the Department of Prints and Drawings in May 1920, where a small team of workers started a scientific study of ancient materials and their reaction to various environmental conditions, and began to evolve methods for treating those objects which had suffered deterioration.

The laboratory was originally sanctioned on the condition that it should be a purely temporary experiment to come to an end in three years, but the work done by Dr Scott was judged to be so successful that the 'temporary experiment' was put on a permanent basis under the aegis of the Department of Scientific and Industrial Research. This continued until 1931 when the laboratory was incorporated as a separate department of the British Museum on the recommendation of the Royal Commission on Museums. The original accommodation in the Department of Prints and Drawings was soon found to be inadequate, and in 1922 the laboratory was accommodated in 39 Russell Square, where it remained until 1947 when it had to be moved to 1 Montague Place, because the building in Russell Square had been rendered unsafe as the result of bomb damage. Both of these buildings were Georgian houses that had to be adapted to laboratory purposes – purposes for which they had never been intended. As the work of the laboratory was developed and extended in succeeding years, a point was reached when this type of accommodation became quite unsuitable. A well-equipped, modern functional laboratory was therefore built behind the Georgian façades of 39 and 40 Russell Square, and in 1961 the laboratory returned to its original site in ideal quarters.

The prime concern of the laboratory in its early days was to develop satis-factory methods for the treatment of those objects in the British Museum collection that showed signs of deterioration. This related chiefly to problems of metallic corrosion and the effects of saline deposits on excavated archaeo-logical material. These original studies have been extended over the years on a wider front by the application of an ever increasing range of chemical and physical techniques aimed at the development of new and improved methods of treatment based on scientific principles and using modern synthetic materials. This aspect of the Research Laboratory's work can best be illustrated by describing in some detail a number of notable examples of such work.

Reference has already been made to the deterioration suffered by museum objects stored in the Underground. Here the main problem was associated with the action of moisture under humid conditions on the soluble salts commonly present in metals and porous materials such as stone and ceramics that have been excavated from salty ground. Under the varying conditions of relative humidity in the Museum these salts tend to move towards the surface where they crystallize out. This effect can be seen particularly in two earthen-ware potsherds – so-called *ostraka* – often used in Egypt for writing on. In 408, 409 order to prevent this crystallization it is necessary to remove the soluble salts by thorough washing; if certain precautions are taken to consolidate the frail surface, this can be successfully achieved. Many thousands of these *ostraka* in 410, 411 the Department of Egyptian Antiquities have been treated in this way. Humidity in the normal Museum atmosphere can also have a devastating effect on certain types of glass – particularly Venetian glass – which may start to 'weep', a phenomenon that shows itself by the formation of droplets of 412 moisture on the surface of the glass. The solution to this problem is to wash the glass objects and then to keep them in very dry atmosphere using a desiccant such as silica gel in the exhibition cases to maintain a relative humidity below 413 42 per cent.

When bronze objects are excavated, they are often covered with a thick unsightly incrustation of copper corrosion products that obscure the finer details of the object and may also conceal inscriptions. A typical example is the statuette of Isis and Horus of the Ptolemaic period. By the use of chemical 414 reagents followed by electrolytic reduction, the corrosion products can be removed so that the fine details of the carving and also an inscription on the 415 base are revealed. The removal of these unsightly corrosion products can be carried out, almost as a routine operation, on many kinds of objects obtained from archaeological excavations, and results in a great improvement in their appearance. Thus the appearance of an ivory plaque of the seventh century BC 416 from Nimrud was transformed by cleaning, and one can see the effect achieved 92, 417 by cleaning and restoring a large silver brooch with gold insets that was found 418, 419 during the rebuilding of a school in Canterbury. Again, the removal of iron corrosion products has revealed beautiful inlay decoration in a black material known as *niello* on the hilt of an iron sword excavated from an Anglo-Saxon 420, 421

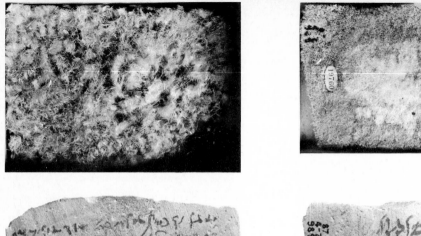

408–411 *Above,* two Egyptian *ostraka* showing crystalline efflorescence; when washed to remove soluble salts the graffi them becomes evident

412, 413 *Left,* a detail of a Venetian glass showing droplets of moisture; *right,* the use of a silica gel to protect a glass gob an exhibition case

414, 415 A corroded Egyptian bronze figure of Isis and Horus before and after treatment. Fine detail and an inscription on the base have been revealed

416, 417 An ivory plaque from Nimrod as excavated and after restoration (cf. Pl. 92)

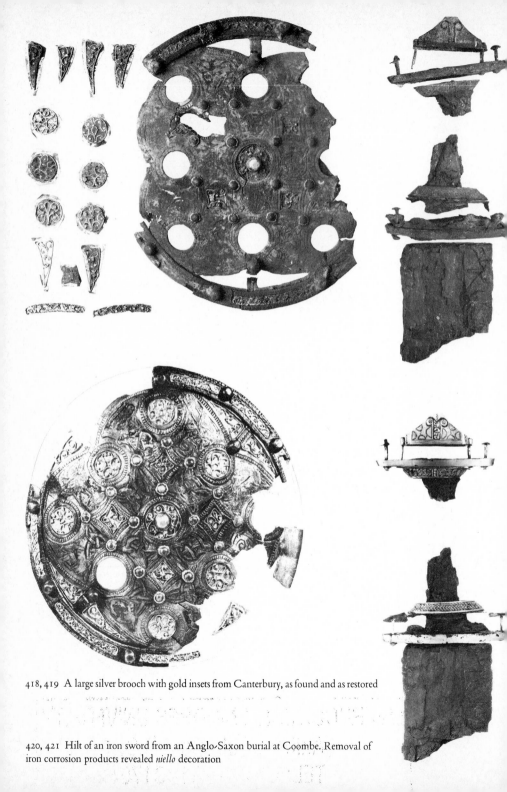

418, 419 A large silver brooch with gold insets from Canterbury, as found and as restored

420, 421 Hilt of an iron sword from an Anglo-Saxon burial at Coombe. Removal of iron corrosion products revealed *niello* decoration

422, 423 The head of Mithras from the Walbrook Mithraeum, as found and with clay accretions removed

424, 425 Synthetic resin was used to strengthen the silver hanging bowl from Ninian's Isle, *above,* after it had been cleaned to produce the restored version, *right*

burial at Coombe. Stone or marble objects do not usually corrode to the same extent as metal objects during burial in the ground, but they often become covered with an accretion of clay, etc., that is disfiguring. This was the case with the well-known marble head of Mithras that was found some years ago on the Walbrook site in London; it is seen here as it was found and then after it had been treated to remove the accretion of clay.

The above instances illustrate typical examples of straightforward restoration that can be carried out by using simple chemical reagents or mechanical methods to remove the corrosion products. These methods were evolved in the early days of the Research Laboratory, but in recent years attention has been devoted to the development of improved methods of conservation using new synthetic materials and employing scientific aids to assess the nature of particular problems before attempting any treatment. This has introduced what may be called the concept of scientific conservation. A striking example of the use of a modern synthetic resin in conservation arose in the case of a silver hanging bowl found during the excavation of the site of a ninth-century church on St Ninian's Island in the Shetlands. When the unsightly corrosion products had been removed, the bowl was left in a very fragile condition because the silver was thin and extremely brittle. However, by using a specially formulated synthetic resin to act as an internal reinforcement it was possible to strengthen the bowl so that it could be handled without risk of damage.

This use of synthetic materials has been extended to other problems of conservation in the Research Laboratory. Thus the water soluble polyethylene glycol waxes have provided an ideal method for treating wooden objects excavated in a waterlogged condition, and a special preparation of soluble nylon, having a unique combination of chemical and physical properties, has been successfully used for the consolidation of objects in a friable condition. By using these synthetic materials it has been possible to carry out satisfactory methods of conservation that would otherwise have been virtually impossible.

Scientific aids, such as radiography, X-ray diffraction analysis, micro-chemical analysis and metallography, are employed in the Research Laboratory to obtain information about the actual condition of an object so that a correct method of treatment can be worked out. Radiography, for example, is used to ascertain whether decorative inlays may be hidden under corrosion products. A typical example of this is provided by a base silver cup of c. 1500 BC date that was excavated at Enkomi in Cyprus. Examination of the object under the microscope showed fragments of gold and a black material (a form of *niello*) embedded in the corrosion, thus suggesting the presence of an inlay on the silver. This was confirmed by taking an X-ray of the cup. The presence of this inlay meant that a special procedure, using a hot 50 per cent solution of formic acid, had to be adopted to remove the corrosion products (which were actually copper salts derived from the copper in the base silver alloy that had corroded preferentially). The inlay was then revealed and it was found to have survived in a remarkably fine state of preservation.

Metallography is often used to examine corroded metal objects to obtain information about the actual condition of the metal and the extent of corrosion. This technique has been used in dealing with the problem of ancient silver objects in cases where annealing is necessary before a crushed or fragmentary object can be repaired. Thus, in the case of a silver libation vessel excavated at Nuri in the Sudan in a fragmentary condition, it was established by metallo-graphic examination that an alteration in the structure of the silver characteristic of annealing only took place at 900° C – a temperature just 50 degrees below the melting point of the silver. A special procedure had, therefore, to be adopted whereby the brittle silver became sufficiently malleable so that the vessel could be reshaped and repaired. Another example of the value of radiography and metallography in the study of antiquities is provided by the shallow bronze Phoenician bowl found by Henry Layard during excavations at Nimrud. This bowl was so extensively corroded that there was no indication of the existence of any decoration, and when a metallographic cross-section was made of a small fragment it was evident that the original bronze had suffered almost complete corrosion. This meant that no chemical method could be used to remove the corrosion, but radiography gave an exciting result, because it revealed an elaborate system of decoration that had been incised in the original bronze, *i.e.* not an inlay executed in a different metal. From the technical point of view the interesting feature about this decoration was that it could be re-vealed by radiography despite the fact that the original bronze had been completely corroded. In cases such as this radiography is of great value because it is the only means of revealing decoration on completely corroded bronze objects thus bringing to light information that confers archaeological in-terest on objects that might otherwise be regarded as being of no particular significance.

It is often necessary for the Research Laboratory to devise special new techniques for solving specific problems of conservation. One such problem which has opened up a new concept in the treatment of corroded silver arose recently in connection with the silver lyre that was found by Sir Leonard Woolley in 1927 during his excavation of the Royal Graves at Ur. The lyre, which was recovered from the ground in a fragmentary state, was mounted on a wooden framework and was for many years so exhibited in the Museum. Although the form of the lyre had been restored by Woolley it did not have the appearance of having once been made of silver. This was, indeed, not surprising, because the original silver had been completely converted during the long period of burial into dirty grey silver chloride. It was therefore desirable that an attempt should be made to restore the silver appearance. This was, however, a difficult problem, because it was necessary to develop a special procedure for converting the silver chloride back into massive metallic silver – something that had not been done before in the treatment of corroded silver objects. Many trial experiments were carried out on small fragments and the problem was eventually solved by developing a special technique of what may

429
430
431

436
438

437

434

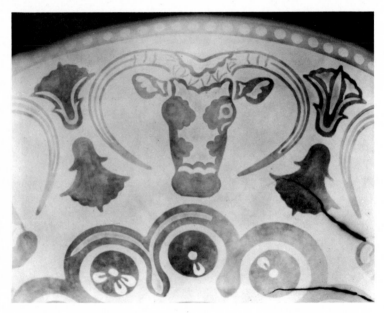

28 *Opposite*, a silver cup from En- Cyprus, *c.* 1500 BC. *Above*, as ated; *centre*, an X-ray detail which ed inlay decoration beneath the ion, and, *below*, after the removal of rosion products

429–431 A silver libation vessel from Nuri, Sudan. *Above,* as found in a fragmentary condition; *centre*, the brittle silver being annealed and reshaped; *below*, after reshaping and repair with its inscription showing clearly

 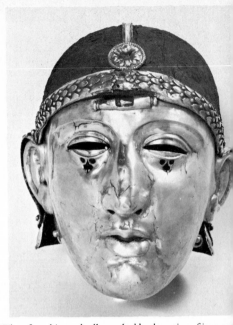

432, 433 Ceremonial silver Emesa helmet from Homs, Syria. When found it was badly cracked by the action of iron co[...] from an inner lining. This was removed and the helmet reshaped and repaired

434, 435 The silver lyre from Ur as found and as subsequently restored for a second time to bring back its silver appea[...]

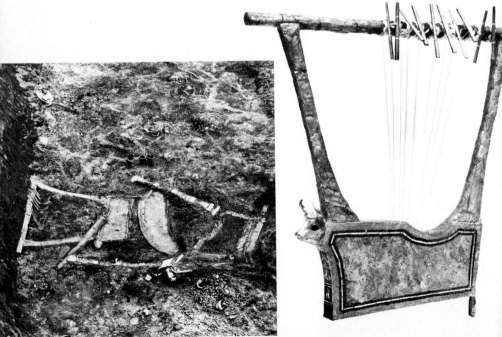

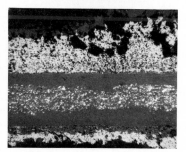

436–438 A corroded Phoenician bronze bowl from Nimrud. A metallographic cross-section, *left*, showed its complete corrosion but an X-ray revealed its interesting decoration surviving in the corrosion products

439 A view of the Radiocarbon Laboratory showing equipment for benzene synthesis

suitably be called consolidative reduction, in which the silver chloride was electrolytically reduced very slowly at a low current density using partially rectified current. Under these special conditions it was possible to reduce the silver chloride throughout its thickness to massive silver. The silver fragments were then mounted on a perspex framework using a special synthetic wax-resin mixture.

435

Another object which necessitated the development of a special method of treatment was the ceremonial silver Emesa helmet found at Homs in Syria. Its distorted, cracked appearance was brought about as the result of the expansion that took place when the internal iron lining corroded. In this case it was necessary to remove the corroded iron and to reinforce the inside of the helmet with silver mesh so that the cracks could be reshaped and repaired, and the helmet restored to its original appearance.

432

433

As well as developing improved methods for the conservation of antiquities, the Research Laboratory is also concerned with the scientific examination and analysis of antiquities to obtain information about the materials of which ancient objects were made and the methods used to make them. As the result of the precise methods of microchemical analysis that have become available in recent years considerable advances have been made in this field. The principal methods of analysis used in the Research Laboratory include emission spectroscopy, atomic absorption, polarography, X-ray diffraction and metallography, and a wide range of problems can be investigated. One such problem of particular interest arose in connection with the Lycurgus Cup, now in the Department of Medieval and Later Antiquities. This elaborately cut glass cup exhibits a striking dichroic effect, showing a turbid green colour by reflected light and a deep magenta colour by transmitted light. The explanation of this dichroic effect was elucidated by analysing the glass and showing that, while the general basic composition corresponded to a typical soda-lime-silica glass of the Roman period, an unusual feature was the presence of minute amounts of silver and gold. It was the presence of the gold and silver in colloidal suspension in the glass matrix that was the cause of the remarkable dichroic effect. Other problems investigated include the nature of opacifiers used in ancient glass at different periods, the causes of the embrittlement of ancient silver objects buried in the ground and the examination of ceramics, especially porcelains, to determine the precise nature of the body paste.

212

These techniques can also be used when the question arises of the authenticity of objects on offer to the Museum. In many cases it may be difficult to arrive at a definite conclusion on stylistic or art-historical grounds, and in such cases a technical examination may produce evidence that is either consistent with the alleged date, or may, on the other hand, reveal anachronisms in the composition or the method of fabrication of the object or show that the apparent signs of age have been recently induced by artificial means.

As an off-shoot of its main activities, research on the technique of radio-carbon dating was started in 1951 in collaboration with the Atomic Energy

Research Establishment at Harwell. At first the method of gas proportional counting was employed, and a special method for converting the samples into acetylene gas for filling the counters was developed. This technique has recently been abandoned in favour of the technique of liquid scintillation counting, in which the samples are converted into benzene and the necessary measurements of the radioactivity are carried out using a Packard Liquid Scintillation Spectrometer. In 1969 a mass spectrometer was acquired for measuring the C^{12}/C^{13} ratios so that dates can be determined with the highest possible precision. This service has been of considerable value to archaeologists in providing information about problems of chronology.

Another technique recently introduced in the Research Laboratory is that of thermoluminescent dating which can be used for dating pottery. This depends upon the fact that the breakdown of radioactive impurities (uranium, thorium, and the isotope potassium 40) in clay builds up energy in certain crystalline components of the clay. When clay is fired to make pottery the accumulated energy is released, but as the radioactive impurities are still present the building up of energy restarts; by measuring this newly acquired energy, and knowing also the content of radioactive impurities in the clay and the susceptibility of the clay to radiation, it is possible to estimate the time that has elapsed since the clay was fired, i.e. to determine the age of the pottery. This sophisticated technique was developed in the Research Laboratory for Arch-aeology and the History of Art in Oxford, and provides a method for the absolute dating of pottery with a present accuracy of about ten per cent. It is also of particular value in dealing with problems of the authenticity of terracotta objects. The technique can also be used in the authentication of bronzes by dating samples of the clay core round which the metal was cast.

A. E. WERNER

PLANS OF THE MUSEUM

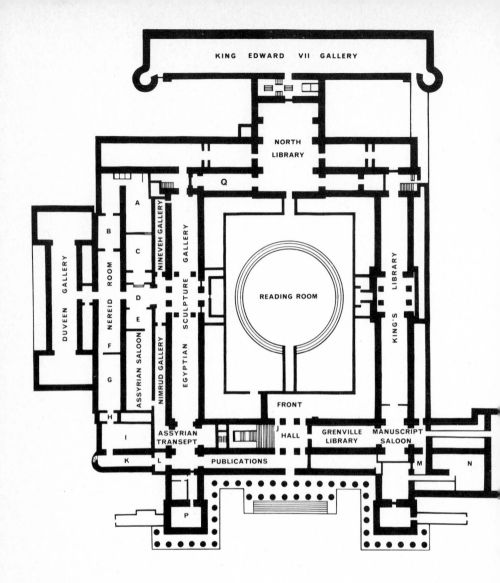

KING EDWARD VII GALLERY

NORTH LIBRARY

Q

A
B
C
D
E
F
G
H
I
K   L
P

DUVEN GALLERY

NEREID ROOM

NINEVEH GALLERY

ASSYRIAN SALOON

NIMRUD GALLERY

EGYPTIAN SCULPTURE GALLERY

READING ROOM

KING'S LIBRARY

FRONT HALL

ASSYRIAN TRANSEPT

J

GRENVILLE LIBRARY

MANUSCRIPT SALOON

M   N

PUBLICATIONS

A	Mausoleum Room	I	Early Greek Room
B	Room of the Caryatid	J	Information
C	Hellenistic Room	K	Bronze Age Room
D	First Roman Room	L	Cycladic Room
E	Second Roman Room	M	Bible Room
F	Bassae Room with Mezzanine Room above	N	Manuscript Students' Room
G	Room of the Harpy Tomb	O	Oriental Printed Books Students' Room
H	Room of the Kouroi	P	Director's Office
		Q	Palestine Room

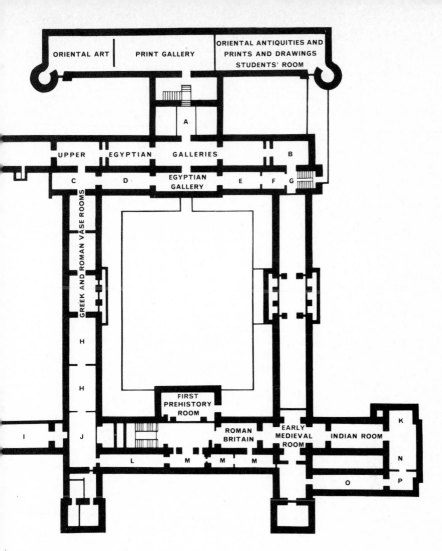

A Coptic Corridor
B Babylonian Room
C Persian Landing
D Hittite and Syrian Rooms
E Room of Writing
F Prehistoric Room
G Maya Landing
H Greek and Roman Corridor

I Coins and Medals Students' Room
J Greek and Roman Life Room
K Medieval Pottery and Tile Room
L Terracottas and Bronzes
M Prehistory Rooms
N Horological Room
O Renaissance and Later Corridor
P Waddesdon Bequest

Sources of the Plates

Unless otherwise acknowledged below, all the photographs are reproduced from British Museum sources and are published by courtesy of the Trustees of the British Museum.

1, 68, 101, 335, Edwin Smith; 12–27, 30–39, 163, John Webb (Brompton Studios); 57, 64, 71, 90, 144, Peter Clayton; 72–76, 80, 157, 161, 217–220, 222, 223, 232, 237, 252, 254, 257, 258, 262–264, 269, 270, 272–282, 284–286, 288, 290–316, 350–353, 384–407, Peter J. Davey; 81, courtesy of Oscar White Muscarella, from the Herzfeld Collection of the Department of Ancient Near Eastern Art, Metropolitan Museum of Art, New York; 92, 93, 162, Eileen Tweedy; 156, courtesy of Dr Reynold Higgins; 207, courtesy of Peter Scott; 336, courtesy of J. V. S. Megaw; 424, courtesy of Professor R. D. Lockhart and the University of Aberdeen, Anthropological Museum.

Vinča, 265; *319*
Viner, G. H., 293
Vyse, Col. Howard, 66

Waddesdon Bequest, 201; *242, 245*
Walbrook Mithraeum, 338; *422, 423*
Wales, National Library of, 22
Walker, Sir Emery, 318
Walpole, Horace, 209, 319
Wanley, Humfrey, 10, 153; *2*
Warwick Gitterne, 200; *235, 236*
Waterloo helmet, 271; *327*
Watteau, Antoine, 307–8; *371, 372*
Weber, F. Parkes, 29
Wedgwood, John, 205
Wedgwood, Josiah, 205; *249*
Wegener collection, 292
Weightman, J., 29
Welford cup, 197; *232*
Wellcome Historical Medical Museum,
Trustees of, 121
Wellcome, Sir Henry, 121
Wessex culture, 26; *321*
Western Asiatic Antiquities, Depart-
ment of, 25, 78–104; *11*

White, John, 293
Whitehead, R. B., 29
Wigan, Edward, 29
Wilding Bequest, 205
Willett, Henry, 204
Wilson, John, 201
Wise, Thomas James, 23, 158, 310
Witham shield, 270
Wodehouse, Mrs Edmond, 209
Wood, J. T., 132
Wood-blocks, 256; *312*
Woodhouse, James, 29
Woolley, Sir Leonard, 22, 92, 94, 339;
81
World War, First, 22, 57, 60, 92, 292,
332
World War, Second, 22, 23, 53, 60, 94,
132, 226, 264
Wright, Nelson, 29

X-ray diffraction analysis, 338; *427, 438*
Xanthus, Lycra, 20, 132, 140; *169*
Xipe, 109; *123*

Zimisces, John, 40; *25*